ROADS IN A MARKET ECONOMY

To Ellen Carmen, so aptly described in Proverbs, Chap. 31, verses 10-22, 24-29.

Roads in a
Market Economy

Gabriel Roth

Civil engineer and transport economist

with a Foreword by James M Buchanan
and an Epilogue by Milton Friedman and Daniel J Boorstin

'Good roads, canals and navigable rivers, by diminishing the expence of carriage, put the remote parts of the country more nearly upon a level with those in the neighbourhood of the town. They are upon that account the greatest of all improvements' (Smith, 1776, p. i, 165).

Avebury Technical

Aldershot • Brookfield USA • Hong Kong • Singapore • Sydney

Published by
Avebury Technical
Ashgate Publishing Limited
Gower House
Croft Road
Aldershot
Hants GU11 3HR
England

Ashgate Publishing Company
Old Post Road
Brookfield
Vermont 05036
USA

British Library Cataloguing in Publication Data

Roth, Gabriel
    Roads in a Market Economy
    I. Title
    388.049

    ISBN 0 291 39814 6

Library of Congress Catalog Card Number: 95-79273

Printed and bound in Great Britain by
Biddles Ltd, Guildford and King's Lynn

Contents

Figures

Tables

Boxes

Foreword

Worldwide momentum toward privatization, depoliticization and devolution surrounds us, aided and abetted by spillouts from the communications-information revolution in technology. But what form can, and should, institutional transformation take in the case of 'public roads' which, at least since the times of the Romans, have been supplied, maintained and managed socialistically?

Since the problems became acute with the advent of motor vehicle mobility, economists have proffered their familiar efficiency-based solutions. Idealized congestion pricing can effectively ration demands for road usage and at the same time generate revenues sufficient to construct and maintain the network. But economists' arguments have been politically persuasive only in part. We observe congestion on roads and streets everywhere, suggesting institutional failures both to restrict the demand for and to increase the supply of road facilities.

Are the arguments of the economists more likely to find receptive audiences in the post-socialist politics of the 1990s and beyond? My skeptical public-choice instincts suggest a negative answer, but who among us predicted the events of 1989? Technology itself imposes a barrier to genuine privatization as a generalized institutional solution. Separated private ownership of most components of the road network remains a dream only for the most utopian libertarians. The possibilities and limitations of free enterprise involvement in the provision of road services were described over forty years ago by two of America's most distinguished scholars, in a prescient essay, published for the first time as an epilogue to this book. But depoliticization via commercialization is both economically and politically realizable, as the existing modes for monitoring road usage come to seem increasingly primitive in comparison with the highly sophisticated methods that could readily replace them.

Public and political attitudes remain stubbornly resistant to explicit price rationing, for roads as for anything else. The challenge is that of organizing an effective coalition of interests in support of an efficient road system. Is it possible that the time is ripe for some combined semantic and institutional entrepreneurship here? By replacing 'taxes' with 'prices', irrelevant issues might be more readily removed from political debate.

As political economists, we are obligated by our discipline to lay out schemes that are within the technologically possible. The basic facts are available, as offered in this book. Most people can be made better off by a revolution that would allow more rationality in road usage.

Who are we to say that such a revolution will not take place?

James M. Buchanan
Buchanan House
Center for Study of Public Choice
George Mason University
March 1995   Fairfax, Virginia

Preface

When I bought my first car — an ex-London Austin taxicab — in 1952, my first reaction to inadequate roads was to ask why the government was not doing more to meet my needs as a road user. I was 'paying my road taxes' and expecting to get something in return. But further reflection brought the realization that no government, not even in California, could build sufficient roads to meet the demands of all road users for unimpeded travel at all times.

I started to do serious work on roads in 1956. In that year the British Government decided to build the M1 London-to-Birmingham motorway and — almost as an afterthought — requested its Road Research Laboratory to study the costs and benefits of Britain's first road to be provided for the exclusive use of motorized transport. At that time, the Traffic and Safety Branch of the RRL, under the leadership of Reuben Smeed, was pioneering the development of mathematical and economic models to enable roads to be used to best advantage. As a Rees Jeffreys Fellow, I joined the team undertaking the M1 study and thus received my first exposure to the notion that roads were economic assets.

However, the RRL's approach to making the best use of roads was strictly governmental. No work was done then on the pricing of roads, and Alan Walters' seminal 1954 paper (Walters, 1954) setting out the principles of road pricing was widely ignored, possibly because it was written in the economic jargon that was then in vogue in British academic circles. It was the arrival in England of William Vickrey's 1959 Congressional testimony describing the possibilities of electronic road pricing, that ignited interest in the subject. In 1961, when I was at the Department of Applied Economics of the University of Cambridge, Michael Beesley and I wrote a paper 'Restraint of Traffic in Congested Areas' (Beesley and Roth, 1963) to introduce the concept of road pricing to the Buchanan committee, which was then working on its 'Traffic in Towns' report. The Buchanan team were more interested in engineering and administrative solutions to traffic problems, and had little use for road pricing. But Christopher Foster showed the paper to officials in the Ministry of Transport who were interested, and who set up a formal committee under the chairmanship of Dr. Smeed to 'study and report on the technical feasibility of various methods for improving the pricing system relating to the use of roads'. Those who served on the committee included Beesley, Foster, Walters and myself. Michael Thomson was the committee secretary and bore the main burden of writing the report.

The Smeed committee reported in 1964 that electronic road pricing was technically feasible and potentially beneficial. I was persuaded that this was the economic solution to the traffic problem and, in my 1967 book *Paying for Roads: The Economics of Traffic Congestion*, attempted to show how a benevolent government could use the price mechanism to provide 'optimal' road networks to serve road users paying 'optimal' prices.

Alas, no government, benevolent or otherwise, was able to apply the concept until Singapore did so in 1975 by requiring vehicles entering a central 'Auto Restricted Zone' to display special entry permits on their windscreens, good for a month or for the day. These permits were available to all who wished to buy them, thus establishing a pricing system of sorts. But the authorities in Singapore showed no interest in designing road pricing arrangements to optimize the use of scarce road space; the prices charged for entering the auto restricted zone were so high that the streets there were almost empty, and continued price hikes had the effect of diverting traffic from the less-congested streets inside the zone to more congested ones outside it, which was not what the economists were recommending.

Here was a paradox. While proponents of congestion pricing claimed that it would be beneficial, and their opponents retorted that it was impracticable, Singapore demonstrated that it was practicable, but even World Bank studies were unable to show that it resulted in quantifiable benefits (Watson and Holland, 1978). This contradiction set me wondering whether it was really a good idea to give to monopoly suppliers of roads — which most governments are — the power to charge scarcity rents for their use. What would they do with the revenues? Would they not have a vested interest in maintaining high levels of congestion to generate the revenues needed to keep them in power? The concern I had then was recently confirmed by a 'senior [UK] Transport Department source [who] said there was no reason why some of the money councils raised from congestion charging should not be used "to build a local leisure centre or some other form of enhancement" to help sell the idea to local voters, provided public transport also benefitted' (*The Daily Telegraph*, 1994).

After the introduction of road pricing in Singapore, Walter Block was writing revolutionary articles suggesting that roads should be privatized, and warning that the imposition of congestion pricing on roads without including them in the market sector was unlikely to result in optimal solutions to transport problems (Block, 1979). It was this seed, planted by Walter, that eventually brought me to write this book. The question it asks is to what extent the concepts of ownership, free prices and voluntary exchange — concepts that govern the provision and allocation of scarce resources in free societies — can usefully be applied to roads. The book discusses the possibilities of public roads being privately provided, but its thrust is directed more at the *commercialization* than the *privatization* of roads. This is because I see the commercialization of roads — their provision on a commercial basis by a public or private entity — as a major objective in its own right, as well as a necessary step on the road to privatization.

In addition to my work in the 1960s with William Vickrey, Alan Walters, Michael Beesley, Christopher Foster and Michael Thomson, I also had the good fortune to meet, and learn from, other pioneers such as James Buchanan (who was visiting Cambridge) and Herbert Mohring. My inability to follow all the conclusions of these experts is of concern to me, but I take some comfort from the thought that economists would be unemployed for most of their time if they agreed with each other on all matters.

The ideas in this book were developed over the last few years and some of the material has already appeared in my *Perestroika for US Highways* (Roth, 1990) and *Tomorrow's Way,* co-authored with John Hibbs (Hibbs and Roth, 1992). Re-presentation in this book is with the kind permission of Professor Hibbs and the publishers.

I am also grateful to Ron Allan, Timothy Hau, Ian Heggie, Loyd Henion, Vincent Hogg, Daniel Klein, Keith Lumley, John Rickard, John Semmens, Roger Toleman, and Sam Zimmerman for helping me in various ways with this project, and for providing many of its good points, without in any way representing the views of any organizations with which they were ever associated. But I alone am responsible for the inevitable errors.

1 Introduction

Younger workers in China's capital want to own a car more than any other product ... according to Hori and Co.'s poll of Beijing consumers aged 16-30 ... (*The Wall Street Journal*, May 24, 1994, p. A11.)

This book is about roads, but it is not only about roads. It is about rights to use and provide roads, and therefore it has to be about rights to use motor vehicles within the accepted frameworks of market economies.

Although people fortunate enough to live in market economies are still permitted to buy cars, the rules of the market do not apply to roads, which are generally planned, financed and administered by governments seeking what they perceive to be the public good, rather than by commercial suppliers seeking to please their customers. The methods used in all countries to provide roads are essentially those that failed in the 'command economies' of Eastern Europe, and the results are similar: Congestion in some parts of the system, wasted capacity in others, and widespread deterioration and financial losses.

The provision of a road through economic markets can be illustrated by an example in the country that is now Bangladesh. In the 1960s, while the government of East Pakistan was making painfully slow progress in road development (despite massive assistance from the US Agency for International Development and the World Bank), a Dhaka bus operator, Momin Motors, provided two gravel (Kuccha) roads for its own buses. One, from Hatkhola to Jatrabi, Babur Hat and Narsinghdi was about forty miles long, and the second, from Zinzira to Ruhitput, fifteen miles. The routes for the roads were selected by Momin Motors, which financed and built them, and was reimbursed out of the fares paid by the passengers, much in the same way that railways used to be reimbursed out of fares paid by their passengers. The construction of these roads, which have since been paved and absorbed into the highway network of Bangladesh, shows that private ownership can play a useful role in road provision even under the most difficult circumstances.[1]

But most roads are provided by governmental entities. An instructive example illuminating how the system works can be found in the *History of the Ottoman Turks* (Creasy, 1877). It is reported there that when the Sultan Amurath IV set out to visit his Asiatic dominions in the year 1633, he found the roads beyond Nicomedia in bad repair, and thereupon had the chief judge hanged. In that case the road system was not provided by contracts between willing buyers and willing sellers; it was the Sultan who decided on the requirements for roads and who suspended the official who failed to carry out his orders.

Before exploring the possibilities of roads being provided in accordance with commercial criteria, it may be worth explaining why the mobility of people and their goods is important, and noting some of the ways in which it is constrained in many countries by weaknesses in the roads sector.

1.1 Importance of personal mobility

Travel has a major role in human culture. The first people moved by foot but, in the course of time, other modes were developed, making use of animal power, boats, railways, bicycles, cars, buses, aircraft, etc. They all contributed to the ability of people to move, trade, and meet for social, business and other purposes, and this mobility was closely associated with economic and social development.

Only travel modes comprising motorized road transport are covered in this book. This is not because other modes are unimportant, but because they are not relevant to the main subject, which is the development of road networks appropriate for motorized traffic. However, as I am bound to be criticized for neglecting the non-motorized modes, let me state that I consider the facilities for pedestrians and bicycles to be shamefully neglected in many countries; that safe footways are of vital importance; and that the potential for 'bikeways' — routes reserved for bicycles — merits much more attention than it is getting. But these important topics merit books to themselves.

1.1.1 Role of door-to-door speed

Why is motorized mobility important? Is it, as some experts aver, based on an irrational 'love affair with the automobile', to which Western people have succumbed and which others should avoid? This is a superficial and misleading approach to the problem. People travel to increase the opportunities available to them. Travel allows workers to get better jobs, shoppers cheaper purchases, sellers more customers, and children more suitable schools. It also allows families to live in more congenial surroundings.

As incomes rise, the ranges of people's opportunities expand, and so does their desire to travel to take advantage of these opportunities. How can they travel more? Because all of us are constrained by time, we get to the point where we have to travel more quickly to expand the range of our activities, and it is motorized travel that gives us the possibility of travelling more quickly, and cramming more activities into our limited days. It is significant that as people get richer, they travel more, not less. People in London, on the average, cover more miles than people in Lagos, while people in New York travel more than those in London. They do not travel more by spending more time on travel, but by travelling faster, because their transport systems offer higher speeds.

The tendency for people to travel further and faster as their incomes rise is found in many cultures and will be illustrated by travel data from the US, India, and the UK.

Examples from the US The tendency of Americans to travel more as their incomes increase is shown by data collected in the city of Baltimore. Figure 1.1 shows how average daily household travel, for all purposes, by the main motorized modes, increases with income. Note that the increase in distance travelled is associated with increasing car use.

The increase in travel speed with income, for the same Baltimore population, is shown in Figure 1.2. The travel speeds are 'door-to-door', i.e. they take account not only of vehicle speeds, but also of the time spent walking to and from bus stops and parking places, and in waiting for buses. The association of increasing speed with rising car ownership is clearly shown.

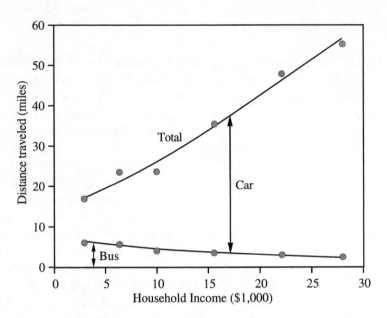

Figure 1.1 Daily distance traveled per household in Baltimore
Source: Zahavi (1982)

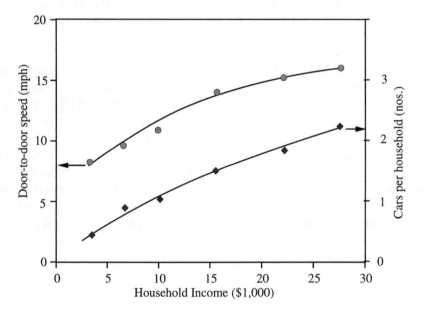

Figure 1.2 Car ownership and travel speed at different incomes
Source: Zahavi (1982)

The relationship between personal income and personal travel, in low- and high-density areas of the San Francisco Bay Region, was investigated by Elizabeth Deakin (Schipper and others, 1994), and the results are shown in Figure 1.3 below. While different relationships apply to the low- and high-density groups (those living in low density travel significantly more than the high density groups), both groups clearly travel more as their incomes rise.

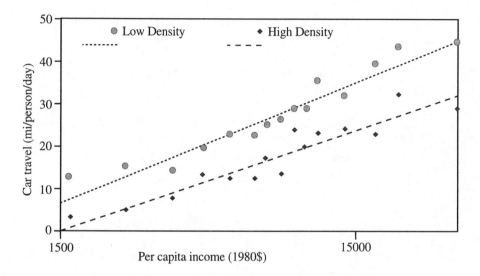

Figure 1.3 Income and car travel in San Francisco in 1991
Source: Schipper and others (1994)

An example from India Data collected in the Indian city of Jaipur, Table 1.1, show a similar pattern of travel to work trips by different income groups. The data are described as follows by researcher Angus Deaton (1987):

> [T]rip time is virtually constant at approximately 20 minutes. All of the adaptation to higher incomes is done through greater distance and faster travel with essentially no effect on travel times. The change in speed with income is accomplished by a switch in modes. As far as employment trips are concerned, the important modes are walking, cycling, special (i.e. works' buses), regular stage buses, and motor

vehicles (including motor cycles, scooters and motor cars). ... The poorest 5% of households make 40% of their trips to work on foot, compared with only 10% in the highest income classes, and 18% overall. Forty to fifty percent of employment trips are made by cycle; this fraction is fairly constant until the top quartile after which cycles are progressively replaced by motorized vehicles ... Trips by motor vehicles increase their share rapidly as income rises, replacing both trips on foot and trips on cycles. As income rises, walkers become cyclists, and cyclists become motor-cyclists or drivers.

Table 1.1
Modes used for travel to work in Jaipur

Mode choice for employment trips

per cent

Percentile	Nos*	Walk	Cycle	Sp. Bus	Bus	Mc/car	Other
All	1.28	18	41	2	10	23	6
5	0.96	40	45	0	10	0	5
10	1.13	27	56	1	8	2	6
15	1.17	31	53	1	7	2	6
20	1.15	19	57	1	13	6	5
25	1.30	28	46	1	12	10	4
30	1.19	23	51	1	10	9	7
35	1.19	16	52	1	12	11	8
40	1.24	14	57	1	10	11	7
45	1.39	19	46	2	10	13	10
50	1.16	18	48	3	10	16	6
55	1.38	19	6	1	11	18	5
60	1.43	16	39	1	11	23	10
65	1.18	16	36	2	11	31	4
70	1.41	14	43	3	11	24	4
75	1.33	15	35	2	13	28	8
80	1.45	15	27	4	13	37	5
85	1.32	17	24	5	10	41	3
90	1.45	13	25	5	7	46	4
95	1.44	11	24	5	7	48	5
100	1.33	10	17	2	11	55	3

* Numbers of trips per household.

Source: Deaton (1987)

An international comparison Some travel relationships are so strong that they transcend national barriers. One such relationship is the one shown in Figure 1.4 below, between distance travelled and door-to-door speed in four cities of the UK and US.

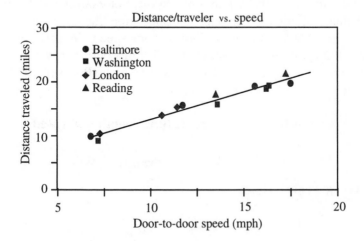

Figure 1.4 Daily distance per traveler related to travel speed
Source: Zahavi (1982)

The existence of such international relationships may suggest that people in all countries share similar travel desires, and that travel characteristics now common in Western countries will be replicated in Asia and Africa as soon as living standards there become high enough to support widespread motorization. Is it possible that the desire for mobility to increase one's opportunities — like the 'propensity to truck, barter, and exchange one thing for another' — may be 'one of those original principles in human nature'?

1.1.2 Public transport as an alternative?

But, say the public transport proponents, granted that people in cities want to get around, why do they not take the bus or the metro? Would we not all be better off if people just used public transport? If it is speed that we want, why do we choose the car, which moves at 14 miles per hour in many cities, in preference to the train that can go at three times that speed? There are several points to be made about this important question.

The first is that the speeds that count are not vehicle speeds in traffic, nor train speeds on their own right-of-way, but the speeds from the beginnings of journeys to their ends. A trip by public transport involves a walk to the public transport route, a wait for a bus or a train and, after leaving the public transport system, a walk to the destination. When all these factors are taken into account, average trip speeds by car in most cities are substantially higher than by public transport. For example, data from the United States Nationwide Personal Transportation Survey, Table 1.2, show that, for trips to work in 1990, door-to-door speeds by privately owned vehicles ('POV') in the US averaged 34.7 miles per hour, while those by bus and train ('transit') averaged 15.2 miles an hour (Pisarski, 1992).

Table 1.2
US work trips by travel time, length and speed

	POV*	Transit	Walk	All
Work Travel Times *(minutes):*				
1983	19.3	46.1	8.9	20.4
1990	19.0	49.9	9.6	19.7
Work Trip Lengths *(miles):*				
1983	10.2	15.1	0.4	9.9
1990	11.0	12.6	0.5	10.7
Calculated Speed *(mph):*				
1983	31.7	19.7	2.7	29.1
1990	34.7	15.2	3.1	32.3

* Privately owned vehicles

Source: Pisarski (1992)

Travel modes in the US are changing, but not in favour of public transport, even for the journey to work. As shown in Table 1.3, the numbers of those driving alone increased between 1980 and 1990, while the number of car-poolers declined. The numbers of those using public transport remained about the same, less than 10 per cent, despite billions of dollars spent in subsidies to urban rail and bus systems.

Table 1.3
How Americans got to their work: 1980 and 1990

	Per cent	
	1980	1990
Drove alone	65.0%	74.0%
Car pooled	20.0	13.0
Public Transit	6.4	5.3
Walked only	5.6	3.9
Bicycled	0.5	0.4
Worked at home	2.3	3.0
Other	0.7	0.7

Source: The Wall Street Journal, June 29, 1993
(based on US census data)

There are exceptions, of course. In cities such as London, New York, and Paris, which developed their underground train systems before the advent of widespread car ownership, many trips can be carried out more quickly by train than by car. But travel conditions in such old-established cities cannot be replicated by the construction of underground railways in newer cities which developed after the car became popular. Thus the lavish 'Metro' rail system of Washington DC, which was superimposed in the last twenty years on a car-dominated city, offers comfort to most of its users but time savings to comparatively few.

A second point is that urban roads are so badly managed that buses are unable to benefit from their main advantage, their economy in road space. A full bus may take up as much road space as three cars, but it can carry thirty times as many passengers, giving it a ten-to-one advantage. If road space were charged for on an economic basis — a point examined at greater length in the following chapters — it would be cheaper for travelers to use buses than cars for many of their journeys. However, except in Norway and Singapore, no additional charges are made for the use of congested roads.

The third factor that hurts public transport is that the services most suitable for passengers in most cities — minibuses and shared taxis operated at high frequencies — are prohibited in most Western cities, though they are successful in Atlantic City, Belfast, Buenos Aires, Caracas, Istanbul, Manila and wherever else they are allowed. For example, taxicab operator Alfredo Santos started a shared taxi shuttle service in Houston in 1983, charging $1 per seat for travel along a fixed five-mile route. The service was popular and profitable, but was closed down by the city authorities because it violated 1924 legislation enacted to protect tram ('streetcar') operators who had long since gone out of business.[2]

In New York City, where formal public transport services are unable to earn even half their operating costs, there are 'swarms of private vans in southeastern Queens' which cover all of their costs, capital and operating, while charging less than the buses provided by the city's Metropolitan Transportation Authority. The MTA does its best to close the unofficial services down, even — thanks to federal and New York taxpayers — providing extra subsidies to buses in competition with them (Faison, 1992).

Public transport enhances the mobility of many, and needs to be developed in response to the demands of its customers. It should be seen as a complement to individual transport, and not as antagonistic to it. Buses on expressways (using dedicated lanes where justified, as at some of the approaches to New York and Washington DC) can provide fast, convenient service without subsidy. But, for many journeys, public transport cannot be an acceptable substitute for individual motorized transport.

1.1.3 Travel in rural areas

It is not only in urban areas that cars improve mobility; their contribution to rural mobility is even more striking. Without motorized transport, rural dwellers depend for their mobility on animals — horses, camels, bullock carts, etc. — which move at three to eight miles in an hour, and need long rest periods. For example, at the beginning of the century, the residents of Oregon, Illinois, had to spend four hours travelling by horse to the neighbouring town of Rockford, 25 miles away. It was possible to do the journey by train, but the timetables made it impossible to make the round trip in one day. So trips of this kind were few. But when cars were acquired, the journey could be made in an hour, and the number of trips multiplied ten-fold (Smith, 1990).

Mobility in rural areas thus impacts directly and profoundly on social and economic development. Not only were physicians prominent as early car owners, but the spread of car ownership enabled growing numbers of patients to be brought to their physicians, a well as to local medical centres, which could not have been viable without widespread motorized mobility. As was noted in a survey of a rural Illinois county:

> Sixteen physicians in 1950 provided more service for more people than 42 physicians had provided in 1920. In the 1920s roads were so poor that physicians spent an hour or two making a call five miles from town and a 40 mile hospital trip took about six hours. Now patients in this rural county can reach town in twenty minutes, and a hospital in an hour or less (Rae, 1971, p. 163).

The effect of motorized transport on rural production and employment may be illustrated by an 1883 instruction given by a Scottish mortgage company not to lend on Oregon farms situated further than 10 miles from a railway station (Rae, 1971, p. 129). On a more positive note, studies by the Brookings Institution on the effects of road improvements in Latin America, India, Thailand and Uganda noted that

> The net increase in mobility implied an increase in both the tonnage of freight and number of people moved during any time period and, in some instances, a lengthening of the average distance traveled. As both cause and consequence of this, a sharp rise in production (mostly agricultural) took place with a growing emphasis on production for the market rather than for subsistence. In other words, the rise in mobility was not simply more movement over longer distances of existing annual volumes of production. In virtually every case, the greater mobility represented a net increase in physical output as well as a higher value of output per unit of weight, as substitutions for both low-valued cash crops and subsistence crops ensued (Wilson, 1966, p. 11).

It may be concluded, then, that travelers and producers have good reasons to choose motorized modes to meet many of their transport needs. Having made this choice, at their own expense or at the expense of their employers, how do they find conditions on the roads provided for their use by their governments? To what extent are the requirements for roads being met?

1.2 Meeting the 'need' for roads

It is of course impossible to generalize about road conditions world-wide; even the term 'road' cannot be defined with any precision. But there is another problem in trying to define the adequacy of road conditions in different places.

When we talk about the adequacy or inadequacy of a commodity or service in a market economy, we assume that the commodity can be bought by people willing to pay for it. Thus, when we say that the supply of lorries or of fuel in any place is 'inadequate', we imply that it is inadequate at a certain price. If the price were high enough, we would expect consumers to want less of it, and suppliers to provide more, until the deficiency is made up.

But prices are not generally applied to roads, the vast majority of which are part of the 'priceless economy'. This leads to the paradox, about which many commentators have written, that supplying more road capacity does nothing to improve traffic conditions because the new capacity attracts so much new traffic that congestion remains as before. Anthony Downs (1992) has even enshrined this proposition as an 'Iron law of traffic congestion', which states that new road capacity quickly gets filled up. Those who write in this vein can get support from the City of London, where day-time traffic speeds have remained unchanged (at 10 miles per hour) ever since observations were first made there in the 1920s.

The solution to this paradox is that road space is not supplied commercially as part of the market economy. It is supplied by governments out of public funds, and it is government officials who determine road 'needs'. The processes used to determine these 'needs' are discussed later (in section 5.2 below), but it may be mentioned at this stage that many engaged in road provision have strong incentives to exaggerate their requirements, in the hope of getting at least some funding from skeptical treasury departments.

> Advocates of each specific use can see little reason to moderate their appetites. ... Winning the battle for funding has a significant payoff without cost. After all, winners do not have to pay higher taxes than losers. Thus, the incentive is to make excessive demands on highway resources.

> In addition, the payment of a tax does not entitle the payer to any specific benefit in exchange for the payment. Those who drive on neglected roads are not relieved of any tax obligation. On the contrary, users of poorly maintained or crowded roads will likely use more fuel

and pay more taxes.

The lack of a direct link between payment and services condemns highways to a persistent imbalance between needs and resources. Public highway agencies cannot help but fall short of delivering everything that people want (Semmens, 1993).

In the light of these difficulties, it is possible to make some comments on the state of roads in different countries.

1.3 The United Kingdom

Almost all motorized travel in the United Kingdom (94 per cent of passenger miles, and 89 per cent of freight ton miles) is by road. There are over 226,000 miles of road there, one for every 104 vehicles, which (except for Italy's) makes British roads the most crowded in Europe. While traffic and road use taxation increased by over 42 per cent in the 1980s, expenditure on roads increased by less than one quarter. There is widespread feeling in Britain that the road system, especially in and near its cities, results not only in substantial waste in travel time and costs, but also in heavy environmental and accident costs, as heavy traffic is routed through towns and villages.

A public opinion poll reported that 29 per cent of road users would be willing to pay for improved roads. However, there is no market system that enables them to do this; road users in Britain still have the freedom to buy cars but, no matter how acute the need for road improvement, or the availability of idle road-building resources, they do not have the freedom to buy, or rent, road space.[3] This is because Treasury officials — who wield immense power — are adamant in their refusal to allow any of the monies collected from road users to be dedicated ('ear-marked', or 'hypothecated') to expenditure on roads. In the financial year 1993/94 road users in Britain paid some £21 billion in vehicle and fuel taxes, but less than 30 per cent of that sum was spent on the roads.

The Treasury's objection to 'ear-marking' is that efficiency in fiscal policy requires funds to be centrally collected and allocated. It is difficult to discern the wisdom of this policy in Britain's post-war transport investments. While road users contributed heavily to general revenues — over £14 billion in 1993/94 — its railways did not have to meet their costs and were supported by government subsidies. Since 1945, successive British governments have held back the development of a modern road system for which users were prepared to pay, by taking from them billions in road use taxation, and spending a substantial proportion of these funds (over £28 billion in the last sixteen years) subsidizing an obsolete technology, which cannot provide door-to-door service, which serves less than a tenth of the transport market, and for which its users are not willing to pay. If this is a typical example of financial allocations made at the centre of government, some might consider 'ear-marking'to be preferable.

Fiscal policies in conflict with the wishes of transport users are not the only obstacle to improving Britain's roads. Road users also have to put up with obstruction from protesters who object to new roads, especially   motorways, ostensibly on 'environmental' grounds. The logic of this kind of objection is not clear, as motorways can enable traffic to avoid local roads, with consequential reductions in pollution and accident costs. And, while it is easy to sympathize with those who lose their property to compulsory purchase, many of the objectors come from other areas to make their point.[4]

1.4 The United States

The USA has a road network of over 3.9 million miles, about one for each fifty vehicles. Its road users might feel that the provision of roads by government has worked quite well, and that political pressure is still the best way to satisfy road needs. They can point with pride to the Interstate Highway System, a network of some 45,000 miles of roads built at a cost of $50 billion,[5] possibly the second greatest public works achievement of all times, the first being the 56,000 mile Roman road system built between 400 BC and AD 200.[6]

However, Americans are concerned about inadequacies in their highway systems. US highway officials reckon that over $300 billion are required to rehabilitate roads and bridges, and that further sums will be needed to increase capacity to reduce congestion, especially in expanding suburban areas. While these numbers probably contain elements of special pleading, there is indubitably a wide public perception that conditions on many US highways are too poor to be acceptable.

1.4.1 Profitability of US roads

If the US road system were operated on a commercial basis, would it show a profit or a loss? If the US road system were operating on a commercial basis, this question would not be important. Questioners would not look at the system as a whole, but at individual sections, seeking to identify those associated with profits or losses. However, as the system is not run on a commercial basis, and as there is widespread dissatisfaction with the performance of some of its parts, it is of some interest to know whether its total costs are covered by payments from road users.

Each year the US Federal Highway Administration's publication *Highway Statistics* includes a table of 'total receipts and disbursements for highways', which summarizes and consolidates receipts and disbursement data from federal, state and local governments.7 Transport economist John Semmens summarized the 1992 figures as shown in Table 1.4.

Table 1.4
Revenues and expenses of publicly-owned roads in the US
$ millions

Revenues

♦	User Taxes & Fees	$51,848
♦	Investment Income	4,677
	Total	**$56,525**

Expenses

♦	Maintenance	$22,878
♦	Administration	7,717
♦	Highway Patrol	7,091
♦	Interest	3,618
	Total	**$41,304**
	Net	**$15,221**

Source: Compiled by John Semmens from FHWA's *Highway Statistics*

These data, which are typical of those produced for US highways, show that road revenues for 1992 exceeded $56 billion while expenditures were below $39 billion. Does this indicate a healthy financial situation?

Unfortunately it does not, because the data are not designed to show financial health. Governmental accounts are generally designed to show only whether receipts are spent honestly, and in accordance with the law, not whether they are spent efficiently. In the words of John Semmens

Transportation agencies do not prepare profit and loss evaluations of their road operations. Accounts are generally kept on a cash flow basis, and no allowance is made for the progressive depreciation of such capital assets as bridges and roads. ... Reserves are not established for the orderly maintenance of facilities. Consequently, as roadways near the end of their design life, there are rarely sufficient funds for replacement or restoration. Hence, the recurring crises in infrastructure finance (Semmens, 1987).[8]

To illustrate what highway accounts would look like if prepared in a more business-like format, Semmens took the *Highway Statistics* data for twenty years, and amended them by adding an item for depreciation, the life of a highway assumed to be twenty years. According to these calculations, the appropriate amount for depreciation in 1992, only for capital expenditure incurred in the previous twenty years, came to $21.587 billion. When this is added to the expenditures in Table 1.4, the surplus of $15.221 billion turns into a loss of $6.366 billion.

Semmens also worked on the data from previous years, back to 1956, the year of the creation of the federal Highway Trust Fund, and graphed the profit or loss figures. This graph is shown in Figure 1.5.

Figure 1.5 Net 'profit' or 'loss' for US roads 1956 to 1992
$ billions
Source: Semmens (1993)

Figure 1.5 shows that since the early 1970s revenues from highway users in the US have failed to keep up with expenditures. This is consistent with the widespread view that the nation faces an 'infrastructure crisis' and suggests that such crises could be avoided by applying to the highway sector the accounting principles which are routinely used in the private sector.

The difference between the commercial and governmental approaches to expenditures is also illustrated by the acceptance by government of the extraordinary rise in the administrative costs of highway provision, which now use up over one fifth of revenues. Semmens points out that:

> From the time that the federal government's role in highway construction expanded with the initiation of the interstate highway program in the mid-1950s, administrative costs have increased. ... As a percentage of construction spending, administrative costs have tripled from less than 7 percent in 1956 to almost 21 percent in 1991 (Semmens, 1993).

There may have been good reasons for the rise in administrative costs, but they are not explained in the relevant tables. And why should they be? So long as expenditures are incurred in accordance with the law, officialdom tends to be satisfied. A commercial operator, on the other hand, would want to know the reasons for such changes in administrative costs.

1.4.2 The federal role: power without responsibility

It is no accident that the divergence between road revenues and costs followed closely the involvement of the US federal government in road financing. The federal 'Highway Trust Fund' (which is discussed in more detail in Chapter 2 below) receives the bulk of highway revenues from dedicated road user charges and distributes them (less amounts retained for 'demonstration projects'[9] and other specified purposes) to the states by formula. This results in excessive demands for expensive facilities, because to the states, which are nominally responsible for expenditure decisions, federal funds are costless, and state officials are accountable to their voters only for state funds.

At the point at which expenditure decisions are made, nobody — neither road users nor state officials nor even federal officials — is responsible for paying the costs that arise from their decisions to spend. The road users have no control over their payments into the federal Highway Trust Fund; members of the federal Congress have control over the total amounts they appropriate for roads, and of the conditions they attach, but no control (which might be to the good) over the distribution of the bulk of the funds between the states, which is by formula; and the states have no control over the amount of federal funds they receive, which they can either spend or lose. In this situation, it is no surprise that the 'needs' for roads always exceed the funds available, and it is difficult to see how expenditures can be controlled as long as the present system persists.

Some might wonder why state officials put up with this arrangement and do not lobby for the return to them of power and responsibility over highway funds. One reason might be that life is much easier for officials at state levels if the power of taxation and allocation is moved up to a higher level. This reduces the differences between tax levels in different states which can signal inefficiencies and even (heaven forbid) cause resources to move from high-tax to low-tax jurisdictions.

> In effect, increasing the power of the central government to tax is a way of forming and enforcing a tax cartel allowing government in aggregate to extract more money from the public. Having extracted more revenue, the government can reallocate the additional money through revenue sharing arrangements so that all governments secure more of the taxpayers' money. ... With local politicians able to provide projects for constituents who can vote them out of office, projects paid for largely by taxpayers in other jurisdictions who can't, a constant demand for excessive and inefficient government spending (all of which enhances the power of central authorities) is assured (Lee, 1993).

It is evident that the use of the federal Highway Trust Fund to centralize the power of financing and providing major roads is part of a wider struggle now taking place in the US. It is being waged between those who want more decisions to be made 'within the [Washington DC] beltway' and those who want to restore to the states many of the powers they held before the 'New Deal' policies of the 1930s. It is not necessary to take sides in this wider struggle to conclude that road users could get far better value for their road money if the financing decisions were made at levels closer to them, and further from Washington DC.

1.4.3 Environmental concerns

A major difficulty facing rational road — and transport — planning in the US is the growing influence of environmental lobbies. These appear to have paramount roles in decisions relating to roads, particularly in California. Americans desire high environmental standards and are prepared to pay for them, and there is no dispute that motor vehicles damage the environment, especially in congested urban areas. A logical approach to the problem would require pollution levels to be reduced to the point at which the costs of additional reductions would be balanced by the resulting additional benefits. This approach is accepted by many in the environmental movement but not by those concerned with transport policy.

The Bush Administration's 1990 Clean Air Act, on which many of the current environmental regulations are based, does not require regulators to consider the costs of regulation. As a result, the federal body responsible, the Environmental Protection Agency (EPA), can require that any improvement of air quality, however trivial, be corrected at any cost, however great. Furthermore, the standards themselves do not seem to have been based on any estimates of costs or benefits, and there is no way of knowing whether the efforts to comply with them increase, or reduce, social welfare. The main sanction used by the EPA to enforce its will is the threat to withhold from states not in 'compliance' with environmental regulations the funds due to them from the federal Highway Trust Fund.

These EPA activities have major effects on personal mobility. They cannot be reviewed here in full, but an example of their flavour can be given. In fourteen areas not meeting the (arbitrary) air quality standards, the EPA is forcing states to mandate firms employing more than 100 people to introduce 'Employee Commute Options' programmes which require employers to reduce the number of their employees' work trips by single-occupancy cars by 25 per cent by 1998. The options proposed to bring about these reductions include compressed work-weeks, taxes on parking facilities, car-pooling programmes and increased taxes on petrol — figures of $2 a gallon are mentioned in Boston and San Francisco (McKenna, 1994).

The effects of these requirements are drastic. In Chicago, for example, the EPA insists that average car occupancy should increase from 1.09 to 1.70 by 1998. Not only is such a target impossible to achieve — London's vehicle occupancy is below 1.5 — but it is by no means clear that its achievement would improve air quality. It is the oldest cars that are generally used for car pools, and those are the most polluting. Because those polluting cars would be driven to different places to pick up car poolers, they could run more miles, and may cause more pollution. And air quality boards do not hesitate to use fines to enforce their demands: The Kaiser Permanente hospital in Los Angeles was fined nearly $1 million because it failed to submit its car-pooling plan in time.

These measures impose large costs and discourage economic growth. For example, according to a study conducted in 1994 in California (the state most affected by environmental regulation), 41 per cent of companies were planning to expand their operations only outside the state, and 14 per cent were planning to move out entirely (Farah and Antonucci, 1994).

It is evident that the Bush and Clinton administrations have chosen to use 'command and control' measures to reduce pollution and mobility to what their regulators regard as appropriate levels. And the regulations used are to a large extent arbitrary, not being based on any clear principles, nor on logically-based standards of mobility and air quality.

1.5 Developing countries

Road conditions are worse still in developing countries where, according to World Bank data, almost US$13 billion worth of roads — one third of those built in the last twenty years — 'have eroded' for lack of maintenance (World Bank, 1994). For example, surveys carried out in Brazil found that, between 1979 and 1984, 6,000 km of new paved roads were built while, in the same time period, 2,000 km of 'good' roads deteriorated to 'fair', and 6,000 km of 'fair' roads deteriorated to 'poor' (Harral, 1988). In Chile, half of the main 3,000 km north to south highway, which was paved in the early 1960s at great national sacrifice, collapsed in the 1970s and had to be rebuilt at enormous cost. Commercial firms wasting their capital assets in this way would soon be out of business, but governmental policies are more difficult to change.

Mismanagement of roads in Latin America is not confined to Brazil and Chile: In the whole Latin American and Caribbean region, deficiencies in the management of inter-city and rural roads is causing them to lose value at a rate equivalent to US$2 billion to US$3 billion each year. Additionally, this deterioration increases annual vehicle operating costs by similar amounts (UN-ECLAC, 1993). When a road is not maintained, and is allowed to deteriorate from good to poor condition, each peso saved on road maintenance typically increases vehicle operating costs by two or three pesos (EDI, 1991, p. 23).

In Africa, roads are in even worse shape. As a result of poor maintenance, nearly a third of the US$150 billion[10] invested in roads in Sub-Saharan Africa (S-SA) has been eroded (Heggie, 1995). In addition to the costs to the road system of poor maintenance there are, as in Latin America, heavy additional costs to road users, which can be illustrated by the annual costs to heavy trucks caused by potholes, which are shown in Box 1.1.

Box 1.1 How potholes affect vehicle operating costs

Potholes cause immense damage to vehicles. To better understand the additional costs associated with potholes, the Federation of Zambian Road Hauliers interviewed truckers to compare the running costs of a truck and trailer combination on a road with potholes with those on a road without potholes. The vehicle considered was a lorry and trailer with twenty-two wheels, weighing between 44 and 50 tons. The costs estimated are those over and above normal running costs. This excess is equivalent to $0.20 per vehicle-km.

On a road with bad potholes, a driver can either pursue a defensive strategy or ignore the potholes and carry on as usual. If he follows a defensive strategy, he first slows down and changes gears. He then has to negotiate the vehicle through the potholes. This causes extra stress on the tires, wheel bearings, spring assemblies, spring hangers, chassis, cross-members, engine mountings, gear box mountings, brakes, steering assemblies, and shock absorbers. Having negotiated the potholes, he accelerates and changes gears again. On the other hand, if he ignores the potholes, he will drive through them at his regular speed, resulting in more damage to the vehicle and tires and increasing the risk of accidents. The axle pressure on the road now increases by at least three times.

The survey resulted in the following annual expenditures over and above normal running expenditures. It ignores extra fuel consumption, damage to goods, down-time of trucks under repair, and accidents caused by potholes and sharp pavement edges.

Quantity	Item	Unit price *(Dollars)*	Annual cost *(Dollars)*
10	Extra tires and tubes	595	5,952
1	Extra clutch and pressure plate	1,071	1,071
4	Extra wheel bearing	201	803
1	Extra set of brake shoes	1,050	1,050
1	Extra set of springs	1,667	1,667
4	Extra spring hangers and bushes	113	452
-	Welding, electrodes/oxyacetylene for: body, chassis and cross member damage, engine, and cabin mountings	952	952
1	Extra steering assembly	1,874	1,874
4	Extra shock absorbers	128	510
	Total annual costs attributable to potholes		14,331

Source: Federation of Zambian Road Hauliers Ltd., February, 1992.
Quoted in Heggie (1995).

It is also estimated that the extra costs due to insufficient maintenance of roads in S-SA amount to about US$1.2 billion per year, which is equivalent to 0.85 per cent of regional economic output (EDI, 1991, p. 9). Many paved roads have deteriorated so far that they have become unusable; their surfaces have to be broken up to convert them to earth or gravel roads which, unlike paved roads, are still passable, at least in dry weather, even when badly deteriorated. Road records in Uganda indicate that, in 1987, over 740 km of the main road network were abandoned as a result of bad maintenance.

Those who attended the 1987 Transportation Research Board Meeting on 'The Road Deterioration Problems in Developing Countries' heard grim reports from World Bank staff on the state of roads in 74 developing countries. It was said that roads financed by the World Bank in 1960s and 1970s were deteriorating so fast that some were expected to become unusable even before the repayment of the funds borrowed for their construction — there can be few worse examples of 'non-performing loans'. While the problem was shown to have a financial dimension (the cost of dealing with the backlog was estimated to have been US$40 billion), the World Bank staff emphasized that money alone could not provide a cure. Much was said of 'institutional failures', e.g.

> despite strenuous and protracted efforts — including management consultancies, technical assistance, and training totaling more than US$1.2 billion over 1971-85 by the World Bank alone — the Bank, its co-financiers, and the recipient countries have had few successes in establishing institutions capable of sustaining cost effective road maintenance with domestic resources (Harral, 1987).

The World Bank authors did not mention that roads on private plantations and estates in developing countries — in Brazil and Liberia, for example — are adequately maintained by their private owners, in contrast to the neighboring roads that are the responsibility of governments. A road in Chile, leading to a private mine, is also perfectly maintained, by the company that owns the mine. Might this not indicate a useful role for the commercial provision of public roads?

1.6 Commercial provision of roads?

Is there then a role for the commercial provision of roads? This is the question to be addressed in this book. Before doing so, it is necessary to define one's terms, and to state what is meant by 'commercial provision'.

The commercial provision of a good or a service, which can be undertaken by public sector entities as well as by private ones, is generally understood to include four major elements:

1. A *management* system to protect the assets of the entity, and to facilitate the production of appropriate goods or services in response to customers' requirements;

2. Freedom to *price* products as desired, except in the case of monopolies, whose pricing powers are constrained;

3. The technical ability to *levy changes* in an efficient manner; and

4. Freedom to *invest* with the objective of expanding profitable operations while reducing loss-making ones.

The next four chapters will examine these elements — management, pricing, charging and investment — in greater depth, and consider their application to roads. Chapter 6 will then discuss the main objections to commercialization, and how they might be overcome. Chapter 7 reviews private sector roles in road provision and Chapter 8 the possibilities for reform.

Notes

1. I am indebted to Dr. Slaheddine Khenissi, IMF Resident Representative in Bangladesh, for information about these roads, which were photographed by consultants to the USAID in the late 1960s.

2. This story had a happy sequel: With the help of the Landmark Legal Foundation, Santos sued the City of Houston and in March 1994 obtained a judgement that allowed him to resume his shared taxi operation.

3. When the Birmingham Northern Relief Road is completed (see section 7.4.2), road users in the UK will have the option of renting space on it, by paying the toll. They will also be able to exercise their powers as consumers by using the roads provided under the DBFO scheme, described in section 8.1.1.

4. For example, a protester who described himself as a 'professional activist', came all the way from Leeds to chain himself to a drain in east London, to hold up the progress of extending the M11 motorway (*The Times*, 1994).

5. But, as a proportion of the size of the economy, the private investments in US toll roads at the turn of the nineteenth century exceeded the public investment in the modern Interstate Highway System (Gunderson, 1989).

6. At the peak of the Roman Empire's power, its road system was about 300,000 km in length. Of these, about 90,000 were main roads, 14,000 km in Italy alone (Forbes, 1934, p. 130).

7. 'Receipts' identified in *Highway Statistics* do not include all taxes paid by road users, but only those considered to have been levied 'because of, or for, ... use of the public highways'. In 1992, these receipts ('highway user imposts') amounted to about two-thirds of the total payments actually collected from road users (Dougher, 1995).

8. It might be considered that the amounts spent under 'Maintenance' were sufficient to keep US roads in good condition for ever. This possibility is excluded by the definition of 'maintenance' which is:

    Costs included under the classification as maintenance are of two types: (1) those required to keep the highways in useable condition, such as routine patching repairs, bridge painting, and other maintenance of condition costs; and (2) traffic service costs, such as snow and ice removal, pavement markings, signs, signals, litter cleaning, and toll collection expenses (*Highway Statistics*, 1990).

9. The phrase 'demonstration projects' has been getting such a bad name that projects voted in 1994 as special favours for members of House Appropriation Committees have been labeled 'high priority Congressional projects' (Anderson and Binstein, 1994).

10. The figure of US$150 billion is calculated as the cost of replacing all existing roads at 1992 prices. It does not include the cost of bridges.

2 Commercial management of roads

So long as government uses any of its coercive powers, and particularly its power of taxation, in order to assist its enterprises, it can always turn their position into one of actual monopoly. To prevent this, it would be necessary that any special advantages, including subsidies, which government gives to its own enterprises in any field, should also be made available to competing private agencies. ... [W]hat is objectionable here is not state enterprise but state monopoly (Hayek, 1960, p. 224).

2.1 Weaknesses in roads management

Most roads today are run like public parks. Central or local government allocates funds for the maintenance or rehabilitation of existing roads, or for the construction of new ones, and the designated government employees expend the funds to the best of their abilities. This kind of arrangement differs from commercial provision in five important respects:

1. Weakness in ownership arrangements;

2. Weaknesses in accountability to customers;

3. Absence of pricing responsive to costs and demand;

4. Absence of competition; and

5. Absence of financial independence.

2.1.1 Ownership arrangements

The essence of the market system is not, as is widely believed, price incentives, but ownership. Experience in Latin America and central Europe (e.g. in Yugoslavia in the 1980s), has illustrated the failure of price incentives in the absence of property rights. Without ownership, managers and workers have incentives to make short-term profits, but not to preserve assets. Anyone observing the deterioration of rented housing in New York, power stations in the Soviet Union and some roads even in the US, will realize that maintenance is at risk without ownership.

To be effective, ownership has to be assigned to a clearly defined entity, which can be private or public. Owners generally find it to their advantage to maintain their assets, but owners also have the right to sell, lease or abandon them. In the case of roads, responsibility under existing arrangements is often unclear, especially (as in the case of the US Interstate Highway System) when nominal owners (e.g. states) depend on others (e.g. central government) for most of the funding.

A key element in property ownership is the existence of individuals who stand to become worse off if their property loses value and to gain if it gains value. Those individuals have strong personal incentives to maintain the value of their assets. In the case of publicly provided roads, although one should not underestimate the power of conscientious, well-trained and well-equipped officials, most of those concerned do not become worse off when the roads in their care become overcrowded or deteriorate. Indeed, in some countries, where road deterioration brings about new contracts for rehabilitation, the handling of big new contracts can actually make officials better off.

2.1.2 Accountability

Road users are usually in no position to reward those who supply them with good roads nor to penalize those who fail to do so. If road users wish to influence the way road systems are managed, they have to go through the political process to obtain changes in budget allocations or in the personnel concerned. This is a time-consuming process beyond the capability of the vast majority of road users. It is also a clumsy way to effect change: when they elect their governments, voters select one particular combination of policies and people over another. The state of the roads is just one issue of many, and voters would be unlikely to change the party in power just to improve the condition of their roads.

The officials responsible for the provision of roads are employed to execute the political decisions of the government. In most cases, their concern is to ensure that monies are spent as appropriated. They are not employed to ascertain whether these expenditures are consistent with the priorities of road users. Furthermore, in many countries, especially in Sub-Saharan Africa and Latin America, the officials concerned with roads are subject to governmental pay scales which are too meagre to allow them to attend to their duties on a full-time basis, so they cannot afford to do their jobs properly.

Matters are done differently in commercial operations, even in public sector ones. Customers dissatisfied with telephone or electricity service can address their complaints directly to the officials concerned. Where services are provided competitively, as in long-distance telephone service in the US, customers can take their business to another supplier, and often do.

2.1.3 Absence of pricing

The pricing of road space will be discussed in Chapter 3. The point to be made here is that, in the absence of commercial road provision, payments made by road users do not fulfil the normal functions of prices in market economies, namely, to enable users to pay suppliers for the provision of scarce resources. Instead, payments for road use are generally taxes paid into the general funds of governments. As a result, there are no price feedbacks from road suppliers to road users; users of high-cost facilities pay the same as those who use low-cost ones, and users of congested roads pay very little more than the users of uncongested ones. The point was put as follows by Tom Deen, a transport planner who later became Executive Director of the US Transportation Research Board:

> When all users of high-cost and low-cost facilities pay the same tax, the result is equivalent to the situation of an electric company which decided to eliminate individual meters and to bill customers not on the basis of their individual consumption, but by measuring total power usage and charging each consumer an equal part of the total bill. Not only is this inequitable; more importantly, it will eliminate incentive for conserving electricity. Many new houses would be heated with electricity, since an individual's cost would not be increased by a decision to install electric heating. Demand for power would soar, and new investment would be needed for new generating facilities. There would be no real basis for determining the proportion of total resources which should be devoted to power generation (Deen, 1963).

In the absence of pricing, public roads are available for all on a 'first-come-first-served' basis, road services being rationed only by congestion. Those whose time is least valuable stay on the roads, while those who cannot afford to waste time in traffic move their work or their homes to other areas. It is difficult to think of a more wasteful criterion for the allocation of a scarce resource — road space.

2.1.4 Absence of competition

The absence of competition is evident in three aspects of the roads sector:

First and foremost, expenditures on roads are determined as part of the periodic allocation of public funds, rather than in direct response to consumer demand. This means that the competition takes place in the political arena, in the tug-of-war for the favour of ministers. It is true that the private provision of additional roads is often allowed, but generally only on unfavourable conditions, as mentioned in section 2.3.3 below.

Second, when decisions are made to construct a new road, it is usually only one design that is considered, though competitive bidding for construction is often invited.

Third, in many countries road maintenance is carried out by full-time government employees, instead of being contracted out to private firms. Many of these employees give good service; but those who do not cannot be removed, and are a burden on those who do, or on taxpayers.

2.1.5 Absence of financial independence

A major result of the points made above is that those who manage the vast majority of roads have no financial independence: they have no sources of funds except government grants, and hence no responsibility to anyone except the government that is the provider of those grants. Managers have too few incentives to exert themselves, and even those who do feel energized to improve their road networks are constrained by lack of resources from meeting the needs of road users.

The significance of this factor can be illustrated by the comparison done by the Congressional Budget Office to determine whether the pavement condition of the tolled sections of the US Interstate Highway System differs significantly from the condition of the non-tolled sections The results showed that, when other factors affecting pavement condition were held constant, the condition of the tolled sections of the Interstate system averaged 17 per cent better than the condition of the untolled sections (Congressional Budget Office, 1985).

2.2 The US telecommunications network as a model for a commercial road system

Is it possible to envisage a management framework that could be applied to roads and which would be an improvement on the current 'public parks' model? Could such a framework offer the roads sector the commercial elements of ownership, accountability to customers, prices that reflect costs and demand, competition at every stage and financial independence? The US telecommunications network provides such a model.

The telecommunications sector resembles the roads sector in important respects. Both serve large numbers of customers, all of whom have exclusive control of privately-owned or rented equipment, and the rights to use their equipment by utilizing infrastructure over which they do not have exclusive control. Both roads and telecommunications are subject to congestion at specific times and places. However, the telecommunications sector — unlike roads sector — has learnt how to avoid the extremes of congestion and over-investment. It does this by adopting the pricing rules and investment criteria developed in market economies to make the best use of scarce resources. In a nutshell: those who provide telecommunications services raise prices at periods of peak demand, and the increased revenues generated thereby attract the required additional investment to expand peak-period capacity.

But are telecommunications systems competitive? In most countries they are operated as government-owned monopolies but, in a few — notably in New Zealand, the UK and the USA — competition is allowed. In New Zealand all services are open to competition, long-distance and local. In the US, competition is freely permitted only for long-distance services, with local services, mostly privately-owned, being operated as 'public utilities' subject to governmental regulation.

For the purposes of this book, the organizational framework to be used as a model for roads is the US telecommunications network: an agglomeration of over 1,300 independent companies, ranging in size from giants with over 18 million access lines to small family firms with fewer than one hundred. Most of these companies are private corporations, but some are municipally-owned and a few are cooperatives. All operate as separate profit centers yet together they provide an inter-connected network to meet the demands of their customers. All have to meet their costs out of revenues. Those subject to competition are able to charge what they please, except the American Telephone and Telegraph Corporation (AT&T) and the local monopolies, which are constrained by regulators.[1]

The US telecommunications system is chosen as a model for organizing roads not because it is ideally suited for the purpose, nor even because it is the most suitable of the telecommunications systems — the New Zealand system seems to be simpler and less restrictive. The US system is chosen because it comprises a wide variety of firms, all financially self-sustaining; because, despite substantial bureaucratic oversight, it delivers first-class services; and because it is well-known. Road systems managed along the lines of the US telephone companies might not be ideal, but they would indubitably be better managed than those we have now.

2.3 Basic requirements of a commercial road system

Readers are bound to object that cars are more difficult to handle than telephones, and that roads are bulkier than switches and cables. Of course they are. But the US telecommunications providers have important characteristics that could be applied to the management of a commercialized road system:

1. They have owners;

2. They are financially self-supporting;

3. They do not discriminate against privately owned companies;

4. Revenues go to those who earn them, not to governments;

5. They operate to common standards to facilitate interconnection.

2.3.1 Telecommunications operating companies have owners

It is difficult to overestimate the importance of ownership in market economies. Owners stand to gain when their assets earn more, and are therefore encouraged to innovate and to look for better ways to employ their assets. For example, telephone companies have developed public telephones that can be operated without coin-boxes; callers can charge calls to charge accounts or use magnetically encoded cards. Similarly, operators of toll roads have developed ways of collecting payments without the use of coins, and even without vehicles having to stop (see section 4.3 below). Not all owners innovate, but some do, and those who do not can learn from those who do. Clearly, the more owners there are, the more innovations there are likely to be; thus the spate of innovation in the US appears to have quickened after the break-up of the AT&T monopoly in 1984.

Ownership also encourages the preservation of assets. Even owners who have no interest in increasing the output of their roads — that is, in increasing the amount of traffic, or its speed, or its safety — are encouraged to preserve the value of their assets by ensuring that their roads are properly maintained. As was shown earlier (section 1.5), poor road maintenance is a major problem in many countries. Under present arrangements, the vast majority of roads do not appear as assets in any balance sheet, their deterioration does not appear as a loss, and those in charge of deteriorating roads suffer no penalties. Effective owners either maintain their assets or dispose of them.

It will no doubt be objected that ownership of roads will be of no consequence because roads do not earn anything. At this stage of the argument this point is well-taken but, as will be shown in Chapter 4, roads can be made to earn revenues almost as easily as telephones.

2.3.2 Telecommunications companies are financially self-supporting

Some of the 1,327 US telecommunications companies serve large or rich populations, while others serve small or poor ones; but all have to meet their costs out of revenues. To enable all households to enjoy 'universal service', there is a tradition in the US for local telephone services to be subsidized by long-distance operations, and these subsidies continue to this day, despite the 1984 break-up of the AT&T monopoly (Marcus and Spavins, 1993). But these subsidies do not absolve the managements of US telephone companies from meeting all their costs out of revenues, within the framework of the rules governing their operations.

2.3.3 No discrimination against private sector suppliers

The rules governing the US telecommunications system do not favour companies in the public sector nor do they penalize privately-owned companies. The situation is different with roads. The rules in the US — and in all other countries — definitely favour public road suppliers over private ones. For example, while most publicly provided roads are 'free', in the sense that payment is not required at the point of use, private providers of roads have to charge tolls which discourage use. To add insult to injury, in many countries (e.g. France, Mexico) toll roads may only be provided in corridors where there is an option to use 'free' state roads. Imagine the effect on retail food shops if they were allowed to open only next to government stores offering free or subsidized food!

Of course, as is shown in more detail in Chapter 4, use of state roads is rarely free, because of the charges made on the purchase, ownership and use of motor vehicles. But payment for roads by means of licence fees and fuel taxes is more convenient than by tolls, and private providers are denied the opportunity of being paid by these means. Furthermore, payment of road tolls is generally supplemental to the standard road use charges, so users of privately-provided roads have to pay twice: tolls to the road provider and road use taxes to the government.[2]

But the biases in favour of publicly provided roads are not confined to ease in payment methods. The difficulty in getting permission to provide roads is probably even more effective in discouraging their private provision. This can be illustrated by the example of the Dulles Greenway toll road in Virginia, which is described in section 7.6.1 below. Non-Americans might be surprised to learn that citizens of the US do not have the right to build public roads in most of their states. This point is not about the need to get planning permissions and environmental clearances, which is not disputed in this volume. In addition to getting these permissions, the promoters of the Dulles Greenway toll road had to get a bill passed by the Virginia legislature before they could get their road built and, having got the permission, they had to go to the state regulatory authority to seek approval for their proposed toll.

In the US, and in other countries, the manner in which public roads are financed also discriminates against private road providers. When US cities, states or counties wish to provide roads they are enabled to borrow funds at preferential rates by the mechanism of selling tax-free bonds, these bonds generally being guaranteed by the states, cities or counties that issue them. Private providers cannot rely on such guarantees (nor should they), nor are they able to sell tax-free bonds. The use by public bodies of their taxing powers to provide 'risk-free' funding enables them to provide roads at lower financing costs than can be afforded by private providers, who have to pay market rates for their funds.

2.3.4 Network charges are not paid to the government

Unlike road use charges that are paid to governments, telephone charges are paid to the telephone companies that provide the service. Many governments impose taxes on the use of telephones, but these are paid to the appropriate tax collectors by the telephone companies themselves; only in totalitarian countries are telephone and electricity charges paid direct to governments, which then decide on political grounds how much of the revenues to remit to the suppliers.

The situation with road user charges is quite different. In almost all cases they are paid directly into the general revenues of governments, which then allot some of the income to the roads sector. Even when governments establish dedicated 'road funds', the monies paid into them are kept in government accounts, where, as in Ghana and the US, they may be frozen or, as in Argentina, Britain, and other countries, the political process enables them to be diverted to other uses.

2.3.5 Interconnection

Another requirement for a road network that is mirrored by the US telecommunications system is a successful protocol for interconnection, which enables calls to be connected even over the lines of more than one company. In addition to physical interconnection, the US system also provides rules for the sharing of revenues paid for calls that use facilities of more than one company. A road system based on the US telecommunications network would have to offer similar facilities.

2.4 Application of the telecommunications model to roads

The argument made in this section is that a management system for roads in a free society should allow roads to be supplied on a commercial basis without discrimination against private providers and without payments for road use having to be made as taxes to governments. How can this be done without major disruptions to existing arrangements? This question comprises two major elements:

1. The organization of the roads and of the staff responsible for them; and

2. The design of appropriate financial mechanisms.

2.4.1 The organization of an effective road management system

To ensure that each road has an effective, unique, owner, the road system should be divided, in a manner appropriate to the country concerned, into sub-systems of appropriate character and size. The ownership of these sub-systems should then be vested in newly-created *Road Corporations*. The manner of system division would vary from country to country and in some cases all roads could be owned by one road corporation. Ideally, each road corporation should own roads used by a readily identifiable group sharing common interests. So long as each segment of road were owned by a clearly defined road corporation, the precise way in which the cake were to be initially cut would not be important, as ownership would give the road corporations the powers to make adjustments, e.g. to sell or transfer roads to one another or to private organizations; to split corporations that were too large; or to amalgamate corporations that were too small.

For example, in the US, ownership of state roads could be vested in state-wide road corporations, ownership of county roads in county-wide corporations, and of city roads in city road corporations. Ownership of existing toll roads could be vested in the toll authorities. A segment of state road could be part of either a state road corporation or a county road corporation.

Road corporations would be required to maintain the roads for which they were responsible, to operate them in a safe manner, or to transfer them to others. They would be empowered to levy charges from road users, out of which they would have to meet all their expenses, including rent for the land occupied by roads, which would be payable to the land owners, which could be public bodies. The precise powers of road corporations formed to own existing roads would have to be determined on a case by case basis. The British Airports Authority, for example, is not permitted to convert airport land to non-aviation uses, but the British Waterways Authority is allowed to convert canal facilities to other uses. Any surpluses of revenues over expenditures could be spent on road improvements or returned to road users in the form of reduced charges. Whether surpluses could be spent for other purposes — such as developing land for recreational or profitable uses — would also have to be determined on a case by case basis. One can envisage circumstances in which a road corporation owning costly lengths of under-utilized roads might wish to give some up to raise the funds needed to maintain those remaining.

The road corporations formed to own existing roads would be managed by directors representing the main interests concerned, including especially the road users, but also property owners and others with legitimate interests in roads. The method of appointing these directors could vary, having regard to the need to have them accountable to road users. They could be elected directly by road users for a limited term of office, or appointed by government on the advice of the various interests involved.

The staff employed by existing road organizations would initially be employed by the new road corporations, e.g. a county road engineer would continue to be the road engineer of a county road corporation. However, after a suitable adjustment period, staff would become the direct employees of their road corporations and would no longer be on the payrolls of their national, state or local governments. Their salaries would come from the earnings of their roads and would not be tied to government pay scales which, in some countries, are too low to attract qualified personnel on a full-time basis. On the other hand, road corporations with low earnings might, after an adjustment period, have to reduce the payrolls of their staffs.

A likely outcome of the creation of publicly-owned independent road corporations would be the emergence of specialist road management firms to serve them. These firms would in all probability recruit their staffs from experts already employed in road management or consultancy.

New, private, road corporations could also be formed, either to provide new roads or to take over roads surplus to the needs of the publicly-owned road corporations. The possibility of the private corporations providing new roads, so long as they meet the same conditions faced by publicly-provided ones, is an essential part of this proposal. For the threat or reality of competition would be the most potent stimulus to good performance by the publicly-owned road corporations.

2.4.2 Keeping the accounts of road corporations

This volume, written as it is by an author who has difficulty in distinguishing between accounting 'debits', and 'credits', cannot deal with the intricacies of accounting. It takes for granted that commercial road corporations will keep accounts designed to show road owners the financial health of their assets. As an example of what the finances of a commercial corporation might look like, Tables 2.1 and 2.2 show the balance sheet of the New Jersey Turnpike Authority on December 31, 1992, and 1993, and the revenues and expenditures for the years 1992 and 1993.[3]

There are however two questions of principle that need to be addressed:

1. How would the capital value of roads be assessed? and

2. Should road assets be depreciated?

Assessment of capital values In a market economy, values of capital assets depend on their earning power. If, for example, a publicly-owned road corporation wished to sell some or all of its roads, it would presumably invite bids and sell to the highest bidder. The bids would depend on the earning power of the road being sold, not on the amounts invested in it in the past. Thus, an expensive bridge that attracts no traffic would be worth no more than its scrap value.

Table 2.1
New Jersey Turnpike Authority: 1992-93.
Assets, liabilities and fund balances

December 31, 1993 and 1992

	1993	1992
Assets		
Cash	$ 33,839,708	$ 41,252,393
Investment, at cost which		
approximates market value	1,181,900,693	1,305,787,509
Receivables	4,587,413	5,257,449
Deposits in condemnation	547,486	547,550
Cost of investment in facilities	2,744,842,503	2,580,397,286
Other Assets	1,198,721	18,064,564
Total assets	$3,966,916,524	$3,951,306,751
Liabilities and fund balances		
Liabilities:		
Accrued interest payable	$ 79,860,479	$ 80,918,404
Withholdings from employees	642,291	577,063
Pension and deferred compensation	42,206,061	32,528,000
Toll revenues received in advance	199,921	201,220
Amounts retained from contractors and engineers	13,909,342	9,573,705
Other liabilities	5,978,310	6,049,631
Bond indebtedness	$2,855,931,751	$2,885,593,264
Total liabilities	$2,998,728,155	$3,015,441,287
Fund balances:		
Applied to retirement of bond indebtedness	53,230,000	31,720,000
Revenues retained	914,958,369	904,145,464
Total fund balances	968,188,369	935,865,464
Total liabilities and fund balances	$3,966,916,524	$3,951,306,751

Source: New Jersey Turnpike Authority (Notes omitted)

Table 2.2
New Jersey Turnpike Authority: 1992-93.
Income and expenditure

	1993	1992
Revenue:		
Toll revenue	$316,519,746	$ 312,535,187
Concession revenue	11,851,766	10,848,377
Income from investments	10,166,441	14,244,293
Miscellaneous	2,003,531	5,895,380
Total revenues	$340,541,484	$343,523,237
Operating expenses:		
Administration	12,324,615	12,696,948
Traffic control and police	18,281,339	17,554,780
Toll collection	55,549,420	55,263,617
Maintenance, repair, re-placement and reconstruction	39,585,380	36,492,606
Engineering	3,205,248	3,146,852
Insurance	24,475,920	18,789,560
Professional	2,154,251	1,812,297
Fiduciary fees	248,627	97,189
Pension, retirement and payroll taxes	14,082,289	9,820,910
Taxes	416,619	380,213
Other expenses		858,622
Cash discounts	(47,683)	(27,478)
Total operating expenses	$170,276,025	$156,886,116
Revenues in excess of operating expenses before interest	170,265,459	186,637,121
Interest expense:		
Turnpike revenue bonds	79,643,253	57,533,422
Total interest expense	79,643,253	57,533,422
Revenues in excess of operating budget and interest	$ 90,622,206	$129,103,699

Source: New Jersey Turnpike Authority (Notes omitted)

When judging the performance of a road corporation one could follow the approach of John Semmens (illustrated in section 1.4) and look at investment undertaken in the previous twenty years, and depreciated over a twenty-year period. But a calculation of this kind would only indicate the lowest acceptable return. A road subject to congestion pricing, as described in the following chapters, might earn revenues far in excess of the return on money invested in the previous twenty years.

How should road assets be depreciated? So long as the owners intend to keep the road operational, funds have to be put aside to replace equipment (e.g. for traffic control) when it becomes worn out or obsolete, and to renew road surfaces and other elements when they wear out. Only the land under the road can be assumed to last forever. So long as owners put aside sufficient funds to keep their roads to the required physical standards, it would not appear to be necessary to set aside reserve funds for replacing them. Indeed, the New Jersey Turnpike Authority does not set funds aside for depreciation, but is required by the State and its bondholders to preserve the long-term integrity of its roadways, structures and other facilities.

In addition to the basic accounting tables, Ian Heggie suggested that it would help road owners and managers to have annual statements prepared showing changes in the value of road assets, indicating losses due to deterioration and gains resulting from maintenance and rehabilitation work. A prototype 'road asset statement' is shown in Table 2.3.

2.4.3 Relationship between government and road corporations

Road corporations formed to take over existing roads would have to be subject to government regulation to ensure that the assets inherent in roads were safeguarded. In particular, decisions to extinguish rights of way would have to be subject to review and appeal. On the other hand, road corporations formed by investors to create new roads should be allowed to enjoy more freedom and less regulation, because the assets at risk would be assets they created themselves. This is similar to the situation with telecommunications, where traditional services to existing customers are regulated more than new ones, such as those provided by cellular phones.

Even under the commercial management of roads there would be important roles for governments. They should obviously have the last word on where new public roads should be permitted (without, however, discriminating against privately provided roads) and on law enforcement.

Table 2.3
Prototype road asset statement for a road agency

(millions of dollars)

	December 31, 1990	December 31, 1991
Fixed assets:		
Total book value at beginning of year	2,030.00	2,035.70
Adjustment for inflation	0	0
New works completed during the year	5.70	3.90
Total book value at end of year	2,035.70	2,039.60
Erosion of capital:		
Rehabilitation backlog at beginning of year	(670.00)	(714.31)
Rehabilitation completed during the year	14.95	6.94
Shortfall in recurrent maintenance	(29.63)	(26.59)
Additional rehabilitation costs	(29.63)	(26.59)
Rehabilitation backlog at end of year	(714.31)	(760.55)
Current value of the road network	1,321.39	1,279.05
Overall erosion of capital (per cent)	35%	37%

Notes:

a. Book values are calculated using the following replacement costs per km: paved, $250,000, gravel, $50,000 and earth $20,000.

b. Calculated for all roads in poor condition using the following costs per km for rehabilitation: paved roads, $230,000, gravel, $36,000.

c. Required maintenance expenditures based on the following values per km: paved, $4,000, gravel, $1,000, and earth, $400. Shortfall is the difference between actual maintenance expenditures (from income and expenditure statement) and required maintenance expenditures.

Source: Heggie (1995)

They should protect road users from exploitation by monopoly suppliers, and standardize and enforce rules relating to safety — it is not helpful, for example, for STOP signs to be used to indicate dangerous crossings in some areas and merely to slow down traffic in neighbouring ones. But the day-to-day operations of public roads could be left to commercial organizations, as are the day-to-day operations of public utilities such as telephone and electricity services.

2.5 Dedicated road funds

Readers who have followed the argument so far are probably wondering how, under the regime proposed, would the roads be paid for. Would the road corporations get their funds by stopping vehicles at toll booths set up at street corners?

Methods of charging for the use of roads are discussed in Chapter 4. All that needs to be said at this point is that one simple financing mechanism that could be used for funding the road corporations is the well-known *dedicated road fund*. With the safeguards to be described below, such funds could be used as effective payment mechanisms for the use of all roads, both publicly and privately provided, and be as separate from government funding as are the current payment mechanisms for electricity and telephone services.

Dedicated road funds were established in many countries, including Argentina, Britain, Colombia, Ghana, South Africa, the US (one federal fund and thirty-three state funds) and Zaire. Honduras recently created a dedicated road fund, the funds being kept outside the government finances. 'Road agencies' supported by dedicated 'road funds' for road maintenance are being set up in several African countries with technical assistance from the World Bank and Finland (Heggie, 1995). There is not the space here to consider the histories, strengths and weaknesses, of all of them, so attention will be focussed on the British 'Road Fund' which existed between 1909 and 1955, and the US federal Highway Trust Fund, which was established in 1956 and still survives. Both offer important lessons in road finance.

2.5.1 Rise and fall of the British Road Fund

The UK 'People's Budget' of 1909 provided for a vehicle tax, based on engine power, and a fuel tax, which was initially three pence per gallon, equivalent to less than a penny a gallon at 1994 prices. The revenues from these sources were intended to be used for improving the road system and to transfer the costs of roads from the rates (local property taxes) to the actual road users. While some road improvement was done, no relief whatsoever was provided for the rates. A 'Road Improvement Fund' (which later became the 'Road Fund') was set up, as a sub-account in the Treasury. According to Sir Edgar Harper, economist and Chief Valuer to the Inland Revenue (the UK tax authority):

> [The Road Fund] is not fed by taxation in the strict sense. It provides machinery by which the owners of motor vehicles in combination and under State guidance are enabled to spend money on roads for their mutual benefit (*The Times*, 5 February 1926, quoted in Rees Jeffreys, p. 58).

This solution to the problem of road finance was a total failure. The semi-autonomous Road Board, which had been set up to administer the Road Fund, was wound up in 1919 and the responsibility for administering the fund was transferred to the newly-created Ministry of Transport. Nothing was done to spend the monies accumulated in the Road Fund until, in 1926, the government repudiated the principle of linking road taxation to road finance, and 'raided the Road Fund' to get more general revenues for the state. In 1936 road use taxes were diverted directly to the Exchequer, and the Road Fund became only a convention in the government's accounts. It was eventually wound up in 1955.

The reasons for the failure of the original Road Fund were:

1. Both Parliament and the Treasury were hostile to the idea of having no control over monies raised by taxation;

2. Members of the Road Board, who were appointed by the Treasury and were not accountable to road users, had neither the enthusiasm nor the mandate for action, and allowed the Road Fund balances to accumulate unspent;

3. As the funds were raised on a national basis, and were to be spent nationwide, there were no linkages between payments by specific road-users and the expenditures made on their behalf; and

4. Unlike the toll roads and canals of the eighteenth century, and the railways and ports of the nineteenth, there was no private sector entrepreneurship in the selection of investments, in the maintenance of assets or in the pricing of their use. The Road Fund was an attempt to

improve a government operation, with road users providing the funding but having no control over the way their payments were spent.

2.5.2 The US federal Highway Trust Fund

For many years, American engineers and highway administrators led the world in promoting the idea that those who use roads should pay their costs. Thirty-three states have highway trust funds, and in thirty-two of them all the revenues collected from road use have to be spent for road purposes only (TRIP, 1994).

The US federal government was involved in building roads as early as 1802. In the nineteenth century Congress passed hundreds of laws providing federal funds for specific roads, but the arrangements varied from case to case and did not conform to any system. The amounts spent were comparatively small, totaling $17 million by 1891. Laws passed in 1916 and 1921 established the federal Bureau of Public Roads (the predecessor of the Federal Highway Administration, the FHWA) and defined a cooperative relationship between the states and federal governments which remains in effect today: 'The States' role was to select, plan, design and construct highway improvements while the Federal Government's role was to review and approve work done with the assistance of Federal funds' (Federal Highway Administration, 1988).

Prior to 1956, there was no link between highway-related federal revenues and disbursements for federal highway aid. In 1956 the federal Highway Trust Fund (HTF) was established by Title II of the Federal-Aid Highway Act to pay for the federal share of the cost of the federal-aid highway programme, which included the 41,000 miles authorized for the Interstate Highway System (IHS).[4] Title II increased some of the existing taxes paid by road users, established new ones, and provided that revenues from these taxes were credited to the HTF for the financing of the federal-aid highway programme. The main sources of funds, accounting for about 85 per cent of receipts, are the taxes on motor fuels, which were fixed at 4 cents a gallon in 1956 and have since been raised. The 1994 user fee structure is shown in Table 2.4.

There is a common belief that revenues accumulated in the HTF go directly to the road agencies to be spent on roads of their choice. According to Frank Turner, one of the most successful of the federal highway administrators, 'nothing could be further from the truth' (Turner, 1975). The only way that funds from the HTF can be allocated to expenditure on roads is by going through the normal budgetary processes of the US

Table 2.4
Federal Highway Trust Fund user fees

User Fee	Rate	Distribution of tax				
		Highway trust fund		Leaking storage tank trust fund	General trust fund	
		High-way acct.	Mass transit acct.		Deficit reduction	Not specified

Fuel taxes *(cents per gallon)*						
Gasoline	18.4	10.0	1.5	0.1	6.8	—
Diesel fuel	24.4	16.0	1.5	0.1	6.8	—
Liquefied petroleum gases	18.3	10.0	1.5	—	6.8	—
Neat alcohol (85% alcohol) made with:						
Ethanol from natural gas	11.4	3.15	1.5	0.1	6.05	0.6
Methanol from natural gas	11.4	3.75	1.5	0.1	6.05	—
Ethanol not from natural gas	12.95	4.0	1.5	0.05	6.8	0.6
Methanol not from natural gas	12.35	4.0	1.5	0.05	6.8	—
Gasohol						
10% gasohol made with:						
Ethanol	13.0	4.0	1.5	0.1	6.8	0.6
Methanol	12.4	4.0	1.5	0.1	6.8	—
7.7% gasohol made with:						
Ethanol	14.24	5.84	1.5	0.1	6.8	—
Methanol	13.78	5.38	1.5	0.1	6.8	—
5.7% gasohol made with:						
Ethanol	15.32	6.92	1.5	0.1	6.8	—
Methanol	14.98	6.58	1.5	0.1	6.8	—

Table 2.4 continued on next page

Table 2.4 continued from previous page
Other taxes — All proceeds to highway account

Tires	Over 40-70 lb, 15 cents per lb in excess of 40.
	Over 70-90 lb, $4.50 plus 30 cents per lb in excess of 40.
	Over 90 lb, $10.50 plus 50 cents per lb in excess of 90.
Truck and trailer sales	12% of retailer's price for trucks over 33,000 lb gross vehicle weight (GVW) and trailers of 26,000 lb GVW.
Heavy vehicle use	Annual tax:
	Trucks 55,000–75,000 LSS GVW, $100 plus $22 for each 1,000 lb (or fraction thereof) in excess of 55,000 lb.
	Trucks over 75,000 lb GVW, $550.

Source: FHWA Table SS93-22

Congress. Appropriations from the HTF differ from other appropriations in that the words 'out of the Highway Trust Fund' are used in the bills instead of the usual language 'out of any monies in the Treasury not otherwise appropriated'. The HTF was not formed to ensure that funds collected from road users were spent on roads; it was formed to ensure that 'no more than the yield of these taxes would go into the highway program. In other words, the HTF was originally designed to be a ceiling, rather than a floor, for the size of the program' (Turner).

It follows from this that the HTF was never a trust fund in any meaningful sense, and its custodians are under no obligation to spend its revenues for the benefit of road users. Legally, the HTF is a separate account (with the name 'Highway Trust Fund') maintained in the US Treasury, from which the FHWA can draw amounts determined annually by Congress. The FHWA uses these revenues to reimburse state governments for the federal share of expenditures previously made by the states. But Congress is free to attach any conditions it wishes to the appropriation of HTF revenues, and is also free to decline to appropriate them, so that they can accumulate to reduce the overall budget deficit.

Indeed, Table 2.4 shows that, as of October 1994, only 10 cents out of the 18.4 cents paid on each gallon of petrol (called 'gasoline' in the US) are credited to highways. 1.5 cents go to a 'Mass Transit Account' which was opened as part of the HTF, and 6.8 cents — more than one third of the revenues from the tax on petrol — is used as general revenues for 'deficit reduction'. In previous years, payments out of the HTF were also made to the Land and Water Conservation Fund and to the Aquatic Resources Trust Fund.

Strengths and weaknesses of the Highway Trust Fund The main strength of the HTF is that it has achieved its objective of greatly improving US highways at a low fiscal cost to highway users. Despite its reliance on comparatively low user fees, over a period of 33 years it succeeded in distributing some $213 billion to finance 43,600 miles of the Interstate Highway System and almost 840,000 miles of other highways covered by the federal-aid system. In view of the inherent weaknesses of the HTF, its success has to be attributed to the skills of the people concerned with making it work.

> Engineers and public officials have generally operated with care and good judgement within a process almost entirely dependent on those qualities (Pisarski, 1987).

But the US highway management arrangements, based as they are on federal/state relationships secured by the federal HTF, pose serious difficulties:

Divided responsibilities US highways suffer from the divided responsibility that arises from the 'partnerships' between different levels of government. This means that responsibility for all but local highways usually involves more than one level of government. For example, decisions in respect of federally-financed state highways — for which federal contributions range from 75 per cent to 90 per cent — require the involvement of both federal and state administrations; the states retain formal responsibility for their highways but do not have to foot more than a small percentage of the bills. This allows them to implement low-priority projects at federal expense, i.e. at the expense of the generality of US taxpayers.

Imposition of costly federal regulations Federal funds do not come free. As a condition for receiving them, states have to abide by burdensome regulations. Some, such as the Davis-Bacon Act wage provisions,[5] the 'Buy America' provisions and requirements for 'set-asides' in contracting, are mandatory for all federally financed programmes and are reckoned to raise highway construction costs by 20 per cent (Stanley, 1989), or even by 30 per cent in some states. e.g. Tennessee. Others, such as the imposition of 55 mph speed limits, and mandatory drinking age laws, are specific to highways. This is not the place to argue the pros and cons of these conditions; the point being made here is that the HTF is being used to force states to abide by controversial regulations which the federal government is unable or unwilling to legislate directly. Additionally, the administrative costs of the programme are of the order of 1.5 per cent at the federal level and 5–7 per cent at the state level so that, in total, highways financed through the HTF cost, on average, over 25 per cent more than if they were financed by the states directly.

Mechanical allocation of revenues between states HTF revenues are allocated between states in accordance with a complicated formula which attempts to take into account relevant factors of transport, population and geography. But even if the formula used to distribute the revenues among the states is the best that can be devised, it cannot replicate economic demand, i.e. the willingness of users to pay for road space. Some states receive less than their payments, while others received more. Alaska, the District of Columbia and Hawaii received eight times, almost four times and three times, respectively, of the amounts they paid into the fund since its establishment in 1956.

Leakage of funds In recent years the integrity of the HTF (which, as mentioned above, is not a 'Trust Fund' at all) has been eroded by the allocation of its revenues to non-road use. The most important leak is the dedication of the proceeds of one cent of fuel tax revenue (totaling about $1.4 billion a year) to public transport. The reduced tax on gasohol (which provides a 60-cent subsidy per gallon of ethanol used in the manufacture of gasohol) also represents a leak of funds, amounting in 1992 to $476 million (TRIP, 1994).

Over-emphasis on capital expenditure at the expense of maintenance The HTF was originally designed to finance only capital expenditure, e.g. new construction. Under the 1976 '3R Program', which was extended in 1981 to become the '4R Program', the HTF has also financed the resurfacing, restoration, rehabilitation and reconstruction of highways in the federal-aid system. Nevertheless, a programme which emphasizes cheap funds for new construction is bound to tempt state governments to tilt the balance against maintenance, and this may have contributed to the deterioration of the system. As was shown in Chapter 1, neither federal nor state highway authorities have any obligation to publish accounts showing liabilities for maintenance following new construction.

Backlash from non-highway federal issues The HTF can be affected by federal issues — such as the budget deficit — which are not specifically highway related. This enables Congress to keep HTF balances unobligated in order to reduce the magnitude of the budget deficit. According to one estimate, by the end of fiscal year 1993 there were at least $21 billion in the HTF that could be spent on new projects (Field, 1995). Criticism of this practice is not meant to suggest that highways should escape cuts in times of crisis; the point is that federal 'macro-management' of the HTF makes nonsense of the 'Trust Fund' concept and also freezes the federally-aided highway programme in a way that does nothing to ensure that the cuts fall on the least urgent projects.

2.5.3 Avoiding the errors of the traditional road funds

To avoid the mistakes of the past, modern road funds should incorporate the following features:

Revenues for road funds should not be treated as taxes paid to govern-ments, but as user charges paid to road providers. They should be lodged in special bank accounts, not in government treasuries. This is not to say that governments should not levy taxes on the use of roads — governments obviously have the legal right to tax whatever their laws provide for and, indeed, many tax the use of electricity and of telephones. But clear distinctions should be made between *taxes*, rendered to governments, and *user charges*, paid to service providers. While the disposal of tax revenues should be the responsibility of the relevant taxing authorities, payments by road users of road charges should be under the control of those responsible for providing or maintaining roads, namely the public road corporations described above, or private road providers. Road users should be represent-ed on the boards of the public road corporations, and have roles in deter-mining the levels of road use charges and the disposition of the revenues. The involvement of road users in determining road user charges and the disposition of revenues paid by road users is already well-established in New Zealand:

> User groups — trucking, agricultural, bus and car associations — are consulted when charges are set and are quick to mobilize when attempts are made to undertake inessential expenditures, or to divert funds (Heggie, 1991).

In keeping with Friedrich Hayek's admonition at the start of this chapter, revenues from road funds should be available to fund all roads on equal terms, without discrimination against commercially operated roads, toll roads, or privately-provided roads. Although recent US legislation allows the federal government to finance, out of the HTF, up to 50 per cent of the costs of some privately-provided roads, this funding is determined on a case-by-case basis, carries with it the usual obligations to abide by federal rules, and does not meet the Hayek criterion of non-discrimination against the private sector. It should be emphasized that the users of the privately-provided roads pay into the HTF at the same rate as the users of publicly-provided roads.

2.5.4 Establishing modern dedicated road funds

The arrangements for setting up dedicated road funds would have to depend on the circumstances of each case, but the following general comments could apply in most situations:

Areas to be covered As the funds would be a mechanism for raising money and distributing it within a single community, it would be desirable for them to be based on groups having strong common interests, similar living standards and similar transport conditions. For example, in the United Kingdom, separate funds for England, Scotland, Wales and Northern Ireland could be appropriate, while in the US — which already has thirty-three dedicated state highway funds — there could be separate state funds. In general: in small countries, one country-wide fund could suffice; in large countries, state or provincial funds could be more appropriate.

Criteria for distributing the revenues These should be clearly specified. The simplest would be to base the allocations on vehicle-miles of travel, with special care being taken to ensure that monies paid to cover the damage caused by heavy-axle vehicles should be credited to the areas where the damage occurs. But other criteria could also be agreed, for example, biasing the distribution of funds in favour of rural areas to make more of their roads financially viable.

Counting the traffic If financial distributions are to be based on traffic counts, the counts would have to be of unchallengeable accuracy. It would not be adequate to use human or mechanical counters on the ground, because of the risk and ease of cheating. However, air photographs, taken on a sample basis from aircraft or satellites, could provide reliable counts to any desired degree of accuracy. Traffic counting is, of course, as essential to good road management as is customer and revenue counting to good commercial management.

Collecting the revenues The revenues would not be paid to a government department but lodged in private banks under the care of trustees appointed by representatives of road users. The trustees would have one function only: to organize the traffic counts in their areas and distribute the funds in accordance with the agreed formulae.

Disbursing the revenues On the basis of traffic counts, the trustees would pay the road fund revenues to the road corporations, in proportion to their traffic, or in accordance with other agreed criteria. Thus, each road corporation would have earning power, and the earnings would accrue to its owners, which might be a motorway, city, or county road corporation, or a private corporation such as Midland Expressway Ltd., the company selected to build and operate the Birmingham Northern Relief Road, or the Toll Road Corporation of Virginia, which is constructing the Dulles Greenway near Washington DC.[6]

'Fiscal neutrality' The total amounts paid into road funds by road users would initially equal the total of governmental expenditures on roads, so that the changeover from the present to the new system would be 'fiscally neutral': the contribution of road users to general revenues would remain the same as it was before the change. However, once new systems get established, only taxes payable by road users into general revenues would be determined, as part of the budget, by those authorized to raise general taxation. The amounts payable into road funds should be determined by negotiations between representatives of road users and road providers.

Options of the road corporations While road fund trustees would have no option but to disburse the funds they collect, in accordance with the law, the road corporations would have alternative options within a general requirement to cater efficiently to the needs of road users. They could, for example, as is the case with existing road authorities, raise or reduce maintenance and/or safety standards; they could build new roads; or sell off old ones; they might (which existing authorities cannot do) vote themselves and their staffs increases in salaries. The extent of the freedoms to be enjoyed by road-owning organizations is a question that would need further attention in the countries concerned.

Other revenue sources The road fund is described here as a mechanism to enable all road providers to receive *some* revenues in accordance with arrangements agreed with representatives of road users. It is not suggested that all their revenues should come from such funds. As will be discussed later, there could be good reasons for road providers to seek other sources of funding, and these are not ruled out.

2.5.5 Irrelevance of the 'ear-marked taxation' controversy

Dedicated road funds are generally considered to be examples of 'ear-marked' or 'hypothecated' taxes which are opposed by some economists because they limit the discretion of central governments to spend tax revenues, and supported by others because they can cause expenditures to be more responsive to the wishes of taxpayers (McCleary, 1991; Teja and Bracewell-Milnes, 1991). This discussion is of interest to those who follow tax issues, but it is not relevant to road funds, because, as was stated by Sir Edgar Harper in 1920, road funds are 'not fed by taxation in the strict sense' but provide machinery to enable road users 'to spend money on roads for their mutual benefit'. Those who hold that road users should not be allowed to spend their money on roads must, to be consistent, also hold that electricity users do not have the right to buy electric power nor telephone users the right to purchase telecommunications services. Such people may be admirable citizens, loving spouses, and model parents; but they have little use for the market economy and this book is not for them.

2.6 Responsibility for road accidents

2.6.1 Should owners be legally liable for accidents on their roads?

If roads were to be provided commercially, should the owners be legally liable for accidents occurring on them? It is indisputable that governments do not take all reasonable measures available to them to reduce accidents. There are many ways in which road operators can, if motivated, improve safety. For example, roadside cameras in West London reduced accidents in one year by one third — from 297 to 187. Why are they not used more widely? According to a press report

> [M]ore widespread use of the cameras, which record registration details of a speeding vehicle,[7] is being thwarted because all the money collected in fines, estimated at more than £1 million a month, goes directly to the Treasury. Last night, one senior police officer said: 'If police forces and local authorities were allowed to use the money to spend on more speed cameras and cameras at traffic lights, then road deaths and injuries would decline more rapidly.' (*The Times*, 1994).

If the roads in West London were operated on a commercial basis, with the management held responsible for accidents, such cameras would have been installed, and the resulting drop in accidents would probably have been reflected in lower insurance premiums.

It is not difficult to think of other methods to reduce accidents: improvement of junction layouts, provision of skid-resistant road surfaces and greater efforts to detect and remove intoxicated drivers. In 1993, for example, because of lax law enforcement, only 27 per cent of the 18,330 drivers certified by the Virginia Department of Transportation as 'habitual offenders' had their driving licences revoked (*The Washington Post*, 1994).

2.6.2 Give insurers licensing and testing responsibilities?

There is no reason to believe that Virginia is either better or worse than other governments in keeping drunk drivers off its roads. While it would not be practicable to give road authorities the power to license or de-license drivers, could not insurance companies be given this responsibility?

In an entry which won the first prize in a 'reinventing government' competition, John Semmens suggested (Semmens, 1994) that road safety could be enhanced by removing from governments the power to license drivers and vehicles, and giving this power to the companies that insure them. If this suggestion is accepted, people would get their insurances and licences from competing insurance companies, and vehicle licence plates would no longer bear the words 'Arizona' or 'Maryland', but instead 'Prudential' or 'Equity and Law'. Road users unable to get cover from one company could seek it from another. This proposal has a number of obvious advantages:

First, it would solve the problem of those who take out insurance policies to obtain licences, and then cancel the insurance; under the Semmens proposal, such actions would effectively cancel the licences also. Second, it would make manageable the problem of those who drive while disqualified; the insurance companies would remove the licence plates. To clarify responsibility for compensation under this system, the rule should be that insurers would be held liable for any damage caused by vehicles carrying their plates. Insurers would then have strong incentives to make thorough examinations of the records of those who apply to be licensed, and to remove the plates of those no longer insured. To guard against forged plates, it might be necessary to embed in the plates electronic or other gadgetry which would enable cancelled plates to be quickly located.

Responsibility for licensing would imply responsibility for testing. It should not be difficult for insurance companies to license testing facilities for both drivers and vehicles. As the quality of the tests would have direct and substantial impacts on the profits of the insurers, testing methods would in all probability become more suited to identifying safety risks.

To meet the criticism that such a system would impose intolerable hardship on the uninsurable, Semmens suggested that

> [I]nsurers may wish to encourage or require some or all vehicles they insure to be equipped with safety-enhancing devices (for example, an ignition that can only be activated after the driver passes an automated on-board breathalizer test). Customers may choose to accept some limitation on their driving in exchange for reductions in premiums.

Thus, the proposal opens the way of getting uninsured drivers off the public roads, while offering even high-risk individuals the possibility of getting conditional licences. One of the most interesting aspects of the proposal is that, by privatizing the licensing functions, and placing them in the hands of organizations that would suffer significant penalties from errors and omissions, strong financial incentives would be created to increase road safety.

2.6.3 Are governments good at making roads safer?

Some of the earliest writers on road commercialization and privatization saw the heavy toll of road accidents as a principal reason for removing the ownership and management of roads from government and placing them in the market place, where competition and the threat of legal action would (so it was claimed) raise safety standards. The point was put as follows by Walter Block:

> It may well be that speed and alcohol are deleterious to safe driving; but it is the road manager's task to ascertain that the proper standards are maintained with regard to these aspects of safety. If unsafe conditions prevail in a private, multi-storey parking lot, or in a shopping mall, or in the aisles of a department store, the entrepreneur in question is held accountable. ... It is logically fallacious to place the blame for accidents on unsafe conditions, while ignoring the manager whose responsibility it is to ameliorate these factors (Block, 1979).

Block might have added that, for modes of transport which are commercially provided, such as by rail or air, managers are strictly regulated for safety, and accidents are generally followed by probing enquiries. This point was made more recently by John Hibbs, discussing an accident on the M40 motorway in which a school minibus crashed with a loss of 13 lives. While the exact cause of the accident was not determined, there was reason to believe that the driver had been overcome by sleep. Hibbs commented on the fact that the motorway opened without any rest or service area, due to objections from local residents to such facilities.

> [T]here is an inherent weakness in planning law, which enables a motorway to be opened in what it is reasonable to believe to be an unsafe condition. Were we to be examining the construction of railways, or tramways — or supermarkets or cinemas — there would surely be an outcry against such nonfeasance [omission of duty]. But, sad to say, no action lies against any real or fictitious person, it would seem, since there is no such thing as the beneficial ownership of a motorway (with or without its service areas). And neither does there seem any redress obtainable from the objectors to the planning permission for the M40 service areas, who must surely bear some moral responsibility for any accident arising from the absence of facilities for rest and refreshment (Hibbs, 1994).

Block and Hibbs suggest that road safety would be improved under commercial management, because commercial management would provide accountability, as well as financial incentives to reduce accidents. Whether safety standards under commercial management would in fact be raised would surely depend to a large degree on the safety obligations placed upon them. If, for example, managements were held responsible for accidents involving intoxication, managers would increase their efforts to exclude drunken drivers from their roads.

The idea that governments would be less committed to safety than commercial organizations may be surprising to some, but the Block/Hibbs position is strengthened by the record of the US federal government, which enacted the CAFE (Corporate Average Fuel Economy) legislation, forcing car manufacturers to reduce the average size of the cars produced in the US, making them less safe and increasing fatalities by an estimated 2,000 lives a year.

Legislating for the production of less-safe cars In 1975 the US Congress passed the Energy Policy and Conservation Act which required the fleet of cars produced in the US after 1984 to have an average fuel consumption of 27.5 miles per gallon. This statutory standard represented an approximate halving of the average fuel consumption of US passenger cars which, until then, were designed and produced to meet customer demand which reflected preferences for fuel economy but also for size and for safety. The only way the industry could meet the new standard was by producing many more smaller cars, which were less safe, thus giving new meaning to the gibe that Americans were willing to 'shed blood for oil'.

That smaller vehicles are less safe than larger ones is agreed by all who have studied the issue. For example, a US study (Insurance Institute for Highway Safety, 1990) reported that

> Overall, the death rate in the smallest cars on the road is more than double the rate in the largest cars. For every 10,000 registered cars one to three years old in 1989, 3.0 deaths occurred in the smallest cars on the road, compared with 1.3 on the largest cars. The death rate is at least twice as high in small cars, compared with large cars, in both single- and multiple-vehicle crashes. ... According to a regression equation estimated by Institute researchers from the death rates and EPA fuel ratings of 47 four-door cars, on average every one mile-per-gallon improvement in fuel economy translates into a 3.9 percent increase in the death rate.

And the Administrator of the US Highway Traffic Safety Administration estimated that the 1,000-lb reduction in average vehicle weight, and/or the associated reduction in size, that occurred in the US in the 1970s and 1980s, resulted in 2,000 more deaths and 20,000 more serious injuries per year (Curry, 1991). Note that the higher safety record of large cars is found not only in collisions between large and small vehicles, but also in one-car accidents (e.g. when cars leave the road and hit obstacles) and even when accidents involving only small cars are compared with those involving only large ones.

Another effect of this policy is to increase the cost of accidents.

> The shift toward more small cars with higher collision losses has resulted in higher overall collision losses compared with what the results would have been absent the downsizing. For the 1989 model year, the difference amounted to about $10 per insured vehicle per year or more than five percent of the $192 average collision loss payment per insured vehicle year (Highway Loss Data Institute, 1992).

The commercialization of roads could have had no effect on the results of the CAFE standards, but it could have reduced the casualties arising out of another US legislative disaster, the imposition of 55 miles per hour speed limits.

The imposition of 55 miles per hour speed limits In 1974, in response to the OPEC oil embargo, the US Congress decided that traffic speeds on US roads should be reduced to save fuel. However, the federal government has no authority over speeds on US highways — which are the responsibility of the states concerned — so Congress could not pass the required legislation. Undeterred by its lack of authority, Congress decided to enforce its will by holding hostage the monies paid by road users into the federal Highway Trust Fund. States were informed that their allocations of HTF monies would be cut if they did not enforce 55 miles per hour speed limits on all roads, including the interstate highways which were designed to accommodate speeds of 80 miles per hour.

The 55 miles per hour speed limit was so widely ignored that the laws proclaiming it fell into disrepute. For this and other reasons, Congress relaxed its attitude in 1987, and allowed states to raise speed limits to 65 miles per hour on portions of their interstate highways. Forty states raised the limits to 65, ten kept them at 55. What was the effect on fatalities? To the surprise of most observers, although fatalities rose on the interstates, state-wide fatalities declined by 3 to 5 per cent in the states that raised the limit, compared to changes in the states that did not (Lave and Elias, 1992). Two reasons have been suggested for these unexpected results: First, police activity was shifted from enforcing the 55 miles per hour limit to more productive safety activities; second, the interstate highways on which the speed limits were raised became more attractive, and a shift of traffic to those roads would tend to reduce fatalities because the interstate roads, being limited-access high-standard expressways, are safer than others.

These episodes appear to support the Block/Hibbs contention that commercial road operators would be more sensitive to safety concerns than government operators. It is difficult to envisage a commercial organization getting away, as the US Congress did with its CAFE law, with a policy that would save fuel at the price of increasing fatalities. Commercial organizations held liable for accidents and operating in the public limelight would have clear incentives to seek — and enforce — speed limits which, unlike the 55 miles per hour limit, would take safety into account. And there is evidence to back the proposition that commercial operators would have better safety records than roads operated conventionally: statistics compiled by the International Bridge, Tunnel and Turnpike Association (IBTTA) show the accident rate on roads operated by its members to be 0.6 deaths per 100 million vehicle-miles, compared to 0.9 deaths per 100 million vehicle-miles on the US interstate system, one of the safest non-commercial road systems in the world.

Despite this, it is difficult to recommend that commercial road operators should be legally liable for all the accidents on their roads. The analogy with the airlines and railways, who control those who drive their vehicles, is not strong enough. There are some activities, such as junction design, the enforcement of traffic laws, repairs to pot holes and the replacement of manhole covers, for which road providers could and should be held responsible. But responsibility for all accidents seems to be too heavy a burden for road providers so long as the agencies responsible for driver and vehicle licensing are not more successful in keeping unsafe drivers and vehicles off the public roads.

2.6.4 Risks to unprotected road users

How would commercial managements deal with the even more difficult problem of risks to 'unprotected' road users, such as pedestrians and cyclists? The only sure protection is to provide physical separation from motor vehicles. This would indubitably increase costs, possibly to an unacceptable degree. Decisions of this kind are a matter for the community concerned.

> To determine whether car-free roads, or pedestrian- and bike-free roads in the downtown area, or in a particular residential area, are to be preferred, is a complicated public choice which is best made at the municipality and/or neighbourhood level (Jansson, 1994).

2.6.5 Conclusions on road safety

It may be concluded that there is a strong case for making commercial roads organizations legally liable for accidents occurring on their facilities, where it can be shown that neglect on their part was a factor in the accident. This responsibility should be imposed within a clear framework of legal obligation. For example, unless road providers are clearly obligated to keep their roads free of ice at all times, it would be wrong to allow road users to sue them when cars skid in freezing weather. But, subject to such safeguards, legal liability for the consequences of clearly defined accidents would put managements of commercial road systems under constant pressure to reduce accident rates in accordance with the prevailing laws and the resources at their disposal.

Similarly, if insurance companies were given responsibility for licensing the vehicles and drivers insured by them, they would be under constant financial pressure to identify and remove from the road system those who pose dangers to themselves and to others.

Notes

1. AT&T is suing to have this restriction removed, arguing that it should apply to all long-distance carriers or to none.

2. Some might compare this to the practice of 'corkage', the fee charged to restaurant patrons who bring their own wine to consume with their meals.

3. The New Jersey Turnpike Authority was established in 1948 by the State of New Jersey to own and operate the New Jersey Turnpike, which is now 113.8 miles in length. The Authority is financially independent and its bonds are not guaranteed by its creator, the State of New Jersey.

4. Subsequent authorizations allowed the IHS to be lengthened to 48,000 miles.

5. The Davis-Bacon Act was passed in 1931 when migrant African-American workers competed with union labour for scarce jobs. It requires employers to pay 'the prevailing wages' for federal work, and US courts ruled that 'prevailing wages' meant union wages. The law also imposed union-based job classifications which, with restrictive apprenticeship regulations, sharply limit the ability of employers to hire or train unskilled workers. The effect of the law is to raise the costs of federal projects and to deny many poor people the chance of employment on federally financed projects (Brazier, 1994).

6. As the tolls to be charged by Midland Express Ltd. and the Toll Road Corporation of Virginia were determined on the basis that the companies would not receive governmental funding, any revenues they might get from a road fund should be passed on to road users by a reduction in the agreed tolls.

7. Speed cameras were developed in the 1960s by a Dutchman following a disagreement with the authorities about an alleged speeding offence by his wife.

3 Commercial pricing of roads

Road expenditures should be fully financed with revenues from a fee system consisting of an annual fixed fee for every road vehicle and a variable fee for using the roads. The way we pay for our telephone services could serve as an example of the kind of system I am thinking of. ... Increasing income from increasing traffic, as well as the possibility to raise the fee to pay for new or improved services, would make it possible to turn to the capital market for long-term loan financing (Dan Nasman, Director of Finance, Swedish National Road Administration, 1991).

In market economies prices serve two purposes: They ration available supplies among consumers, and they indicate to producers whether supplies need to be increased to meet changing demands. High prices discourage use and stimulate supply; low prices encourage use but discourage supply. Toll roads are the only kinds of road that use prices in this manner.

Road users are, of course, required to pay a variety of charges before being allowed to buy and own motor vehicles, and to run them on public roads. As illustrated in Figure 3.1, these payments are generally treated as taxes; they bear little relationship to the costs that arise out of road use or to the costs of supplying road facilities. Under a commercial system, the role of prices would be quite different.

How do commercial operators decide how much to charge for the goods or services they sell? Much has been written on this subject but the answer generally boils down to two principles:

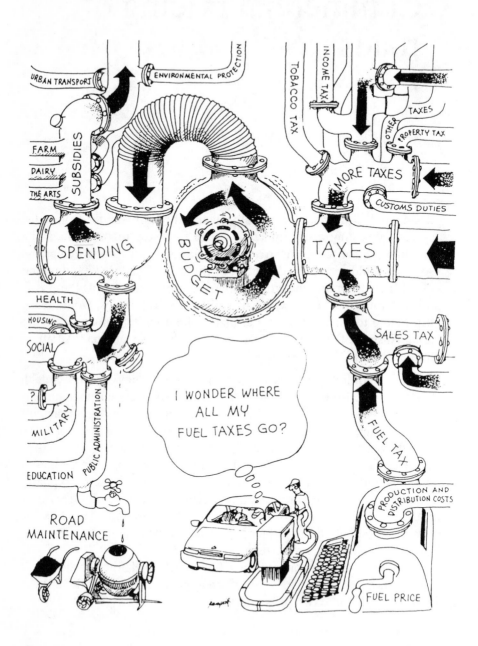

Figure 3.1 I wonder where all my fuel taxes go!
Source: UN-ECLAC, *Roads* (1993)

1. To charge *no less than* the amounts required to meet the 'direct' (or out-of-pocket) costs of providing the item in question, and

2. To charge *no more than* prices that maximize profits.

There is a common fallacy, described by Peter Drucker as one of 'The Five Deadly Business Sins', that prices should be based on some definition of cost. But successful businesses do not 'arrive at their prices by adding up costs and then putting a profit margin on top'; they are more likely to find out first what customers would be prepared to pay, and keep their costs low enough to enable their products to be profitable at those prices (Drucker, 1993).

The ability of merchants to charge different prices for essentially the same products has been recognized for many years and was described by the French engineer J. Dupuit in his essay on the pricing of public works:

> The same commodity in various guises is very often sold in different shops at quite different prices to the rich, the moderately well-off, and the poor. The fine, the very fine, the super-fine, and the extra fine, although drawn from the same barrel and although alike in all real respects other than the superlative on the label, sell at widely different prices (Dupuit, 1844).

This sort of 'charging what the traffic will bear' was also supported by Adam Smith, who wrote that

> When the toll upon carriages of luxury, coaches, post chaises, &c. is made somewhat higher in proportion to their weight than upon carriages of necessary use, such as carts, waggons, &c. the indolence and vanity of the rich is made to contribute in a very easy manner to the relief of the poor, by rendering cheaper the transportation of heavy goods to all the different parts of the country (Smith, 1776, p. ii, 246).

It is evident from the text that Smith's concern here was to help the poor not by general relief measures but specifically by reducing the costs of transporting goods.

Another way in which costs can be irrelevant to prices in a market economy may be illustrated by the bridge tolls in Guangzhou (Canton). New river bridges were built in the 1980s and tolls were imposed on them to cover their costs. Traffic reacted to the tolls by avoiding the new bridges whenever possible and using the old ones, which were still untolled. The authorities, unhappy that their new bridges were only lightly used, imposed charges on the old ones also, by requiring users to display passes that had to be purchased. As a result, traffic on those bridges fell by some 25 per cent and the remaining traffic was more evenly distributed between all of the bridges. As an incidental result, the city coffers also benefitted. The charges for using the old bridges were designed to improve the utilization of the city's road network, and had nothing to do with the historical costs of providing those bridges.[1]

It should be emphasized that the practice of charging 'what the traffic will bear', which is perfectly consistent with the two pricing principles enumerated above, does more than enrich the suppliers. It can also improve the lot of their customers, as is shown in the taxi episode (Box 3.1). By raising prices to those who can afford to pay more, providers of services, such as medical doctors, are often enabled to serve those who can afford only little. Similarly, the ability to extract first class fares from some travelers enables airlines to offer cheap seats to others.

In fact, the operation of a commercial airline illustrates the application of these commercial principles to transport. The conveyance of passengers by air involves unavoidable expenses: the costs of fuel, of food, of linen, etc, costs that can only be avoided by not undertaking the journey in question. Clearly, no rational airline would fly aircraft if it did not recover these out-of-pocket or 'avoidable' costs. Nor would the airline charge so much as to price its seats out of the market. It would observe the rates charged by its competitors and set its prices in the light of the prevailing charges for similar amenities.

Similarly, road corporations should charge prices that cover at least the costs directly caused by their customers' vehicles, which will be discussed later in this chapter. But there could also be good reasons to collect higher charges from those prepared to pay them, to enable the road providers to improve their finances and expand their services.

Costs arising out of road use What, then, are those direct costs arising out of the use of roads, which road users should always be required to pay? They can be categorized as follows:

1. Road damage costs: wear and tear of the road;

2. Congestion costs: delays imposed on other road users;

3. Accident costs: increased risks of accidents to others; and

4. Pollution costs: environmental costs imposed on others, both on and off the road.

These costs are of different kinds, and merit consideration separately.

Box 3.1 Efficient transport pricing in the Himalayas

A more modern example of efficient but 'unfair' pricing that seemingly bears no relation to transport costs was related by P.F. Amos at a conference in 1979 (Amos, 1980). His narrative is reproduced below in a slightly edited version:

Having taken a bus to the Nepal-India border from Kathmandu, and being first through customs, Mr. R.G. Bullock (a transport planner employed by the consultants R. Travers Morgan Pty Ltd) was advised that the bus to Gorakhpur would be delayed by at least two hours until all the other passengers had been processed. He was then approached by an Indian who was in a similar predicament, but in a greater hurry, who asked if he would share the one taxi which was available, going halves on the 60 rupee taxi fare to Gorakhpur. Mr. Bullock was willing to pay only 15 rupees. The Indian decided that he himself wasn't prepared to pay more than 30 rupees so he canvassed other travelers as they came through customs. He found one prepared to pay 10 rupees and another prepared to pay 3 rupees.

They all asked the taxi driver if he would take them to Gorakhpur for 58 rupees, and the driver agreed on condition that he could pick up other passengers en route to try to make up the other two rupees. The travelers agreed to this condition provided they all shared any extra rupees made in excess of the two. They drove to Gorakhpur, picking up and dropping off several short-distance passengers, making 6 rupees in total and sharing 4 of them, as agreed.

So all the passengers paid prices that reflected the intensity of their demand; the driver received his fee, capital equipment (the taxi) and labour (the driver) were fully utilized, and all received compensation for a somewhat slower and less comfortable journey due to the stops on the way.

This unique experience can provide food for thought for transport planners in more advanced economies as they wait in the rain for a taxi late on a Friday evening, while occupied ones drive past in great numbers, their 1.25 passengers per vehicle nervously watching the meters click up.

3.1 Road damage costs

For a road to be available to users it has to be designed, financed and constructed. However, as soon as it is constructed, it starts to deteriorate as a result of adverse weather conditions and the application of heavy loads to its surface, and it requires continuous *maintenance* to preserve it for long periods. If the road carries significant traffic it requires *operating* expenditures — traffic lights or other control devices, and supervision to help road users to cope with breakdowns and with the results of reckless driving.

Some of these costs — notably the damage due to loading — occur only as a result of use. They are known as 'direct' or 'variable' costs, because they vary with the traffic and are not incurred in the absence of traffic. Other costs, such as the original construction costs, do not occur as a result of use but still have to be incurred at some point. These are known as 'indirect' or 'invariate' costs, because they are not affected by the amount of traffic. Road maintenance and operating costs are partly 'direct' and partly 'indirect', depending on the circumstances of specific cases.

The costs of providing roads and keeping them in good order vary with many factors and also with one another. For example, increasing the pavement thickness can substantially increase road life: strong, thick road pavements incur significant fixed costs when built, but comparatively low wear-and-tear costs arising out of use. Road life is also increased by timely, effective, maintenance — road surfaces deteriorate rapidly if cracks are not immediately sealed.

William Paterson and Rodrigo Archondo-Callao (1991) categorized the main costs of road provision, as follows:

1. The costs of operating roads, such as lighting, traffic management (including traffic light operations), policing, incident management, etc;

2. Costs of road maintenance, including routine activities (such as clearing drains) which are continuous, and rehabilitation activities, which are periodic;

3. Costs of road improvement: widening, safety enhancement, etc;

4. Initial costs of construction, including land acquisition and interest on borrowed funds.

Each of these categories includes many different sub-categories of expenditure, as shown in Box 3.2. The extent to which road expenditures, in each of these categories, are related to traffic volumes can be summarized as follows:

Box 3.2 Road expenditure categories

Operation   Traffic management (guidance, control, etc.)
Facilities management
Administration
Policing
Incident management (accidents, hazards, etc.)

Maintenance: Routine maintenance:
*Pavement and shoulder (localized repairs including
    patching, crack sealing, etc.)*
*Reserve and drainage (vegetation control, drainage
    cleaning and repair, etc.)*
*Appurtenances (signs, lighting, pavement, markings,
    barriers, etc.)*
Structures (minor repairs to bridges, tunnels, etc.)
*Snow and hazard control (removal of snow, ice, debris
    and hazardous materials)*
*Emergency work (landslides, washouts, catastrophic
    damage, etc.)*

Pavement maintenance:
Restoration
Resurfacing (surface treatment, thin asphalt overlays)
*Rehabilitation (shape correction and/or strengthening by
    overlay, etc.)*
Reconstruction (replacement, recycling)

Structures maintenance

Improvement *Incremental capacity increases (alignment, widening,
    additional lanes, etc.)*
Facility upgrading (dualization, paving)
*Safety enhancement (barriers, intersection
    improvement, etc.)*

Expansion   *New construction*
Facility construction
Land acquisition

Source: Paterson and Archondo-Callao, (1991).

3.1.1 Costs of operating roads

These were typically 5 to 10 per cent of total road expenditures; about 70 per cent were found to be independent of traffic and only 30 per cent to be traffic-related. Thus, the traffic-related costs of operating roads often do not exceed one third of one tenth of total road expenditures.

3.1.2 Costs of maintaining roads

Table 3.1 shows that the costs of maintaining roads can vary widely, from less than 1 cent to over 8 cents per vehicle-km.

Table 3.1
Costs of road maintenance on different types of road
(US cents per vehicle-km)

	Main roads			Local access roads	
	Paved roads			Unpaved roads	
	Minor arterial	*Collector or arterial*	*High volume*	*High volume*	*Low volume*
Daily traffic	3,000	1,000	300	300	50
Normal loading (8 ton limit), high motorization (20% trucks)					
Variable costs	0.28	0.53	0.65	—	—
Fixed costs	0.29	0.84	2.40	—	—
Total	0.57	1.37	3.05	—	—
Normal loading (8 ton limit), low motorization (70% trucks)					
Variable costs	0.50	1.01	1.92	1.92	3.01
Fixed costs	0.32	0.92	2.68	0.91	5.48
Total	0.82	1.93	4.60	2.83	8.49

Notes:
   — Not applicable
   Based on data from a selection of developing countries that do not
      have any extremes of climate.
   US cents per veh-km is the average cost for all vehicles.

Source: Heggie (1995), based on Paterson and Archondo-Callao (1991)

To examine the extent to which road maintenance costs, over their lifetimes, are related to traffic and to axle loadings, Paterson and Archondo-Callao modeled the costs of maintaining five typical roads showing a wide range of traffic volumes. In all five cases the roads were assumed to have been constructed to 'optimal' configurations, i.e. the pavement thickness and maintenance regime were selected to minimize the total costs of the roads and their traffic. Some of the results are shown in Figure 3.2.

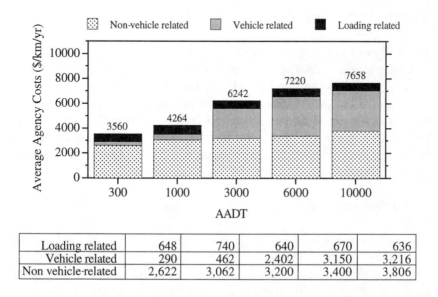

	300	1000	3000	6000	10000
Loading related	648	740	640	670	636
Vehicle related	290	462	2,402	3,150	3,216
Non vehicle-related	2,622	3,062	3,200	3,400	3,806

Figure 3.2 Attribution of maintenance costs to traffic volumes
Source: Paterson and Archondo-Callao (1991)

On light pavements it was found that, as traffic increased from 300 to 10,000 vehicles per day, the share of maintenance costs due to traffic ranged from 24 per cent to 74 per cent of total maintenance expenditures; on strong pavements, for the same variation in traffic, maintenance costs due to traffic varied from 2.5 per cent to 50 per cent of total maintenance costs.

The costs of maintaining unpaved roads were more sensitive to traffic volumes, while the costs of maintaining structures (such as bridges) were almost entirely weather-related, though the passage of heavy vehicles tends to open up cracks and increase the damage due to rain and frost.

A general trend identified by the study showed that only 46 per cent of maintenance expenditures were related to traffic, while 54 per cent of maintenance expenditure were 'fixed costs' in the sense that they would be incurred irrespective of traffic.

3.1.3 Costs of road improvement and capacity expansion

The costs of improving and expanding roads are all, of course, independent of present traffic levels, though they are determined by expected future traffic patterns.

3.1.4 Costs of constructing roads

The costs of road construction depend on so many factors — terrain, cost of land, pavement thickness, number of lanes, number and spans of bridges — that generalizations are not helpful. The only certainty is that new roads do not come cheaply. Costs per mile of modern expressways can be US$4 million in Mexico, US$10 million in China, US$20 million in the UK and $30 million in the US. Table 7.2 in Chapter 7 lists the cost and length of many privately-provided road projects, some completed, most still under study or construction.

3.1.5 Effect of axle weight on road pavements

It is well known that the damage caused by vehicles to roads is related to their axle weights. The most widely used formula suggests that this damage is proportional to the fourth power of axle-weight. For example, a doubling of axle weight multiplies the damage by sixteen, so that an 80,000-lb truck with five axles can do as much damage as 10,240 automobiles each of which has two 2,000-lb axles.[2] For all practical purposes, significant damage to road pavements is caused only by the passage of trucks equipped with heavy axles, and the fourth power relationship results in the heaviest axles causing particularly serious damage. For example, using the above assumptions, it can be shown that a vehicle with two 12-ton axles causes over three times as much damage as a similar vehicle equipped with three axles each carrying only 8 tons, although both vehicles carry a total weight of 24 tons.

A rational charging system for roads would take account of this, and encourage truck operators to reduce road damage by equipping their vehicles with more axles. The state of Oregon does in fact operate such a charging system for heavy vehicles, as does New Zealand. Information about them is given in the next chapter.

3.2 Congestion costs

Congestion costs arise out of the tendency of vehicles sharing limited road space to slow each other down. The sole user of a 'freeway' can travel safely on it at high speed, but congested conditions can bring all traffic to a stop. Although speeds drop as more vehicles join the traffic stream, it has to be recognized that every vehicle in the stream contributes to congestion, not just the latecomers. While it is almost only heavy axles that damage road surfaces, and require road pavements to be strengthened and thickened, all vehicles in traffic contribute to congestion, and to political pressures to increase road capacity.

3.2.1 Calculating congestion costs

Not all vehicles contribute equally to congestion. Measurements in urban areas show that a truck can slow traffic as much as two cars, and a bus (with its frequent stops) as much as three. Traffic engineers use the term *passenger car unit*, or pcu, to indicate the effect of a vehicle on the rest of the traffic. Thus, in the above example, an ordinary car is deemed to have a 'pcu value' of 1; a truck a pcu value of 2, a bus a pcu value of 3, and so on.

The effect of additional vehicles in slowing down traffic can be modeled by a mathematical formula of the type:

$V = V_{max} - Aq$, where:

V = Average traffic speed in miles per hour;

V_{max} = Speed, in miles per hour, when there is no congestion;

A = a constant; and

q = Vehicles per hour

To illustrate the application of this relationship, consider the observations made by the author on a network of ten streets in Cambridge in 1962. V_{max}, the speed at no congestion, was 24 miles per hour, and the constant, 'A', was 0.01091, which gave the following relationship between vehicle flows and traffic speeds in the city:

$V = 24 - 0.01091q$, where:

V = Average traffic speed in miles per hour, and

q = Vehicles per hour

This formula indicates that, because of traffic lights and other factors, a single vehicle could not traverse the network faster than at 24 miles an hour, even when unconstrained by traffic. As traffic built up, the speeds dropped in proportion to the increase in traffic.

By using this relationship, and a little mathematics, it is not difficult to calculate the delay costs that vehicles inflict upon one another. For example, in his paper *The Traffic Problem in Towns* (Smeed, 1961), Professor Reuben Smeed showed that, if speed changes are proportional to increases in traffic volumes, the delay T, in hours per mile, resulting from the addition to the traffic stream of one pcu at speed V, is equal to:

$T = (V_{max} - V)/V^2$, where

V_{max} = speed in mph (24 in our example) at no congestion.

This formula (or another appropriate one) enables us to calculate the delays, in hours per mile, imposed by each vehicle on others in congested traffic. By valuing these delays in terms of £ per hour, based on how time is valued, we can evaluate the delays caused in money terms, in a road network similar to that of Cambridge in 1962. A time value of £5 per pcu per hour is assumed in the following table:

Table 3.2
Congestion costs imposed on traffic by an additional pcu[a]

Traffic volume	Traffic speed	Delay imposed by one additional pcu	Cost imposed by one additional pcu[b]
pcu per hour	*Miles per hour*	*Minutes per mile*	*£ per mile*
600	14.57	2.40	0.222
700	12.99	3.90	0.326
800	11.41	5.82	0.484
900	9.83	8.82	0.733
1,000	8.25	13.86	1.157
1,100	6.67	20.40	1.945

[a] Passenger car unit

[b] Time valued at £5 an hour

Source: Author's measurements and calculations

The relationships shown above, which are typical of those observed in the traffic stream, illustrate the mechanism which causes congestion costs to be imposed by each vehicle on others. Time losses are probably the largest component of congestion costs, but congestion also results in increased fuel consumption and vehicle wear-and-tear, and in additional pollution. As a first approximation, all these costs may be assumed to be proportional to time losses, and they can be allowed for in the calculation shown above by appropriate increases in the value of time. It is however evident that the magnitude of congestion costs is critically dependent on the money values assigned to time savings.

Can such relationships, with the value of time being increased to allow for other time-related losses, help us to calculate the price to charge road users in order to maximize the benefits obtainable from congested roads? Before attempting to answer this question it is necessary to ask whether it is fair to charge road users for the congestion they cause.

3.2.2 Is it equitable to impose congestion charges?

Any discussion of congestion charges is bedeviled by the natural objection to any suggestion that road users already suffering from congestion should be required to pay extra. To require those who are already getting a bad deal to pay more, to enable some to get improved conditions, seems to fly in the face of what is fair. Egalitarians may consider it 'fairer' that all should get equal but poor service, rather than that some would become worse off and some better off. These equity issues are discussed in Chapter 6. All that can be said here is that a congestion charge would make better use of the congested facility, and that the revenues generated could be used to expand it, or to improve the situation of those forced off by the higher price. The following ferry-boat analogy might shed light on this issue:

Consider a situation where passengers crossing a river on a ferry-boat can gain 12 pesos from their journeys, for example by picking apples. Assume that each person values time at 1 peso a minute and that each person on the boat increases its journey time by one minute. How many people will there be on the boat? How many people should there be if economic benefits are to be maximized?

Table 3.3 gives the answer to these questions, and sceptics are invited to check them with their calculators.

Column 1 shows the number of passengers on the boat.

Column 2 shows the resulting journey time, on the assumption that when there is only one passenger, journey time is four minutes.

Column 3 shows the gross benefit for each passenger. This is always 12 pesos (Column 3), the value of the apples obtainable at the other side.

Column 4 shows the net journey benefit for each passenger, that is, the value of the apples (12 pesos – Column 3) less the cost of the journey time (Column 2), valued at 1 peso a minute.

Column 5 shows the total net benefit obtained by all the passengers; it is calculated by multiplying the number of passengers (Column 1) with the net benefit per passenger (Column 4).

Column 6 shows the total delay costs due to each additional passenger when time is valued at 1 peso a minute.

Table 3.3
Benefits and costs on a ferry-boat

(1) Number of Passengers	(2) Journey time	(3) Gross journey benefit to each passenger	(4) Net journey benefit to each passenger	(5) Total net benefit	(6) Delay cost due to each additional passenger
	Minutes	*Pesos*	*Pesos*	*Pesos*	*Pesos*
1	4	12	8	8	—
2	5	12	7	14	1
3	6	12	6	18	2
4	7	12	5	20	3
5	8	12	4	20	4
6	9	12	3	18	5
7	10	12	2	14	6
8	11	12	1	8	7
9	12	12	0	0	8

Source: Author's imagination

How many passengers will there be in the boat? It is clear from the table that there will be eight, each benefitting one peso from the journey. For if there were only seven passengers it would still be to the advantage of an eighth to join them. But if there were nine, the total journey time would become 12 minutes and, with time valued at a peso a minute, there would be no journey benefit to anyone, so the journey would not take place.

But Column 5 shows that eight would not be an efficient arrangement, because benefits are maximized when there are only four or five passengers making the journey. When the number of passengers exceeds five, the costs imposed by each passenger on the others exceed the net benefits that each additional passenger gets. Nevertheless, the boat will still be loaded with eight passengers because each, when considering only the benefit to themselves individually, would still find the journey worthwhile.

How could a better solution be reached? If passengers could bargain among themselves, seven of them could gain four pesos by paying the eighth two pesos to stay behind and that passenger, who would be getting two pesos for not making the trip instead of one for making it, would also be better off. But if there are large numbers of passengers, bargaining would not be practicable.

In a 'command economy' rules could be passed forbidding boats carrying apple pickers to carry more than five passengers. The fortunate five might be deserving party officials, or selected by lottery, or else the boatman could be instructed to leave as soon as five passengers were in place, in which case queues would form.

In a market economy the problem would be solved by the ferryman imposing a surcharge on the fare of, say three and one half pesos. Any fee less than 4 pesos would result in five passengers being in the boat, each imposing delay costs of four pesos on the others. A three and a half peso surcharge would give the ferryman 17.5 pesos extra revenue. If he were to make a large profit at that price, he might replace his boat with a bigger or faster one because, if he did not, a competitor would be likely to do so. Note that a bigger and faster ferry-boat would benefit many more passengers than the four or five who, in our scenario, agreed to pay the surcharge.

Another solution might be for the passengers to get together and buy the ferry-boat from its owner. But, once they become the owners, it would be to their advantage to operate it as profitably as possible, and to distribute the profits among themselves, rather than to allow the ferry-boat to be operated in an overcrowded and less profitable manner.

This analogy shows that there are situations in which users of a scarce resource, if left to follow their own individual interests, would not use it to best advantage. Operational efficiency requires a suitable institutional arrangement. In the case of the congested road, as in the case of the ferry, such an arrangement could be provided either by 'command' or by ownership of the scarce resource. Ownership has the advantage that it would generate funds which could be used to improve the service, or in other ways preferred by the owners. A 'command' solution would not generate funds, nor would it generate 'willingness to pay' information which would help to assess the need for further investment.

3.2.3 Calculating benefit-maximizing congestion charges

Congestion costs are not ordinary costs. We do not often hear of 'congestion costs' as posing problems in the hotel and theatre business, nor even in respect of telephone and electricity supply. If there were congestion in those commercial sectors — manifested for example by long queues of customers waiting to be served — prices would be raised to expand supply and dampen demand. Congestion costs arise on roads because those who use them are not confronted with prices that take account of the delays they impose on other road users.

The calculations made for Table 3.2 show that, at a flow of 900 pcu per hour, 'traffic speed would be 9.83 mph and the congestion costs imposed by each vehicle on the rest of the traffic would be at the rate of £0.733 per pcu per mile. Careful road owners, whether in the private or the public sector, would attempt to keep off their roads any vehicle whose journey was of less benefit than the costs of £0.733 per mile imposed on the rest of the traffic. The simplest way to ensure that the network was only used by those to whom the journey was worth more than £0.733 would be to charge that amount. The effect of such a fee would be to reduce the traffic, because not all road users would pay it. The new flow might be 700 pcu per hour, at which the speed would rise to 12.99 mph and the congestion cost imposed on others would fall to £0.326 per mile, well below the imposed fee of £0.733. Under these new circumstances, the fee would be too high, and all-knowing road-owners would lower it, trying to find the price which just equalled the costs imposed on the rest of the traffic *in the conditions prevailing after the charge was imposed*. At this price the benefits to the traffic would be maximized, in the sense that a higher price would deter too many vehicles — including some imposing costs that were lower than the fee they were charged — while a lower price would allow road use to too many vehicles, including some imposing on the rest of the traffic costs in excess of the benefits which they themselves received.

Note that, in this scenario, the 'correct' price for the use of congested roads would be influenced by the value assumed for time. In situations where time values were high, delay costs would be higher and so would be the prices for the use of congested roads. These high prices would force some traffic off the congested road, so the speed of the remaining traffic would rise as traffic volumes fell. Where time is cheap, road prices should be set at lower levels to allow roads to accommodate higher traffic volumes moving at lower speeds.[3]

Congestion charges in a market economy The method described above for calculating the 'proper' prices for the use of congested roads would not be appropriate in a market economy, where prices are fixed by interactions between willing buyers and willing sellers. If roads were operated like other productive assets in a market economy, they would have owners, and the owners would charge fees for their use. How would a market economy determine the fees to be charged on congested roads?

It was suggested at the start of this chapter that, in a market economy, owners of assets would be likely to charge amounts that would maximize their profits. In the case of roads, charges would depend on what users were prepared to pay, which, in turn, would depend on the alternatives available to them. If the road owners were subject to competition — if the traffic could readily take alternative routes — the road charges could not, in the long run, exceed the total costs of providing similar road facilities, because competition would drive down the charges to the point at which the facilities could earn only 'normal' profits.

If the owners enjoyed monopoly power, they could, if they were allowed to, charge more than the costs of providing the required facilities, and collect more than the amounts required to keep them in the roads business.[4] In market economies, the prices that may be charged by monopolists are generally regulated, to protect consumers.

Two approaches have been described in this section for calculating the appropriate charges for the use of congested roads: one, based on the costs of delays imposed by road users on one another, the second on the interest of competitive road owners to maximize their profits. Would calculations based on these different approaches lead to the same result? If not, which is to be preferred?

It is beyond the scope of this book, and the abilities of its author, to plumb the depths of this problem. It was noted, however, that the calculation of congestion charges on the basis of delay costs requires assumptions to be made about the value of time, which is itself a highly contentious issue. It could be argued that, in a competitive market economy, the value of time to choose in estimating delay costs is the one that would result in the same answer being produced by both approaches. This is because willingness to pay high congestion charges is a reflection of high valuations of time. As to the preferred method of arriving at the optimal congestion charge, readers can take their choice. Those of us who support market economies are likely to prefer valuation methods based on the interactions of buyers and sellers in competitive markets to prices determined by governments on the basis of academic studies.

Recent estimates of plausible congestion charges Some will feel that conditions in Cambridge in 1962 are no longer relevant to decision-making in the 1990s. More up-to-date estimates of congestion charges can be found in reports of the London road pricing study commissioned by the Department of Transport in 1991. Table 3.4 shows some of the charges that were modeled and preliminary assessments of their possible effects on travel in the area by car, rail and bus.

The estimates in Table 3.4 indicate that charges based on mileage would produce higher revenues, but lower benefits, than cordon charges. This is surprising as, if the prices were right, one would expect higher benefits from mileage- than from cordon-charges, because vehicles would not pay congestion charges while using roads within the cordons. In practice, the benefits and revenues would be sensitive to such factors as the spacing between cordons and the levels of the mileage charges, and the best system could only be found by trial and error. These preliminary results were regarded as tentative by all concerned, but they may well indicate the effects to be expected from congestion charges in a city such as London.

3.2.4 Are congestion-free roads desirable?

Should governments aim to provide roads that are free of congestion at all times? This would not be an economic solution. If road users do not impose any congestion costs on one another, the benefits generated by the road network could be increased by allowing more traffic on it, up to the point at which those who find it least worthwhile to use the network receive benefits from using it equal to the costs imposed by them on the rest of the traffic. At this point the network would be operating at its 'optimal economic capacity' (Roth, 1965). Admitting more traffic to the network at this point would reduce its usefulness, as some vehicles would be imposing costs in excess of the benefits associated with their presence in the congested traffic.

Congestion-free roads are also unsatisfactory from the point of view of the road providers, who would stand to benefit from congestion charges to generate the payments required to pay for the capital costs of the congested facilities. Thus, a more efficient solution than congestion-free road networks would be networks congested to the extent that efficient congestion charges (i.e. charges equal to the costs imposed on the rest of the traffic) yield sufficient revenues to pay their capital costs. This aspect is discussed in more detail in Chapter 5.

Table 3.4
Effects of hypothetical congestion charges in London, 1991

	Assumed charges			
	Inbound cordon		Distance, per mile	
	£2	£4	40p	80p
Change in car km (%)				
— centre all day	−16	−29	−13	−23
— centre am peak	−16	−29	−14	−26
— centre pm peak	−17	−30	−15	−27
— inner London all day	− 2	− 3	− 1	− 2
— inner London am peak	− 2	− 3	− 1	− 2
Rail demand (i)	+ 2	+ 3	+ 2	+ 3
Bus demand (ii)	+ 7	+13	+ 6	+11
Revenue from congestion charges *(£m p.a.)*	150	260	210	400
Economic benefit *(£m p.a.)*	110	160	100	150
% change in				
— Fuel consumption	− 2	− 3	− 2	− 3
— Pollution (iii)	−23	−40	−20	−32
— Accidents (iv)	− 3	− 2	− 1	− 1

Notes:
  i)   % change in trip-km for peak period rail trips with destinations in the central area.
  ii) % change in trip-km for peak period bus trips with destinations in central/inner area.
  iii) In charged area.
  iv) Based on changes in vehicle-km.

Source: Department of Transport (1994)

Charging for the use of congested roads To be efficient and effective, charges for the use of congested roads should be applied selectively, with the prices reflecting congestion levels at different places and at different times of the day, as is done with telephone charges. For this reason alone, collection at conventional toll booths would be impracticable. Conventional toll booths would also impose unacceptable delays to traffic. However, electronic charging systems, which are described in Chapter 4, can vary prices from one place to another and from time to time.

3.3 Accident costs

3.3.1 The magnitude of road accident problems

The World Health Organization estimates that about 600,000 people are killed on the world's roads every year, and that about three-quarters of the deaths occur in developing countries. There can be few readers who have not felt direct personal loss from road accidents. They clearly pose problems of the utmost gravity. In high-income economies road accidents are one of the leading causes of death in the 5- to 44-years age group, typically accounting for 15 per cent of mortality and of hospital bed occupancy. Figure 3.3 shows that, in the UK, road accidents were the leading cause of accidental deaths in 1992, despite reductions compared to 1991 levels.

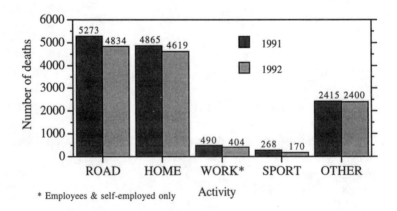

Figure 3.3 UK accident fatality rates: 1991 and 1992
Source: Royal Society for the Prevention of Accidents

But, while the situation is slowly improving in the high-income countries, it is getting worse in the developing ones, where road death and injury rise in relative importance as death from disease is reduced. (Downing and others, 1991). As shown in Figure 3.4, the numbers of fatalities per motor vehicle can be over ninety times as high as in Western countries.

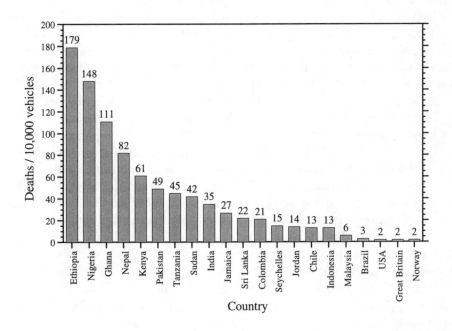

Figure 3.4 Road accident fatality rates 1988-1990
Source: Transport Research Laboratory, Ref. TRL20978
      Based on Downing and others (1991)

In Thailand, for example, more years of potential life are lost through road accidents than from tuberculosis and Malaria combined; in Mexico accidents as a cause of death rose from 4% in 1955 to 11% in 1980, with traffic accidents playing the leading role (Yerrell, 1992).

How should accidents be dealt with in a market economy? Should our policies be designed to eliminate them entirely?

While many would be willing to expend all their available resources to avoid specific accidents to themselves, to relatives or friends, and even to other identifiable individuals such as lost mountaineers or injured children, it is quite a different matter to devote resources to reducing the chances of accidents to people not identified, or even to oneself. People can get killed by falling out of windows, yet not all windows are barred, even when children are at risk. Skiers could avoid accidents by giving up skiing, but they keep skiing in increasing numbers.

Similarly, road users take risks. Do we always use our car seat-belts? Do motor-cyclists always don their safety helmets? Do we always use pedestrian crossings? In the UK only 89 per cent of pedestrians use them; in Bangkok only 48 per cent; and in Karachi only 20 per cent. In their daily activities, most people will go so far — but no further — to avoid accidents, some being more risk-averse than others. This is because accident avoidance is not free. It involves either giving up pleasurable but risky activities, (such as skiing) or spending money (buying more expensive equipment) or being continuously vigilant (buckling up safety belts).

Furthermore, reducing accidents in some areas can increase them in others. Chapter 2 gave the example of the freeway 55 mph speed limits which reduced accidents on the freeways themselves but increased accidents on other roads and overall. The US aviation authorities withdrew a proposal to require increased safety for infants in aircraft after it became convinced that the increased costs would induce some passengers to switch to car travel which is generally more dangerous than air travel.

Given the fact that the use of roads is bound to result in some accidents, what should we do to minimize their incidence? If economists were all-powerful, they would introduce accident avoidance measures that do not exceed the costs of the accidents avoided. This might be a correct approach in theory, but not one that can be readily applied. There are however two principles that could guide the daily actions of road managers:

1. Those who cause risks to others should purchase sufficient insurance to enable them compensate victims in the event of an accident, and

2. All concerned with road conditions should be under the pressure of strong incentives to reduce accidents.[5]

3.3.2 How much insurance? The costs of accidents

In a market economy the costs of accidents should be borne by those who cause accidents, or who make them more likely. The previous chapter suggested that road providers should have some legal liability for accidents occurring on their roads and, of course, road users should also be able to meet claims against them arising out of road accidents. As the sums involved can be high enough to bankrupt most people, the only practicable way of ensuring that payment is made is to require road users to insure themselves. The insurance approach has the advantages that those who succeed in reducing accidents pay lower premiums while those considered more likely to cause them can be charged higher premiums. In market economies, insurance can be provided commercially and competitively.

Accident costs Accidents can involve death, injury and property damage. Injuries range in severity from those involving permanent disability (e.g. brain damage or loss of limb) to the insignificant, and there is also a wide range of property damage. For this reason, many accident studies focus on fatal accidents, usually defined as accidents in which death occurs within thirty days

The costs of fatal accidents, and indeed of all accidents, are dominated by the costs attributed to loss of life. The old way of estimating this cost in the UK (as followed by the author in the Road Research Laboratory in the 1950s) was based on net contributions to 'gross output'. This was obtained by calculating the lost value of the future output of accident victims over their lifetimes, and deducting from those sums the value of the resources they would have consumed. The inadequacy of this methodology is evident from the fact that the deaths of those retired from gainful employment were treated as benefits!

More recent methodologies base fatality costs on what road users themselves would be prepared to pay to reduce the risk of a fatal accident. For example, people observed to pay $1,000 to reduce the risk of death by 1 in 2,000 are assumed to value their lives at $2 million. This approach, which, in a free society, seems more appropriate than attempts to measure changes in total output, indicate that people in Western countries are prepared to pay US$1–12 million to reduce the probability of one fatal accident, and therefore 'values of life' are considered to lie in this range. In the UK, the value of a 'statistical life' was taken by the Royal Commission on Environmental Pollution to have been £744,060 in 1994, while in New Zealand, it was NZ$2.0 million (about £775,000 or US$1.2 million) in 1993. Estimates in the US range from $2.1 million to $11.3 million at 1992 prices, with a geometric mean of $4.87 million (Small and Kazimi, 1995).

Determination of premium levels The premiums payable depend on the risks involved which, in their turn, depend on the chances of accidents occurring and on the amounts payable in the event of accidents. The chances of accidents depend on distances covered, and on driver and vehicle characteristics. For example, in Great Britain in 1987, the average driver faced a risk of 8 in 100,000 of being killed, and of 100 in 100,000 of being seriously injured. Drivers of ordinary motorcycles faced above-average risks of accident, while drivers of motorcycles with side-cars faced below-average risks. Having regard to considerations such as these, M.W. Jones-Lee (1990) calculated that the appropriate premium to meet accident risks in Great Britain in 1987 was £140 a year, or about 1.4 pence per mile for a vehicle covering 10,000 miles a year. Jones-Lee pointed out that £140 was substantially in excess of premiums paid at the time by motorists in Britain enjoying 'no-claims bonus', and that a tax of about 14 pence per gallon of fuel (over and above the insurance premium) would have been appropriate to raise the cost paid by road users to the level required to cover accident costs. This amount was compared by Jones-Lee to the petrol excise duty of over 92 pence per gallon that road users in Britain were already paying at that time.

It does seem therefore that, at least in Western countries, premiums to cover the accident risks of drivers with good records need not be out of line with amounts already being paid for car insurance. If it is considered necessary, various arrangements could be made to enable road users to pay accident costs not covered by their insurance policies, for example, costs due to 'hit and run' drivers. One way of charging for such costs would be to create an insurance fund financed by a surcharge on fuel.

Insurance for accident-prone individuals Some drivers have such poor safety records that it is impossible to find insurance companies that agree to insure them. The costs of allowing such individuals on public roads may be so high that society would benefit from their exclusion but, perversely, arrangements can be made by the insurance industry (as in the US, under state government pressure) to accommodate even those who cannot get insurance on a commercial basis, to allow them to continue to be a menace to themselves and other road users. This is another example of the way in which governmental actions reduce road safety. As mentioned in the previous chapter (section 2.6) a better way of dealing with accident-prone road users might be to make their insurers responsible for conditionally licensing them and their vehicles.

Conclusions on accidents Road accidents pose serious problems, especially in developing countries, but commercial insurance, affordable by most road users, could mitigate the financial risks and also exert pressure to raise safety standards. Risks not covered by personal insurance policies could be covered by a surcharge on fuel.

More questions Should road users be required to insure against the loss of their own lives to protect their dependants? If they have no dependants, should they still be required to insure their own lives? Such questions, and many others concerning safety and mobility, cannot be pursued in this chapter, which must now consider the environmental costs resulting from road use. These costs are due to many effects including noise and visual intrusion, but this book will consider only the ones receiving the most publicity: the costs arising from air pollution.

3.4 Pollution costs

For reasons that are not clear, pollution costs attract much more attention than accident costs, though the latter are generally considered to be significantly higher. For example, according to one of the best known studies on pollution costs (Hall and others, 1989), the risk of premature death in a car accident in California is twice as high as the risk of premature death from pollution in the Los Angeles area, reportedly one of the most polluted areas in the US. Studies carried out in France (Quinet, 1989) and England (Royal Commission on Environmental Pollution, 1994) confirm that road accidents impose higher measurable costs than pollution from motor vehicles.

Air pollution has many ramifications, and the subject is too big and too difficult to be fully covered here. The points to be discussed below are:

1. The damage caused by atmospheric pollution.

2. Should polluters be required to pay for the damage they cause?

3. How should payment be made?

3.4.1 The costs of pollution from motor vehicles

Although the desire to reduce environmental pollution plays a major role in transport planning, there are few firm data on the magnitudes of the costs that arise from it. The air in Los Angeles is indubitably more polluted than in (say) Santa Barbara but, with the significant exception of damage caused by lead, there is no agreement about the consequences in terms of increased illness or lower life expectancy. Whether a society wishes to reduce pollution by pricing or by regulation, estimates of the magnitude of the damage it causes have to be obtained for sensible control decisions to be made.

When considering the damage caused by pollution, it is useful to distinguish between 'local' effects, which impact people in the vicinity of the polluting vehicles, and 'global' effects, which impact on people everywhere as a result of changes in the earth's atmosphere.

Local effects The main health effects of pollutants from motor vehicles have been listed in a World Bank working paper (Faiz and others, 1990) and are shown in Box 3.3. It has proved difficult to quantify the costs of these effects, and it may be significant that neither the UK nor the US governments, nor the World Bank, have given any indication of their magnitude. However, studies have been made in California and Scandinavia, and some of the results will now be reviewed.

Professor Kenneth Small and Dr. Camilla Kazimi calculated the costs of vehicle-related pollution in the Los Angeles region (Small and Kazimi, 1995). Their method was to assess the tonnage of pollutants emitted by vehicles in the Los Angeles area; to relate this to consequential deaths and illness; and to cost the incidence of death and illness on the basis of what people would be prepared to pay to reduce their risk. They found that the results were dominated by the 'value of life' which (as discussed in the previous section) is based on the amounts that people are willing to pay to reduce the risks of death. They concluded that, if people in Los Angeles valued their lives at $4.87 million (their best available estimate, at 1992 prices), the average pollution costs resulting from a vehicle-mile of travel were 3.28 cents for an average petrol-engined car, which compares reasonably well with the 2 cents per car-mile calculated as the average for the whole of the US by Douglass Lee (1995). For an average heavy-duty diesel lorry, the Small/Kazimi finding for Los Angeles was 52.70 cents per vehicle-mile. These costs took no account of lead poisoning, because the use of lead in petrol is prohibited in the US by regulation.

Box 3.3 Health effects of pollutants from motor vehicles

Pollutant	Health Effects
Carbon Monoxide	Interferes with absorption of oxygen by hemoglobin (red blood cells); impairs perception and thinking, slows reflexes, causes drowsiness, brings on angina, and can cause unconsciousness and death; it affects fetal growth in pregnant women and tissue development of young children. It has a synergistic action with other pollutants to promote morbidity in people with respiratory or circulatory problems; it is associated with less worker productivity and general discomfort.
Nitrogen Oxides	Can increase susceptibility to viral infections such as influenza; irritate the lungs and cause oedema, bronchitis and pneumonia; and results in increased sensitivity to dust and pollen in asthmatics. Most serious health effects are in combination with air pollutants.
Hydrocarbons and other Volatile Organic Compounds	Low-molecular wight compounds cause unpleasant effects such as eye irritation, coughing and sneezing, drowsiness and symptoms akin to drunkenness; heavy-molecular weight compounds may have carcinogenic or mutagenic effects. Some hydrocarbons have a close affinity for diesel particulate and may contribute to lung disease.
Ozone (Precursors: H.C. and Nox)	Irritates mucous membranes of respiratory system causing coughing, choking, and impaired lung function; causes headaches and physical discomfort; reduces resistance to colds and pneumonia; can aggravate chronic heart disease, asthma, bronchitis, and emphysema.
Lead	Affects circulatory, reproductive, nervous, and kidney systems; suspected of causing hyperactivity and lowered learning ability in children; hazardous even after exposure ends. Lead is ingested through the lungs and the gastrointestinal tract.
Sulfur Dioxide	A harsh irritant, exacerbates asthma, bronchitis and emphysema; causes coughing and impaired lung functions.
Particulate Matter	Irritates mucous membranes and may initiate a variety of respiratory diseases; fine particles may cause cancer and exacerbate morbidity and mortality from respiratory dysfunctions. A strong correlation exists between suspended particulates and infant mortality in urban areas. Suspended particulates have the ability to adhere to carcinogens emitted by motor vehicles.
Toxic Substances	Suspected of causing cancer, reproductive problems, and birth defects. Benzene and asbestos are known carcinogens; aldehydes and ketones irritate the eyes, cause short-term respiratory and skin irritation and may be carcinogenic.

Source: Faiz and others (1990).

The pollution costs attributed to a private car in Los Angeles is of the same order as that obtained in the Institute of Transport Economics in Norway (Larsen, 1994): In Norway the local environmental cost for an average petrol-driven car was estimated to vary from 2.4 to 4.8 US cents per vehicle-mile. When comparing the Los Angeles with the Norway figures it should be borne in mind that the air in LA is particularly polluted, and that the Norway figures include all local environmental costs (e.g. noise), not only those due to atmospheric pollution.

Small and Kazimi reckoned that, on the assumption that fuel consumption in Los Angeles averages 23 miles to the (US) gallon, the appropriate fuel surcharge to cover the polluting cost of private cars in Los Angeles would be 60 cents per gallon, equivalent to about 41 pence per Imperial gallon. For reasons discussed later in this chapter, a surcharge on fuel does not appear to be the appropriate way to deal with avoidable pollution costs, but even the 60 cents per gallon mentioned by Small and Kazimi would not pose insuperable problems to the use of passenger cars. They can be compared to the current US taxes on petrol, typically 30 cents per gallon, and to European taxes on fuel, which can be ten times as high in countries less rich than the US. However, a fuel tax to deal with the pollution due to heavy commercial vehicles could cause their owners to use larger numbers of smaller vehicles.

Global effects The earth's atmosphere contains some 3,000 billion metric tons of CO_2. This total is reported to increase each year by about 0.5 per cent as a result of human activity. This 'enhancement' of CO_2 levels is said to augment naturally occurring 'greenhouse' effects (mainly due to water vapour), and to produce harmful 'global warming'. Whether human activity enhances 'global warming' is debatable and, even if it does, there are no reliable estimates of its costs to humanity. Despite the absence of such estimates, many governments approved the United Nations Framework Convention on Climate Change, which requires the developed countries to reduce the emission of man-made ('person-made'?) 'greenhouse gases' (mainly CO_2) to 1990 levels by the year 2000.[6] The cost of reaching this arbitrary target, which has yet to be scientifically justified, is often used as a proxy for the cost of global pollution.

It is difficult for the outsider to assess the arguments in this specialized scientific field, but some comments may be in order.

First, as is evident from Figure 3.5, there has been a rise in the climatic temperature from 1880 to 1940, followed by a decline. There is no firm evidence of recent 'global warming', though temperatures have increased in the vicinity of large urban areas, for reasons which have nothing to do with climate change.

Second, it is by no means clear that global warming would do more harm than good to the majority of people. Global warming might cause sea levels to rise (due to the melting of polar ice) which could cause flooding, but it would also have beneficial effects, e.g. it would enable some marginal lands to be cultivated. In any event, there is evidence that the earth may be in the midst of a cooling trend, which could be more damaging than a warming one.

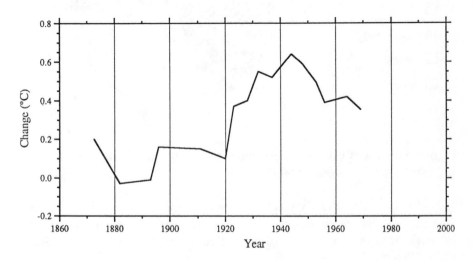

Figure 3.5 Global temperatures for the 0-80° latitude band
Source: National Defense University (1978)

Third, to the extent that people affect the environment, it is not only by using motor vehicles but by other means, such as the use of coal and chemicals. Some of these factors are shown in Figure 3.6, which indicates that petroleum use worldwide accounts for only 17.2 per cent of man-made 'greenhouse enhancement', and petroleum use for cars and light trucks in the US for only 1.6 per cent (General Motors, 1994). The contribution of motorized transport in Britain to worldwide greenhouse emissions has been estimated by the Royal Commission on Environmental Pollution to be 0.7 per cent. While environmentalists are concerned even about these small percentages, the main growth in motorized mobility is going to come not from Western countries, but from those in Asia, whose governments have refused to be bound by the UN greenhouse targets.

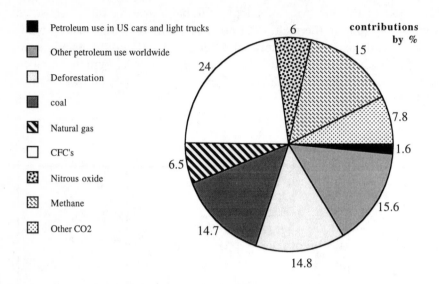

Figure 3.6 Contribution of petroleum to greenhouse emissions
Source: General Motors (1994)

Fourth, measures already taken to improve vehicle engines have resulted in dramatic falls in engine emissions. For example, cars made today in the US emit only 3 to 10 per cent of the pollutants emitted by cars built in the 1960s (Peters, 1994).

Fifth, the global warming predictions are generated by computer models which cannot adequately simulate the heating or cooling effects of clouds, nor the relationships between the atmosphere and the oceans, and which have not proved to be even good predictors of current temperatures.

Sixth, many of those calling for government intervention to protect the global environment agree that the computer predictions are uncertain, and justify the effort in terms of insurance against possible risks. But insurance is costly, and many of the policies recommended to deal with global warming would significantly reduce living standards, which would also cost lives. In his 1994 book *Breaking the Vicious Circle: Toward Effective Risk Regulation* Judge Stephen Breyer (now serving on the US Supreme Court) calculated that each $7.25 million spent in the US on environmental regulation induces one fatality due to the loss of economic growth, and that regulatory costs of $115 billion (his estimate of their annual cost in the US) cause some 15,000 deaths while saving at most 6,600 lives.

Ozone depletion While atmospheric ozone is treated as a pollutant at ground level, it is considered to be a desirable component of the atmosphere because it provides insulation against ultra-violet (UV) radiation from the sun. In recent years observations have shown that the earth's ozone layer is thinning, especially over the poles. It is suggested that the loss of ozone is due to pollutants, particularly CFCs (chloro-fluorocarbons) which are used in refrigeration, and that this loss can lead to excessive global warming and also to skin cancers. The destruction of ozone is said to be due to its interaction with the hydrogen fluoride (HF) produced as a result of the chemical breakdown of CFCs in the atmosphere.

It is not disputed that ozone holes have appeared above the earth's south pole, as they have been observed there as early as the 1950s. What is disputed is the importance of CFCs in creating them, because HF is created naturally in massive quantities. For example, measurements made in the 1920s showed that steam emitted each year from the Katmai region of Alaska (one of the world's hundreds of volcanic regions) contained 200,000 tons of HF, as well as 1,250,000 tons of hydrogen chloride and 300,000 tons of hydrogen sulphide (Gilmour, 1995). More recently, one active volcano on Mount Erebus in Antarctica was reported to be spewing into the atmosphere 40 to 480 tons of HF each day, equivalent to 15,000 to 175,000 tons a year (Towe, 1995).

There is also no agreement about the harm (if any) resulting from the increased radiation. Some experts assert that the segment of UV radiation associated with skin cancer is not absorbed by ozone at all. But these questions have not stopped the adoption by Western countries of the Montreal Protocol of 1987 which obligated them to cut down on CFC emissions, at a cost to US citizens estimated at over $100 billion.

Caution The issues discussed in this section give rise to high emotions, and it is difficult for those of us who are not environmental scientists to judge between conflicting claims. As some environmentalists in this debate protest that those who disagree with them represent vested interests with axes to grind, one might be permitted to point out that the environmental groups themselves have enormous vested interests in government controls to reduce motorized mobility: their staffs and representatives depend for their living on the acceptance of their arguments. Furthermore, many of the environmental groups claiming to be concerned about carbon emissions undermine their own position by opposing a readily available and potentially safe source of carbon-free energy: nuclear power.

Contention there certainly is, but it is not between 'goodies' and 'baddies', but between opposing groups holding different positions.

Readers can only be advised to seek the best evidence, and to listen to all sides, before coming to conclusions.

3.4.2 Should polluters pay?

How should these local and global costs be dealt with? Societies interested in the well-being of their members attempt to devise rules that encourage individuals to promote this societal well-being. Market economies use prices to limit the use of scarce resources so that the benefits from using them exceed their costs. For example, to the extent that the prices of land, bricks, timber and the other components used in house construction correctly signal their costs to society, the willingness of a buyer to pay for the house ensures that the benefits from the use of these products are greater than their costs.

Pollution is undesirable because it depletes the commodity 'good environment'. As 'good environment' is not priced, those who use it up ('consume' it) are not required to take its costs into account. Unless road users are charged for the damage they do to the environment — the costs due to pollution — the costs of their trips could exceed the benefits, even if road users pay for the road, congestion and accident costs occasioned by them. This, in brief, is the case for pollution charges. It involves assessing charges against polluters, charges equivalent to the damage they cause, and leaving it to each of them to decide by how much to reduce their polluting activities.

Another approach — favoured in 'command and control' economies — is for government to decide which polluting activities are to be permitted, and which not, and to issue and enforce regulations to bring about the desired results. Many, in the environmental movement and elsewhere, argue that pollution should be prohibited by regulation and that offenders should not be allowed to buy 'licenses to pollute'.

There is, even in a market economy, a case for regulations that prohibit some activities absolutely — drunken driving on public roads, for example. Where toxic substances are clearly identified — e.g. lead in drinking water — laws can be passed to prohibit their use, though such laws can also do harm — by raising the costs of pipes or water, they make sanitation less affordable. Thousands of low-income people died from a cholera epidemic in Peru after the government (learning that the US authorities were considering a ban on chlorine) decreed that water should no longer be chlorinated.

The prohibition of polluting activities by regulation has other drawbacks:

First, it can be horrendously expensive. A regulation requiring US pulp mills to prevent the release of carcinogenic chloroform was estimated to cost $99.4 billion for each life-year saved. This was because the chance of a cancer was so remote it would be necessary to spend $30.3 million a year for 33,000 years to avert a single fatality (*The Wall Street Journal,* July 6, 1994).

Second, regulation is more costly to those being regulated than pricing, because those made worse off by the regulation do not have the option of reducing their losses by making the required payment.

Third, pricing produces revenues, which could, in principle, be used to compensate those who are hurt by the pollution or those who purchase equipment to reduce it.

In the US, especially in Southern California, enormous efforts are being made to reduce pollution levels by 'command and control' methods that do not relate costs imposed to benefits gained. Indeed, because US, environmental laws do not require costs to be balanced by benefits, public policies appear to be based on the proposition that any improvement in air quality, however trivial, is worth any cost, however great. This approach can lead to significant waste in that the costs due to the regulations exceed the benefits they are intended to confer.

3.4.3 Targeting polluting vehicles directly

While the pricing approaches — trying to assess costs and to make users pay them — are more appropriate in market economies than 'command and control' methods, even they fall short if they target *average* costs rather than *actual* ones. It is as if a government, concerned that its people were, on average, ten per cent over-weight, taxed the price of food to ensure that average consumption fell by ten per cent. Such a tax would indubitably improve the health of some citizens — as well as the health of the government's finances — but it could make some people, especially those both thin and poor, much worse off. A better policy for 'nanny-state' governments applying this kind of social engineering would be to identify overweight individuals, and target them directly for weight-reducing measures.

Similarly with polluting vehicles. Some vehicles pollute more than others, and it is wasteful to treat them all equally. For example, vehicles could be classified by age. Cars built in the US since 1983 are equipped with catalytic converters that remove about 96 per cent of all emissions. Pre-1983 cars emit about 3 grams of volatile organic compounds (VOCs) per mile; cars built since then emit 0.40 grams per mile. Pre-1983 cars in the US account for over 85 per cent of car emissions, and their removal would be a comparatively easy way of reducing local pollution effects. An appropriate way to encourage the scrapping of these vehicles would be to levy an annual charge on them, equivalent to the costs they impose. Such a tax need not be confined to old vehicles, but could also be applied to engines that pollute, thus encouraging the development of cleaner engines.

An even better way than targeting classes of vehicles to reduce car pollution is to target *individual* vehicles on the road, and identify those that exceed pollution standards for any reason, for example, because of poor adjustment or of deliberate tampering with catalytic converters. Studies carried out in California indicate that 'most of the total emissions are produced by only 10 to 15 per cent of all autos' (Lave, 1993). Figure 3.7 shows that just 10 per cent of cars tested in California produced over 72 per cent of idle exhaust hydrocarbon emissions, while Figure 3.8 shows that only 7 per cent of cars were responsible for 50 per cent of all carbon monoxide emission. How can these gross polluters be found?

In the US, the EPA encourages states to find polluting vehicles by Inspection and Maintenance (I/M) programmes which require all vehicles to be tested at government-supervised centres at intervals ranging from six months to two years. The average costs to the state of inspecting one vehicle at these stations vary from $5 in New Jersey to $27 in California. Vehicles have to be brought to the testing stations, which are generally open only during working hours set for the convenience of the testing staff. If periodic tests were effective, the costs might be acceptable, but these 'clean-for-a-day' systems have been compared to controlling drunken driving by requiring drivers to report periodically for breathalyser tests (Lave, 1993). They appear to be singularly ineffective in detecting the 10-15 per cent of gross polluters who are responsible for most of the pollution by cars in the US. Is there another way?

The Stedman Remote Sensing Device Common sense suggests that it would be more effective to seek out polluting vehicles on the public road, and to do so continuously, rather than to expect the polluters to appear every six months to two years at the testing station. Can this be done? With the help of the Colorado Office of Energy Conservation, a team at the University of Denver headed by Dr. Donald H. Stedman developed an infra-red remote sensing system for monitoring car carbon emissions. This system, which is called FEAT (Fuel Efficiency Automobile Test) consists of a source emitting an infra-red beam; a detector that can assess the strength of the beam, and a computer to make the required calculations. When the beam is broken by a passing car, some of the light is absorbed

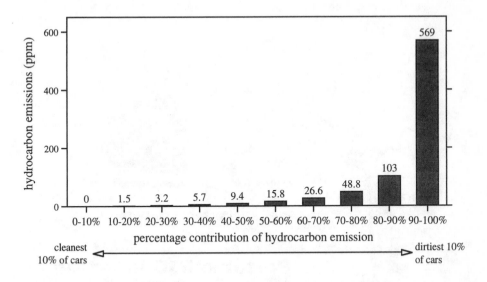

Figure 3.7 Average idle exhaust hydrocarbon emissions
Parts per million
Source: Breedlove (1993)

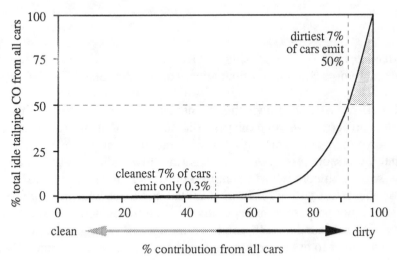

Figure 3.8 Carbon monoxide emissions from all cars
Source: Breedlove (1993)

by its pollutants, and the polluting effect can be assessed by the measuring device and its computer, as shown in Figure 3.9.

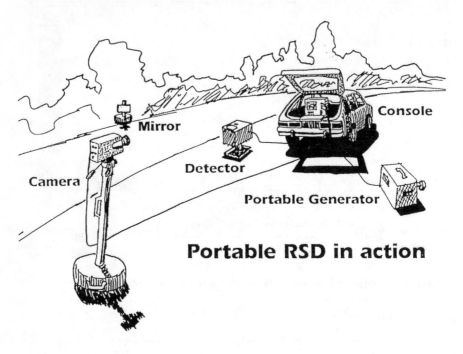

Figure 3.9 How remote sensing works
Source: Remote Sensing Technologies, Tucson, Arizona

The EPA has not shown much enthusiasm for remote 'on-the-road' testing, preferring to rely on periodic 'universal' testing at ever more expensive official testing stations. One objection put forward by the EPA is that the remote testing devices might not always be reliable, and could miss some polluters while wrongly identifying clean cars as dirty ones. That some errors will occur is not disputed, but those who advocate remote testing do not propose to base enforcement on the evidence of single tests. Their recommendation is to employ a number of testing devices working as a team, and to assemble a computer file of persistent offenders. While one bad reading could be false, it is unlikely that a clean vehicle could trigger five or six false alarms. A remote testing regime would be mainly concerned with getting the persistent offenders off the roads, and it is likely to do this more quickly, effectively and cheaply than the 'universal', 'periodic', checks promoted by the EPA.

3.4.4 Paying for automotive pollution

How then should road users pay for the pollution they cause? As comparatively few vehicles are responsible for significant proportions of pollution, it would be good public policy to target the heavy polluters and to encourage them to repair or replace the offending engines. This objective would not be achieved by a fuel surcharge imposed on all vehicles indiscriminately. The following four-tiered approach seems appropriate.

1. *To cover the costs of emissions due to vehicles that perform well within current specifications, using the least-polluting fuels:* A surcharge on fuel, payable by all road users, equivalent to the emission costs imposed by the cleanest vehicles, those with well-tuned systems conforming to latest specifications. This 'floor' charge would cover the minimum pollution costs emitted by all vehicles on the road. As modern vehicles emit less than three per cent of the pollutants emitted by vehicles made before 1974, this 'floor' is likely to be small.

2. *To cover the costs of emissions from vehicles that perform within current specifications, but which are not those with the lowest emissions:* A surcharge on the annual license fee, specific to each vehicle model, corresponding to the additional (the excess above the 'floor') pollution emitted by well-tuned vehicles of that model. This surcharge would have two purposes: to recover from road users pollution costs in excess of the minimum, and to encourage manufacturers to produce low-emission engines.

3. *To cover the costs arising from the use of fuels which pollute more than the minimum (e.g. leaded fuel):* A fuel surcharge corresponding to the additional costs imposed by these types of fuel.

4. *To cover the costs imposed by 'gross polluters', i.e. by engines that do not meet specifications or which malfunction:* Punitive fines high enough to force the owners to get their vehicles properly tuned, or to remove them from the public roads. These gross polluters would be identified by remote sensing devices, of the kind described in section 3.4.3 above.

3.4.5 Conclusions on commercial payments for pollution

There is a strong case for requiring road users to pay for the pollution costs caused by their vehicles, but there is still much work to be done to evaluate their magnitudes, and the level of the charges payable.

The Small and Kazimi work on pollution costs in the Los Angeles area suggests that the *local costs* resulting from passenger cars (averaging 3.28 cents per miles in one of the most polluted areas in the US) could be absorbed without much difficulty by users, but that the costs resulting from heavy lorries (averaging 52.7 cents per vehicle-mile) could cause problems to the trucking industry. A similar result can be deduced from the 1994 report of the UK's Royal Commission on Environmental Pollution.

But even if the Small/Kazimi value of life figure of $4.7 million is accepted, the pollution costs due to most passenger cars with well-maintained engines are likely to be well below the 3.28 cents per mile calculated as being the average in the Los Angeles area. This is for two reasons:

1. Atmospheric conditions in the Los Angeles basin produce excep-
    tionally severe air quality problems, and

2. The Small/Kazimi findings relate to averages but, because of the effect
    of the 10–15 per cent of vehicles that are gross polluters, the others
    produce less than the average.

Charges to cover the *global costs* of pollution should, by definition, be the same everywhere per unit of damaging pollutant emitted. But this author is not convinced that a case has been made for any charges to be payable on this score. If and when the reality of global damage from vehicular emissions is established and quantified, appropriate charges would have to be worked out for those emissions shown to be harmful.

3.5 Payments of more than direct costs

3.5.1 Theoretical considerations

While there appears to be an overwhelming case for requiring road users to pay the direct costs — including congestion and pollution costs — that arise directly out of their choices, the position is less clear in respect of indirect costs, i.e. the costs that do not arise directly out of road use (e.g. construction costs, and costs arising out of weather conditions) but which nevertheless have to be paid for if the roads are to be made available.

Why might road users not be required to pay road costs that do not arise directly from their journeys? Because raising prices is likely to reduce the amount of road use. This might not be a problem on congested roads, but can be wasteful where roads are uncongested and have spare capacity. If this approach is consistent with economic theory, it leads to strange paradoxes.

Consider for example a group of vehicles waiting to use a road closed by snow, in a society that follows the rule that road users pay only the direct costs arising out of road use. In this situation, payment has to be made only for the first vehicle to use the cleared road for, once the snow is cleared for the first vehicle, it costs nothing to let the others through. Imagine, if you can, the following unlikely scenario, where the road users, and the idle snow-plough, wait until one of them decides to make the payment. The road is then cleared, the vehicle for which payment was made goes first, and the others follow. In this scenario, costs were incurred to enable the first vehicle to pass, but no additional expenditures were incurred for the passage of the others. Should the other road users have been required to share in the costs of snow clearing, costs that did not arise directly from their passage?

Take another example: a gravel road suffers significant wear as a direct result of the passage of each vehicle. Say these costs are ten cents a mile. They are 'direct' costs and most people agree that they should be paid by all road users. Then the road gets paved, and the costs of using it fall to, say, a tenth of a cent a mile. Should we argue that users of the paved road — whose vehicle operating costs drop significantly — should only pay one tenth of one cent a mile, while those using the gravel road must pay one hundred times as much, despite the heavier vehicle operating costs they incur?

Strange as it may seem to non-economists, some economists argue that those who enjoy the results of snow-clearing and road paving should *not* be required to meet those costs, which do not arise directly out of use, because, if such charges were imposed on uncongested roads, those unwilling to pay would be denied the use of available facilities, which would therefore be under-utilized and, to that extent, wasted. The basis for this mistaken view can be illustrated by quotations from distinguished authorities:

Maurice Clark (Clark, 1923) wrote that

> [O]nce a well-paved road is built, reasonable use costs nothing at all, and any charge which limits the amount of such traffic [traffic which benefits] would result in unused capacity and the loss described by the phrase 'idle overhead'.

Christopher Foster in *The Transport Problem* (Foster, 1975), wrote that

> The marginal cost of supplying something is the total addition to the expenses of an enterprise resulting from the production of the last (marginal) unit of output. ... [T]he equality of all prices to marginal cost is a necessary condition for the optimal allocation of resources.

Alan Walters, in the World Bank publication *The Economics of Road User Charges* (Walters, 1968) wrote that

> If ... user charges exceed the sum of the variable maintenance cost [that part of maintenance cost that arises directly from road use] and the congestion cost, then the vehicle owner will be dissuaded from undertaking certain vehicle journeys although the true cost is less than the returns. Taking into account the user charge, he may find that the sum of the operating cost and user charge exceeds the returns he expects from the trip ... Consequently, potentially valuable services of the road are wasted.

But that is not the whole story. Pricing to make the best use of existing facilities may well maximize the welfare of some, but commercial operations in free markets have to have all their costs covered by users or beneficiaries, such as land-owners. If commercial operators are to provide roads that are not congested, they will have to be paid more than just the costs arising directly from road use. Those waiting for roads to be cleared of snow might prefer systems that require all travelers to share in the cost of employing snow-clearers, even though this could result in some road users being denied passage because of their inability to pay. As a practical matter, a system under which all payment for snow clearing had to be met by the first traveler would be cumbersome to implement, as no one would wish to be the first. Given the choice, road users would probably get together voluntarily and agree to share the costs of clearing the snow 'for their own mutual benefit'.

Similarly, those waiting for gravel roads to be paved may be prepared to pay (i.e. use the commercial approach) to get the work done quickly, because vehicle operating costs on unpaved roads are so much higher than on paved ones, that the costs of paving are often completely off-set by savings to users.

Is it possible to reconcile the commercial approach with the proposition that 'equality of all prices to marginal cost is a necessary condition for the optimal allocation of resources'?

The first thing to be said is that the marginal price proposition requires that *all* prices be equated to marginal costs. In the examples given above, the snow-clearing and road construction industries were assumed to have spare capacity — equipment and workers waiting to start work — so the prices payable for employing them must have been below their own marginal costs, so the marginal conditions were not met.

Second, although the writers quoted above declared that under-utilized resources result in waste, all realized that other considerations applied also. Thus, Clark continued his exposition by recommending that

> [T]he overhead costs of streets and highways [should be organized] so that they will fall on the users, but *not solely or chiefly as a direct cost of use*. Rather it should still take the form of an overhead charge, such as an annual license fee. A moderate tax on gasoline might also be justified, especially as there are still some highway costs which vary with the general volume of travel, but if the tax were made heavy enough to raise a large part of the highway overhead, it would check traffic whose 'variable cost' to the public would be far less than the tax (Clark, 1923 p. 304).

Christopher Foster wrote:

> We cannot do without a rate of return to decide investment problems where capital is scarce or capital investment significantly indivisible. The social surplus rate of return is what is logically entailed by MSC [Marginal Social Cost] pricing but it is not capable of being used by us in our present state of knowledge (Foster, 1975, p. 325).

Alan Walters wrote:

> For the *use* of the highway each user should be charged the marginal cost. Then if further revenue is required to cover the costs, we ask simply which would be the best way to raise such finance; and if it were decided that, for political or institutional or even economic reasons, the tax would do least harm if raised from the road users, the problem is to create or increase taxes that interfere least with the normal cost-minimizing decisions taken by the truck owner or motorist (Walters, 1968, p. 5).

It seems, then, to be generally agreed that there are welfare losses when users of a road — or of any economic asset — are charged more than the direct costs arising out of such use. But it is also agreed that the avoidance of welfare losses should not be the only guide to economic policy. Societies seeking economic growth also need efficient investment rules, and such rules can conflict with the objective of avoiding welfare losses. Sir Alan Walters has been heard to remark that efficiency in resource use has sometimes to be sacrificed for efficiency in investment.

Going back to the previous examples, the time lost by potential snow clearers and motorists waiting for snow to be cleared, and the damage to vehicles prior to roads being paved, and the wastes arising from idle resources in the road construction industry, could be much greater than the losses due to the exclusion of those unwilling to pay the full costs of snow-clearing or road paving.

It may be significant that Dupuit, who pioneered the study of public works pricing, did not teach that prices should be designed only to make the best use of existing facilities. In his path-breaking essay 'On the measurement of the utility of public works' (Dupuit, 1844), he discussed the effects of toll charges and showed how the usefulness of a bridge declines as its tolls are raised, to the point at which it becomes completely useless when the toll is raised so high that no one can afford to cross it. 'Does this mean', he asked 'that there should only be very low tolls or even that there should be none at all?' To his own question he responded

> That will not be our conclusion when we come to speak of tariffs; but we hope to show that their height needs to be studied and operated according to rational principles, in order to produce the greatest possible utility and at the same time a revenue sufficient to cover the cost of upkeep *and interest on capital*

In the same essay he remarks

> No doubt the Pont des Arts does take 5 centimes' worth of utility from all those who cross over it, but in so far as this is merely *a repayment of capital advanced* it is a law of human nature and of the present state of progress of the human mind to which we must needs resign ourselves (author's italics).

Dupuit did not argue that uncongested bridges should be run at financial deficits; he sought the lowest tariffs that would enable bridges to be paid for by their users.

The principle that road users should pay only costs arising out of road use is not, by itself, sufficient to generate the funds required to provide the facilities that road users are prepared to pay for. A mechanism to generate additional funds is required if uncongested roads are to be provided by the market. One that readily comes to mind is the 'club' which is concerned with a definable group sharing an economic interest and joining together 'for their mutual benefit', with powers to exclude non-members. 'Club goods' are typically financed by charges relating to direct costs incurred by members and by 'subscription charges' which are paid irrespective of use

(Buchanan, 1965). As road users share an economic interest (improved roads to enhance their mobility); are often prepared to pay more than the costs arising directly from use (to reduce their total transport costs); and, as non-payers can be excluded; it seems that roads have the characteristics of club goods. It follows that allowing commercial providers to charge more than direct costs need not reduce societal benefits over the long run and can often even increase them.

3.5.2 The magnitudes involved

'But' the reader must be asking 'why is this important? What is the magnitude of road costs that do not arise directly out of use? Are they significant?' Congestion, pollution and accident costs arise only out of road use but, as was shown in section 3.1, a large proportion of road maintenance costs, especially on strong pavements, are independent of traffic. Additionally, the original road construction costs are independent of traffic. If we make the plausible assumption that the costs of constructing a road can equal the costs of maintaining it over its lifetime, it follows that at least half of the costs of road provision can be independent of traffic, i.e., they need not arise directly out of road use.

This might not pose a problem on congested roads, because the revenues from congestion charges imposed on their users can be high enough to cover their total costs, including their original construction costs. The problem arises on roads that do not generate sufficient congestion charges to cover their total costs.

3.5.3 Conclusion on recovering all road costs

It has to be concluded that there is a strong case, even in theory, for devising payment systems to enable road providers to recover all costs arising out of road use; not only those arising directly from journeys, but also those that have to be expended to have roads available to meet the demands of users. Some of the available methods are described in the next chapter.

3.6 Should road charge levels be controlled by government?

The question of whether government should determine the charges for the use of congested roads has intrigued economists since the 1920s, when Frank Knight, in a celebrated article (Knight, 1924), suggested that, if

roads were privately owned, the market itself could be relied on to determine socially-optimal prices. This assertion was challenged by (among
others) James Buchanan (1956) and David Mills (1981). Both argued that
Knight was right only to the extent that roads were provided competitively.
They pointed out that road providers with monopoly powers would be
interested in pricing roads at levels that maximized their profits, and that
the resulting prices would be higher than prices prevailing under competition.

One hesitates to follow such heavyweights in this discussion, but the
extreme situations seem clear: where there are many competing private
suppliers, as in the case of US long-distance telephone services, governments do not have to be involved in the prices charged. Where there is one
monopoly supplier, there can be a case for government intervention to
protect the public interest.

But these extreme situations rarely arise in practice. The more usual
scenarios are likely to be those now being played out in California, South
China and Virginia (see Chapter 7), where private providers are adding
high-capacity links to existing road networks. In those situations the
provision of additional road facilities by private suppliers would reduce
monopoly powers in roads, so the public welfare would be increased even
if the new suppliers were allowed to charge at profit-maximizing rates.
Should they be permitted to do so?

To answer this question, it might be useful to distinguish between
circumstances of two kinds. On the one hand, where a public road is
privately provided as a result of voluntary transactions — where, for
example, no governmental powers are used to purchase land, and where
providers of new roads are given no protection from competitors. In those
circumstances, it is difficult to justify government interference in the rights
of the owners to set any fees they please. On the other hand, where
government powers are used to obtain land, or where a private supplier is
given protection from competition, an arrangement to limit the profits of
the enterprise would seem to be reasonable.

As a practical matter, in places where those who fix prices 'in the public
interest' know the prices that maximize social welfare, and have the
freedom to set them accordingly, and where it is also commonly believed
that prices will continue to be set in this manner in the future, it could be
argued that it would be in the public interest to do so. But in places where
prices are politically determined, the gains in public welfare resulting from
government-imposed charges might be more than off-set by the reluctance
of private investors to commit their funds to projects of which the profits
are politically determined. Experience in the 1990s in China, Mexico,

Thailand and the US suggests that it is not easy to interest investors in roads. Until markets are more forthcoming, it might be counter-productive to add politicized road charges to the impediments already obstructing the flow of private funds to the provision of roads.

3.7 Conclusions on the commercial pricing of roads

The purpose of this chapter is to review the principles governing commercial pricing and the application of these principles to roads. The main elements to be charged for were identified as:

1. *Road costs* — the costs arising out of road use and the costs of providing roads;

2. *Congestion costs* — costs imposed by slowing down other road users;

3. *Accident costs* — those not covered by insurance; and

4. *Pollution costs* — costs imposed on others by vehicular emissions and other environmental effects.

  It may be concluded that:

Road costs arising out of road use are fairly well known and that meeting them does not pose special difficulties except, possibly, for lorries with heavy axle loads;

Congestion costs can be extremely high in urban areas and could be difficult to collect from users, but that revenues from congestion costs could be used to pay for the road infrastructure costs that do not arise directly out of use;

Accident costs not covered by insurance could be paid for by a modest fuel surcharge; and that

Known *pollution costs* can readily be met and that the unknown ones do not have to be met until they are identified and quantified.

  It should be pointed out that these costs can be related to one another. The relationship between congestion and road costs has already been mentioned, but there is also a connection between congestion and pollution costs. To the extent that a congestion change results in higher traffic speeds, pollution costs may be expected to fall and accident costs to rise.

It may also be concluded that, in a market economy, ways have to be found to enable all road costs to be paid for by those who use, or benefit from, roads, and that the amounts payable need not be determined by governments except when road users face monopolistic road suppliers.

Notes

1. In New York, in contrast, the river crossings west of Manhattan are tolled, but the ones to the east are still toll-free, despite heavy traffic congestion in their vicinity. This difference in municipal attitudes might help to explain why the economy of New York City (which faces a deficit of $1.1 billion in 1995) is declining, while that of Guangzhou is rapidly expanding.

2. 5/2 times $(16,000/2,000)^4$ equals 10,240.

3. In situations where congestion is so heavy that traffic is almost at a standstill, the effect of the increased price could be to increase speeds and flows simultaneously.

4. Surpluses in excess of what is necessary to keep factors of production in existing uses are dubbed 'economic rents' by economists.

5. In India in the 1960s motorists involved in road accidents in rural areas were reported to have been killed by villagers. Travelers were advised, if involved in an accident, to leave their vehicles and join the crowd calling for the blood of the driver. This advice provided a strong incentive to drive carefully.

6. Reducing CO_2 *emissions* to 1990 levels would not be sufficient to reduce its atmospheric *concentration* to 1990 levels.

4 Charging for road use

It does not seem necessary that the expence of those public works should be defrayed from that public revenue, as it is commonly called, of which the collection and application are in most countries assigned to the executive power. The greater part of such public works may easily be so managed, as to afford a particular revenue sufficient for defraying their own expence, without bringing any burden upon the general revenue of the society (Smith, 1776, p. ii, 245).

The previous chapter reviewed the principal costs payable for the use of roads, and it is now necessary to consider how a commercial road organization might receive appropriate payments from road users.

4.1 Requirements to be met by a road pricing system

A useful starting point for reviewing the means available to charge for the use of roads is the report 'Road pricing: The Economic and Technical Possibilities' published by the UK Ministry of Transport in 1964. It is known as the 'Smeed Report', because the panel of engineers and economists that produced it was chaired by Dr. Reuben Smeed, then Deputy Director of the Road Research Laboratory. The panel was supported by staff of the Laboratory who prepared pioneering papers on the technicalities of different pricing methods, of their likely effects on traffic speeds and volumes, and on the expected costs and benefits. In considering the amounts that should be paid for road use, the panel proposed (in Para. 2.2.4) that 'the road user should pay a sum equal to the costs he imposes

upon others', i.e. the direct costs arising out of road use. It then identified
seventeen 'operational requirements of a road pricing system' which, if
followed, would enable this objective to be achieved. These were:

1. *Charges should be closely related to the amount of road use.* This
requirement would be best met by some kind of metering device. In the
absence of meters, surcharges on items such as fuel, which relate to the
amount of road use, are preferable to charges such as vehicle ownership
fees, which do not vary with road use.

2. *It should be possible to vary prices for different roads at different times
of day, week or year, and for different classes of vehicle.* This requirement
could be roughly met by the use of daily licences, which would entitle
holders to enter designated areas at hours of high demand, when congestion and pollution costs are high. But only electronic charging methods
(discussed in sections 4.3.2 and 4.3.3) can enable this requirement to be
met with anything approaching precision.

3. *Prices should be stable and readily ascertainable by road users in
advance of their journeys.* As an important function of charges is to enable
road users to weigh the consequences of their journeys before undertaking
them, prices should be known in advance. This requirement conflicts with
proposals made at one time for road pricing in the City of Cambridge,
under which charges would depend on traffic speeds at any particular
instant, so that (for example) road users stuck behind a broken-down
vehicle would be charged additional fees.

4. *Payment in advance should be possible.* It would be undesirable for
road users to fall into debt to road providers, as road providers could not
'forgive' the debts of some without forgiving the debts of all, and the costs
of collection could be prohibitive.

5. *The system should be regarded as fair.* Enforcement of any system
regarded as unfair is difficult. Road providers would have to ensure that
price levels are defensible, and that the collection methods do not discriminate haphazardly between road users. Public relations campaigns to
explain their positions may be appropriate.

6. *The method should be simple for road users to understand.* A balance
has to be struck between sophisticated systems designed to pursue benefits
to the last penny, and rough-and-ready ones that are easily understood but

respond poorly to cost changes. Telephone charges vary by zone, and by time of day, but no attempt is made to have every cost element represented in the scale of charges.

7. *Equipment used should be highly reliable.* The occasional failure of a metering device to collect can be forgiven, but an error resulting in a road user being inadvertently overcharged could prove fatal to a new pricing system.

8. *Payment should be difficult to evade.* There is little point in introducing payment systems that cannot be enforced.

9. *The method should be capable of handling millions of vehicles.* As the vehicle population within reach of busy road systems can be numbered in the millions, pricing methods involving individual accounts will have to be smart enough to recognize millions of them.

10. *Payment in small amounts should be possible.* Requirements for large payments — for monthly licences for example — would unnecessarily restrict the travel of those who need to use high-price roads only occasionally. These travelers could include shoppers, tourists, and others who do not travel regularly on the roads being priced.

11. *Drivers in high-cost areas should be aware of their payment rates.* Information about road prices, displayed either inside vehicles or outside them, could help road users to react to different prices — to avoid travel in high-price periods, for example.

12. *Drivers should not be 'unduly' distracted from their driving activities.* Drivers should not have their attention diverted from road conditions by having to switch pricing devices on and off when, for example, crossing boundaries of different pricing zones.

13. *The method should be able to accommodate users from other areas.* As vehicles are, by their nature, mobile, all road systems are liable to be used by vehicles based long distances away. In the same way that car phones can be used over wide areas, with their owners receiving just one monthly bill, so road users should be enabled to pay road bills from just one account.

14. *Enforcement should lie within the capacities of non-police staff.* As in the cases of payments for gas, electricity, and telecommunications,

enforcement should be by officials of the services concerned, the police only being summoned in cases of fraud.

15. *The method could be used to charge for street parking.* It would be desirable that pricing methods employed to charge for the use of scarce road space could be applied not only to moving vehicles but also to parked ones.

16. *It should indicate to planners the strength of demand for road space.* To provide helpful investment indicators — for example, the desirability of a new ring road — the pricing system should be able to give information about the extent to which travelers are prepared to pay for using specific routes.

17. *It should be amenable to gradual introduction, starting in pilot areas.* While pricing systems for roads should be considered as ultimately embracing whole networks, pilot schemes in limited areas would enable critical segments to be tackled first, and experience to be gained on the performance of different items of equipment.

These requirements still seem to be valid, but a further one needs to be added, to protect the privacy of road users :

18. *The payment process should not necessarily identify payers or vehicles.* A road pricing system proposed for Hong Kong would have rendered a monthly account to each household showing the roads used by each vehicle. This in itself was considered an unacceptable invasion of privacy, but even more damaging was the fear that all vehicular movements would be traceable by the authorities from government computers.

Having regard to the above requirements, what are the available pricing methods and how can they be classified? Figure 4.1, based on a diagram that appeared on the Smeed report, presents an overall picture of the main possibilities. It classifies road charging methods as being either *indirect*, in which charges are imposed not for using specific roads, but on associated factors, such as vehicle ownership or use, or *direct,* in which road use is charged for directly, as on a toll road.

'Indirect' charging methods, which are by far the most common (see Table 4.1 below), are subdivided, e.g. by whether the charges relate to vehicle ownership (purchase charges, annual fees), or vehicle use (surcharges on fuel or tyres). 'Direct' charging methods are subdivided by

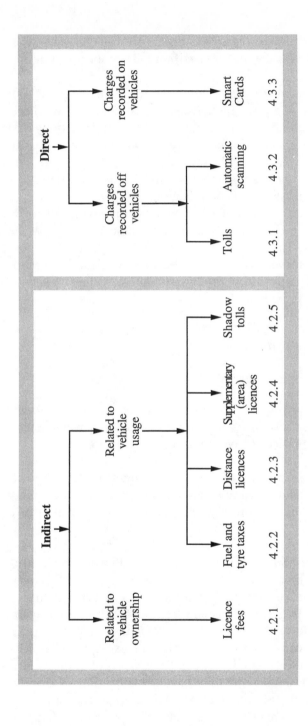

Figure 4.1 Methods of charging for the use of roads
Source: Adapted from Ministry of Transport (1964)

whether the charges are registered on or off vehicles, and whether the charges are made for the use of specific roads or for traveling in a specified area.

The division between 'direct' and 'indirect' charging methods is not always clear-cut. The test applied here is to consider as 'direct' those methods that would allow a road owner to be paid directly by a road user traveling along a specified piece of road. On this basis, New Zealand's 'distance' charges payable by heavy lorries, Singapore's system of cordon pricing, and the proposals for 'shadow tolls', are all classified as 'indirect'. Others may prefer a different classification.

The following discussion relates to methods of paying for roads which, as recommended in Chapter 2, should be distinguished from payments into general revenues. Thus, purchase or import taxes on motor vehicles, at a carefully selected level,[1] can be a useful way of raising general revenues, but this has nothing to do with their suitability to meet the expenses of commercial road providers.

4.2 Indirect charges for road use

4.2.1 Indirect charges: charges related to vehicle ownership

It is useful to distinguish between *purchase and registration charges* which are incurred just once for each vehicle, and renewable *licensing fees* paid on a regular basis, e.g. every year or every quarter.

Purchase and registration charges These one-time charges bear little relationship to road use and thus fail the first Smeed requirement, which is one of the most important. For this reason, they are inferior to other methods.

Renewable licence fees While not directly related to vehicle use, licence fees that have to be renewed at regular intervals — typically every month, quarter or year — bear some relationship to it, e.g. vehicles that are not in use do not usually get their licences renewed. While inferior to charges directly related to use, they can be a useful way of charging to recover costs specific to certain types of vehicle. For example, when it is known that certain kinds of vehicles cause excessive pollution as a result of engine design, or damage to road pavements by dint of axle weight or configuration, surcharges on renewable licences can encourage the owners to switch to other vehicles or, if they cannot, to pay for the damage caused.

Table 4.1
Proportions of taxes and charges paid by road users
(Per cent of total revenues paid by road users)

Country	Year	Taxes/charges on Vehicle use				Vehicle ownership	Vehicle acquisition
		Fuel taxes	Tolls	Other taxes/ charges	Sub- total		
Africa:							
Burundi	1986	72.74	1.17	—	73.91	0.13	25.96
Kenya	1986	63.29	0.00	—	63.29	9.16	27.55
Niger	1986	40.20	0.00	27.20	67.40	4.90	27.70
Rwanda	1984	41.26	11.48	12.25	64.99	13.05	21.96
Tanzania	85/86	26.10	2.27	—	28.37	6.66	64.97
Europe, Middle East and North Africa:							
Cyprus	1984	33.29	—	—	33.29	35.61	31.10
Hungary	1986	62.00	0.00	—	62.00	16.00	22.00
Pakistan	84/85	32.59	0.86	—	33.45	26.89	39.66
Yemen A.R.	1985	15.81	0.00	—	15.81	17.55	66.63
Yugoslavia	1987	70.00	9.50	—	79.50	9.50	11.00
Latin America and Caribbean:							
Argentina	1987	63.90	0.10	20.19	84.19	1.70	14.30
Chile	1986	58.53	3.36	—	61.89	0.00	38.11
Colombia	1986	35.69	12.54	12.21	60.44	0.00	39.56
Costa Rica	1986	88.71	0.54	—	89.25	0.00	10.75
Domin. Rep.	1984	89.18	1.97	—	91.15	8.25	0.60
Asia:							
India	87/88	48.64	0.00	16.40	65.04	22.32	12.64
Indonesia	85/86	51.09	4.00	—	55.09	25.74	19.13
Malaysia	1985	58.42	2.22	2.26	62.90	9.84	27.26
Sri Lanka	1985	60.27	0.00	2.54	62.81	5.85	31.34
Thailand	1985	66.83	0.00	0.19	67.02	3.74	29.24
France	1987	65.13	6.97	8.98	81.08	7.79	11.13
W.Germany	1987	75.13	0.00	—	75.13	24.87	0.00
Japan	1985	38.96	19.07	—	58.03	26.08	15.89
UK	1987	63.88	0.00	—	63.88	16.33	19.79
USA	1984	64.59	7.26	—	71.85	12.67	15.48

Source: Heggie (1992)

Prevalence of charges on vehicle ownership and use Table 4.1 indicates the importance of charges on vehicle ownership and use. In the sample of countries shown, the percentage of these charges ranges from a tenth to two thirds of taxes and charges paid by road users.

4.2.2 Indirect charges: charges related to vehicle use

Surcharges on fuel Surcharges on fuel are probably the method most widely used to raise revenues from road users. Their importance is shown in Table 4.1. Typical rates, for both petrol and diesel fuel, are shown in Figures 4.2 and 4.3.

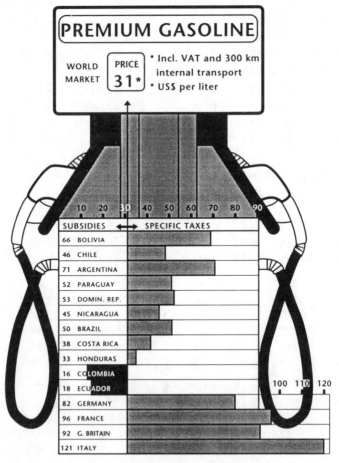

Figure 4.2 Surcharges on petrol in different countries
Source: UN-ECLAC (1993)

Fuel surcharges meet the Smeed Committee's requirement for comparative ease of collection, though, even in the US, ways been have found to cheat the tax authorities. Fuel charges have gained public acceptability, and the amounts paid relate to distance traveled. Their main drawback is that they cannot be varied much by time of travel or by place of travel, and therefore they cannot be used to charge for congestion.

The diesel surcharge has an additional drawback as a source of funding for roads: It is used in industry, and for home heating, as well as for transport. To surcharge diesel fuel as a source of funding for roads, it is necessary to distinguish it from diesel fuel used for other purposes. The standard approach is to apply a dye to non-road diesel, and to exempt the

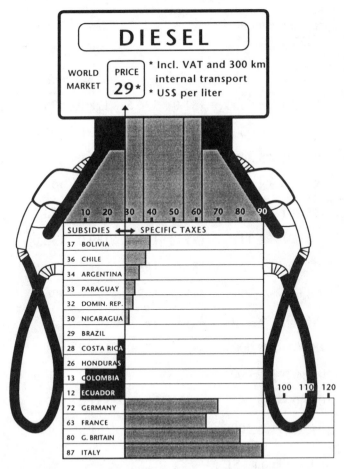

Figure 4.3 Surcharges on diesel oil in different countries
Source: UN-ECLAC (1993)

dyed product from the road charge, while ensuring that it is not used on the road. This is not easy in all countries.

Surcharges on tyres These are used in a number of countries, including the US. Because they discourage tyre renewal they pose a safety hazard, and are not generally recommended. They could be used without danger for heavy tyres of slow-moving vehicles (such as tractors and earth-moving equipment) and may be appropriate in areas, such as are to be found in China, where bicycle users require expensive infrastructure.

Table 4.2
Oregon: Axle-weight mileage tax table

Declared combined weight group	Number of Axles				
	5	6	7	8	9 or more
(Pounds)	*(Mills per mile)*				
80,001–82,000	151.0	136.5	128.0	123.0	117.5
82,001–84,000	1550.	139.5	130.0	125.0	119.0
84,001–86,000	159.5	139.5	132.0	126.5	120.5
86,001–88,000	165.0	142.5	134.0	128.5	122.0
88,001–90,000	172.0	146.0	136.5	130.0	123.5
90,001–92,000	179.0	150.0	139.0	132.0	125.0
92,001–94,000	187.0	158.0	141.5	134.5	126.5
94,001–96,000	195.0	163.0	144.0	136.5	128.0
96,001–98,000	204.0	169.0	147.0	138.5	130.0
98,001–100,000	—	175.0	150.0	141.0	132.0
100,001–102,000	—	—	153.0	144.0	134.5
102,000–104,000	—	—	157.0	147.0	137.0
104,001–105,500	—	—	161.0	150.5	140.0

Note: 1,000 Mill equal $1

Source: Oregon Department of Transportation (1992)

4.2.3 Indirect charges: charges related to distance traveled

The damage done to roads by heavy axles was mentioned in the previous chapter, as was the fact that Oregon and New Zealand both impose special charges to recover these costs.

The Oregon axle weight-distance tax Oregon's first weight-mile tax, which applied to all vehicles weighing more than 26,000 lb, was introduced in 1948. The payments depended only on gross vehicle weight and distance traveled. Since 1990, motor carriers operating vehicles heavier than 80,000 lb pay an axle weight-distance tax which also takes into account the number of axles on a vehicle. There are separate schedules for five-, six-, seven-, eight-, and nine-or-more-axle-vehicle, with each schedule requiring higher payments for higher gross weights. But — as can be seen from Table 4.2 — the rates are structured in such a way that, at any registered gross weight, carriers can obtain a lower per-mile rate by adding axles to their vehicles (Oregon Department of Transportation, 1992).

Vehicle owners are responsible for paying the applicable taxes on a monthly or quarterly basis, their declarations being subject to audit by state inspectors. Since the introduction of the system in 1990 a significant number of carriers have added axles to their vehicles, but it is too early to judge the effects of the added axles on the condition of Oregon's roads.

New Zealand's 'Distance Licences' In New Zealand, vehicles with a manufacturer's gross laden weight of more than 3.5 tons are required to carry 'Distance Licences' which are bought for distances of 1,000 km, or multiples of 1,000 km. After the licensed distances are traversed, new licences have to be bought, so that vehicles are continuously licensed while on public roads. The rates charged for some of the distance licences are shown in Table 4.3 below, and some of the axle configurations in Figure 4.4.

As in Oregon, licences vary by vehicle weight and axle configuration, so that (as shown in Table 4.3) the addition of axles to heavy vehicles reduces the fees payable. However, unlike Oregon, where the enforcement depends on reading the vehicle milometers, visible only on their instrument panels, in New Zealand vehicles operating with distance licences have to be fitted with approved hub odometers. These devices are distance recorders which are fitted to the hubs of heavy vehicles to facilitate the enforcement of distance licensing.

Table 4.3
Rates for distance licences in New Zealand

Dollars per 1000 kilometers (621 miles) of distance to which licence relates

Vehicle type numbers

Maximum weight (tonnes)	1	2	5	6	14
1	13.61				
2	16.43	16.43	16.31	16.31	16.31
3	20.36	20.14	19.91	19.91	19.80
4	25.43	24.64	23.74	23.63	23.40
5	31.95	30.15	27.68	27.56	27.11
6	41.06	37.35	32.18	31.95	30.94
7	53.78	46.91	37.35	36.79	35.10
8	71.44	59.63	43.43	42.41	39.60
9	95.51	76.50	50.51	48.94	44.44
10	127.69	98.78	59.18	56.81	49.84
11	169.88	127.58	69.64	66.26	55.91
12	224.21	164.36	82.24	77.40	62.78
13	292.95	210.60	97.43	90.68	70.76
14	378.56	267.75	115.65	106.54	79.54
15	483.98	337.84	137.25	125.44	89.89
16	611.78	422.66	163.01	147.60	101.70
17	765.23	524.25	193.39	173.70	115.20
18	947.59	644.85	228.94	204.19	130.61
19	1,162.35	786.60	270.23	239.63	148.28
20	1,413.34	951.98	318.04	280.46	168.30
21	1,704.26	1,143.56	373.05	327.15	190.91
22	2,039.51	1,363.95	435.83	380.70	216.56
23	2,423.03	1,616.06	507.38	441.56	245.36
24	2,859.64	1,902.83	588.26	510.30	277.76
25	3,353.74	2,227.39	679.73	587.70	313.99
26	3,910.50	2,592.68	782.21	674.55	354.26
27	4,534.88	3,002.40	896.74	771.64	399.26
28	5,232.15	3,459.71	1,024.54	879.75	448.99
29	6,007.95	3,968.44	1,166.18	999.68	504.00
30	9,867.90	4,532.18	1,323.00	1,132.31	564.64

Note: The licences purchased at the rates shown in the screened blocks, would normally exceed the maximum legal weight for that vehicle type on a Class 1 Road.

Source: New Zealand Ministry of Transport.

POWERED VEHICLES

No. of axles	Types of axles	Example vehicles	Vehicle type No.
2	2 spaced axles, both single tyred	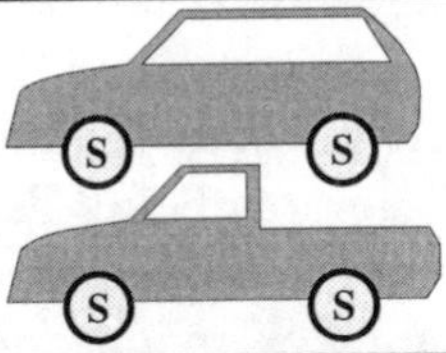	1
	2 spaced axles, 1 single tyred and 1 twin tyred	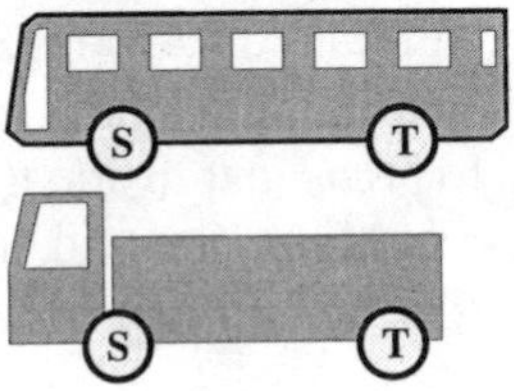	2
	Any other configuration		1
3	3 axles, 1 single tyred and 2 twin tyred	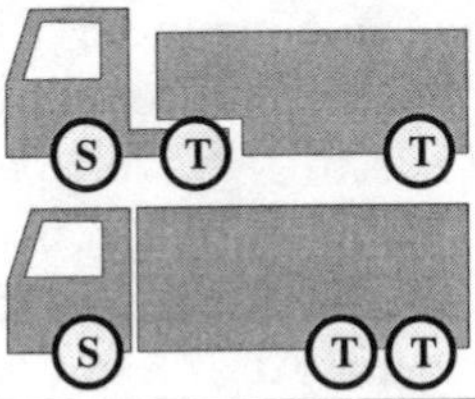	6
	Any other configuration		5
4	Any configuration		14
5 or more	Any configuration		19

Key:

Single tyred axle: **S**	Twin tyred axle: **T**
Spaced axles ◯ ◯ ◯	Close axle groups ◯◯ or ◯◯◯

Figure 4.4 Axle configurations of different vehicle types
Source: New Zealand Ministry of Transport

4.2.4 Indirect charges: supplementary licences

Daily, weekly or monthly licences displayed on vehicles within designated zones, or at their borders, offer simple and cheap means of charging for the use of roads. Such licences can be sold in a variety of ways. For example, the Smeed Committee suggested that dated daily licences could be sold in books, with refunds obtainable for tickets not torn out. It is even possible to envisage different rates of charges for different zones. For example, areas of heaviest congestion could be designated 'red', and require costly red licences, while in less congested 'blue' areas, road users would have to exhibit less costly licences coloured blue. Variations by time could also be accommodated, with an area being declared 'red' in peak periods, 'blue' during the rest of the day and free at night-time.

Despite their advantages of cheapness and simplicity, such systems suffer from two significant disadvantages. First, in most areas the fixing of the zone boundary would be to some extent arbitrary, leading to anomalies and injustices due to areas just inside the zone being treated quite different-ly from areas just outside. Second, road users traveling long distances within the priced zone would pay no more than those traveling only short distances.

The Singapore Area Licence Scheme (ALS) Windscreen licences were first used for road pricing in Singapore. Since June 1975, road users entering the 'Restricted Zone' in the centre of Singapore in the morning peak period (7.30-10.15 a.m.) have had to display on their vehicles' windscreens a daily or monthly licence. Under the original scheme, buses, lorries, motorcycles, taxis and cars carrying four people or more were exempted from payment. After a few weeks taxis were required to pay half the regular fee. The authorities expected the restriction during the morning peak to result in reduced traffic in the afternoon peak but, for reasons never properly understood, the afternoon peak remained heavy and, in 1994, the afternoon peak traffic was restricted also. To avoid queues building up at the zone entrances, licences are purchased at booths else-where, or by mail. Enforcement is by visual inspection at the zone entranc-es, with police personnel using tape recorders to note the licence-plate numbers of vehicles lacking the proper windscreen licences during the times of restriction. Owners of offending vehicles are then billed for the appropriate fines and, it being Singapore, they pay.

Singapore's ALS worked smoothly, with negligible administrative problems, thus disproving the frequent criticisms made of road pricing, that though economically beneficial, it would be administratively impracticable. Singapore showed road pricing to be not only practicable, but also profitable — annual revenues were over 94 per cent of the capital costs of the ALS, the bulk of which were spent on the construction of fringe car parks. However, economists should not crow too loudly about Singapore; although the ALS was shown to be practicable, no one was able to show that it produced net economic benefits. This can be explained by the relatively high daily licence fee of three Singapore dollars a day (equivalent then to a daily fee of US$1.25), which was raised in December 1975 to four Singapore dollars (US$1.67). At these rates the streets in the restricted area were less congested than those outside, and subsequent raising of the fees had the effect of diverting traffic from less-congested to more-congested streets, which was not what the economists recommended.

The Singapore authorities are in the process of selecting an electronic system (of the type described in section 4.3 below) to replace the manual one introduced in 1975.

Cordons in Norway Since 1986 the Norwegian city of Bergen has been levying a charge of 5 Krones (equivalent to US$0.65) for automobiles entering the business district; the revenues being used for road improvement. Possibly because the revenues are used for this purpose, there has never been significant opposition to them. The Bergen charge raises revenues but has had a negligible effect on traffic volumes. Later, cordons were also established in Oslo and Trondheim (Hau, 1992b).

4.2.5 Indirect charges: shadow tolls

'Shadow tolls' are amounts paid to road providers in respect of traffic on their roads, but without immediate payment from the road users concerned. This feat can be achieved by means of vehicle counts, which are used to assess the payments due to the road provider. This method of payment does not seem to exist anywhere at the present time, but needs to be discussed because of its simplicity and potential importance. Two examples of 'shadow tolls' are described here: the method adopted by the Associations Intercommunales in post-war Belgium, and the proposal for financing the UK 'Black Country' route in 1980.

Financing the Associations Intercommunales in Belgium In 1962 the Belgian parliament passed legislation to enable local authorities to associate for certain purposes, e.g. to operate public utilities. Under this law, a local authorities' association ('Intercommunale vereniging voor de autoweg E3') was formed in 1963 to construct and operate the E3 motorway from Eindhoven to Lille, a distance of some 180 km. On January 2, 1963, the Association was granted a concession by the Belgian government to build and operate the E3. The contract required the Association to construct the E3 in accordance with a specified timetable, to equip it with specified lighting and other safety facilities, and to install and operate equipment necessary to count the numbers of vehicles using the motorway. For its part, the central government undertook to pay the Association an agreed amount for each vehicle-km traveled on the E3, this amount being intended to cover all costs incurred over a thirty-year period, including principal and loan charges. It was agreed that if the payments were insufficient to cover these costs the rate per vehicle could be increased or the concession period extended.

Subsequently six more 'Intercommunales' were formed to provide motorways and these associations were responsible for the majority of motorways being built in Belgium in the 1970s. However, the system of payments proportional to traffic, which involved laborious traffic counts, and resulted in different payments for different roads, was considered to be too complicated. In July 1973, the system of 'shadow tolls' was abandoned and replaced by a system of state grants to repay the obligations assumed by the communal associations.[2]

The UK 'Black Country' proposal In the early 1980s UK government funding for roads was cut back and much of its road construction industry idled. One consequence of this was an intense interest in private road financing, which resulted in a novel proposal for financing the Black Country route, a seven-mile road in the West Midlands. The proposal was submitted to the Ministry of Transport in July 1983 by the West Midlands County Council (WMCC), which prepared it in conjunction with TNS, a consortium consisting of Tarmac Construction Ltd., National Westminster Bank PLC, and Saturn Management Ltd.

The essence of the proposal was that TNS would provide a road to the design and specifications of the WMCC, which would pay the consortium an agreed amount for each vehicle-mile traveled on the new road and another amount for each square foot of new development in the vicinity of the new road. The payments were to start as soon as the road was open to traffic and to cease twenty-five years later. Funding for the project would have been in two stages: Interim funding for the construction period, to be provided by a commercial bank, and long-term funding for the 25-year operating period, to be provided by a financing institution such as an insurance company. This division was proposed because banks in the UK are reluctant to commit their funds for long periods, while long-term lenders (such as insurance companies) do not support uncompleted projects. The main advantage to the WMCC from the proposal was to have been the earlier completion of the road, and the advantage to the Ministry of Transport that the risk of insufficient traffic to justify the road would have been taken by the private sector. The financing to the WMCC would have been at a higher interest rate than available from government funds, but TNS claimed that this disadvantage would have been off-set by lower costs and quicker completion.

In the event, this type of financing was not then tried in Britain because the Minister for Transport, David Howell, who was interested to try it, left the Ministry. His successor, who was less interested, enabled the WMCC to get conventional financing for the Black Country route.

However, in 1994, following submissions from the Automobile Association, an organization representing British road users, and a report prepared at the London School of Economics (Glaister and Travers, 1994), the Department of Transport (successor to the Ministry of Transport) announced that private consortia are to be invited to bid for contracts to design, finance, build and operate four new road projects in England, and that the successful contractors would be paid by 'shadow tolls'. The implications of this important announcement are discussed in Chapter 8.

4.3 Direct charges for road use

4.3.1 Direct charges, registered off vehicles: conventional tolls

Road tolls are at least 2,500 years old, as they had to be paid for using the Susa–Babylon highway under the regime of Ashurbanipal, who reigned in the seventh century BC (Gilliet, 1990). It is known that tolls on roads and bridges were common in England in the twelfth century (AD), because a royal decree in 1189 freed the burgesses of Northampton from the obligation to pay them (Jackman, 1966, p. 9). They were still common five hundred years later: in his diary for 1653 John Evelyn reported that

> On April 11th I went to take the air in Hyde Park. There every coach was made to pay a shilling and sixpence for every horse, by the sordid fellow who purchased it of the so-called state (Francis, 1963).

The word 'Turnpike', which originally meant a revolving spiked bar, attests to the age of the concept of holding up travelers until the road or bridge charge was paid.

Tolls were never popular with travelers and were abolished in London in 1871. However, as described in more detail in Chapter 7, tolls facilitated the creation of countrywide networks of roads in Britain and the US before the railways and, in more recent years, they enabled high-quality roads to be provided in Asia, Europe and Latin America.

According to the International Bridge, Tunnel and Turnpike Association (IBTTA, 1992), there are currently over 400 toll facilities operated by their members. Of these, about one third are in the US and most of the remainder in Western Europe, Japan and Mexico — see Table 4.4.

Drawbacks of conventional toll roads While enabling roads to be provided despite shortages of government funds, toll roads have been criticized as being inefficient in three ways:

1. By requiring vehicles to stop or slow down, manual toll collection wastes time and raises vehicle operating costs.

2. Collection costs can absorb up to a third of revenues, and revenue theft is considered to be comparatively easy.[3]

3. Where the tolled roads are less congested than the parallel 'free' roads, the traffic diversion resulting from the tolls increases congestion on the road system and reduces its usefulness.

These criticisms are generally valid. They can all be overcome by the use of 'shadow tolls', which were discussed earlier. The first and second can also be dealt with by the use of electronic pricing methods, which are discussed in the following sections. Electronic pricing is particularly important in situations where the objective is to improve the usefulness of roads by diverting traffic from congested to less-congested roads, an objective which cannot be achieved by the use of shadow tolls.

4.3.2 Direct charges, registered off vehicles: electronic road pricing

Electronic road pricing depends on vehicles being equipped with electronic identifiers, known as *Transponders*, which reflect unique identification signals when passing — even at high speeds — through radio beams emitted by *Readers*. The readers send out low-level radio signals, and a transponder within range reflects the signals back which the readers then decode to obtain its unique identification code. Within a fraction of a second the system carries out security tests and, if all is well, receipt of the

Table 4.4
Number of principal toll roads, bridges and tunnels

Country	Roads	Bridges	Tunnels
England	0	3	3
France	49	1	3
Ireland	1	2	
Italy	37	0	3
Norway	3	0	0
Portugal	6	1	0
Scotland	0	1	0
Spain	14	0	2
Canada	0	4	0
Mexico	19	0	0
USA	63	70*	9
China	2	0	0
Hong Kong	0	0	3
Indonesia	9	3	0
Japan	70	8	2
Malaysia	7	0	0
Taiwan	1	0	0
Thailand	2	0	0
South Africa	14	0	1
Australia	2	1	1

* Operated by IBTTA members.
Sources: Author's estimates, based on reports of the IBTTA, *Public
Works Financing,* and the Reason Foundation.

identification code is reported to a central computer which can debit a
specified account. If the signal received is not satisfactory — if, for
example, the code is associated with an account that has no credit — a
photograph of the vehicle's number plate, or other appropriate action, can
be taken. A schematic diagram of a proposed site equipment layout is
shown in Figure 4.5.

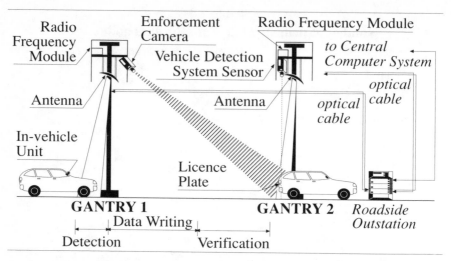

Figure 4.5 Layout for identifying transponders in motion
Source: SEEL-Marconi SpA-GEC Consortium, Singapore

Equipment of this kind is routinely used to identify aircraft, railway wagons, and containers, and has been tested on vehicles for more than twenty years. In the 1970s, for example, Southern California Rapid Transit equipped its Los Angeles buses with transponders to enable management to keep better control of their movements. In the same period the New York Port Authority was testing transponders with a view to using them for non-stop toll collection at the busy tunnels through which vehicles enter Manhattan from New Jersey.

In the 1980s 3,000 vehicles in Hong Kong were equipped with transponders, to test the technical possibilities of road pricing there. The equipment performed well, but political difficulties prevented its general application.

Fixed and moveable transponders In the 1960s and 1970s, and in the Hong Kong tests, the transponders were fixed securely to the undersides of the vehicles and the readers were activated by sensors located under the surface of the highway. In the late 1980s the Amtech Corporation of Dallas introduced portable transponders for non-stop toll collection. These were credit-card sized windscreen units, which they named *TollTags*™.

One advantage of the moveable transponders over the ones permanently fixed to their host vehicles was that vehicle owners could mount and unmount the moveable units themselves, enabling (for example) one transponder to be used by a family or a firm possessing more than one vehicle. However, the portable transponders had another subtle but significant advantage: as they were not fixed to specific vehicles they stopped threatening the privacy of their users. Amtech TollTags could be rented on payment of a monthly fee without the owners having to be identified. Although the movements of the TollTags were recorded on the toll road computers, the identity of the people concerned was not revealed. So long as their accounts were in credit, they could be used to pay tolls. When their credit was exhausted, the TollTags became as useless as out-of-date credit cards and, like out-of-date credit cards, subject to confiscation when presented.

The issue of privacy on toll roads is one of the major concerns affecting public attitudes to road pricing. Many road users (including the author of this book) object to their movements having to be recorded on traffic control devices. The Amtech TollTags were the first to give them the option of anonymity.

Introduction of the Amtech TollTags TollTags were introduced in 1989 in New Orleans, to enable 13,000 users of a toll-bridge to pay their tolls without having to stop. Amtech opened distribution outlets near the toll bridge to enable the bridge users to prepay not less than $10 for toll payments. As they passed toll points, their accounts were drawn down and they could then either go to the sales outlets and make further prepayments, or they could arrange for their credit cards to be automatically charged for replenishment, and thus avoid having to return to the sales outlets. As TollTags reduced toll collection costs, New Orleans offered users a 30 per cent discount on the regular toll rate.

Following the successful introduction of their system in New Orleans, Amtech took on a more ambitious assignment in their home town of Dallas: offering TollTags to users of sixty-two of the toll collection points of the seventeen-mile Dallas North Tollway. As the Tollway Authority does not provide TollTags without charge, the 21,000 or so TollTag users in Dallas have to pay $2 a month rental, and a five-cent surcharge on each toll payment, to cover all or part of equipment costs. Despite this, over 24,000 TollTags were issued in Dallas in the first ten months of the system's operation, and over 36,000 transactions a day were recorded there. Eighty per cent of users arrange for the transfer to the toll authority's account to be made automatically by credit card, so that once their accounts are set up, TollTag holders need do nothing to keep them open, except to pay their credit card bills. The Amtech TollTags were reported to have performed well.

An off-vehicle electronic pricing system is to be introduced in 1995 in the Washington DC area, on the Dulles Toll Road, which was built alongside the access road from the Washington Beltway to Dulles Airport. As in the case of the Dallas North Tollway, use of the system will be voluntary, but a high response will be encouraged because the Virginia Department of Transportation, which operates the Dulles Toll Road, expects to make substantial savings in operating costs from automated non-stop toll collection. It therefore proposes to establish dedicated lanes to those using electronic toll collection to maximize time savings to road users and minimize toll collection costs to the Commonwealth of Virginia.

Modern Example The system illustrated in Figure 4.5 was designed and extensively tested for use in Singapore by the consortium SEEL, Marconi SpA and GEC Singapore. If selected for implementation, it will cover sixty separate entry points to Singapore's expressway system and central business district, and replace the 1975 Area Licence Scheme described above (section 4.2.4). Using high frequency (5,800 Megahertz) radio communication, the new system is designed to detect and react to all vehicle types from motorcycles to trucks, whether traveling at high-speeds (up to 160 km per hour) or in congested traffic. Unlike some of the earlier systems, it can perform these tasks in the absence of lane barriers, with vehicles unconstrained from carrying out manoeuvres such as lane-changing and overtaking, even while under the gantry-mounted equipment. The equipment can handle two opposing streams of vehicles passing simultaneously under the same gantries. Charges can be recorded either on computers connected to the gantry equipment or on in-vehicle units, equipped with 'smart cards' of the type described in section 4.3.3 below. Vehicles have to cross two sets of detectors; those that do not complete a valid charge transaction get their rear licence plates photographed automatically (*Traffic Engineering and Control*, 1994).

4.3.3 Direct charges, registered in vehicles: electronic charge cards

In contrast to systems that register charges on centrally managed computers, other electronic systems have been proposed, which would register charges in the vehicles themselves, thus eliminating the need for centralized accounting.

The development of plastic cards that can store data and perform calculations through the medium of embedded computer chips has stimulated interest in the concept of the personal road pricing meters. Such cards are used on modern subway tickets, which lose value as they are used up, and also by the plastic phone-cards for UK public telephones, which are sold by many outlets and thrown away when exhausted. The latest version of these cards — known in the trade as 'Smart Cards' — do not have to be thrown away but can be reprogrammed for further use by suitable equipment.

'Smart cards' enable systems of two kinds to be operated: 'point pricing' and 'continuous pricing'. Both systems use in-vehicle equipment that is triggered by stimuli received as vehicles pass 'pricing points'. Under 'point pricing' systems, the charges payable depend on the number of pricing points triggered, with some points triggering higher charges than others. Under 'continuous pricing', in-vehicle meters are switched on or off (either manually by the drivers, or automatically by road-side beacons) as zones are entered or left, and the charges are based on the times elapsing while the meters are on.

The application of these smart cards to road pricing can be illustrated by the UNIPASS™ system, unveiled in 1994, and presented as a low-cost, flexible system for use in a wide variety of situations. The heart of the system is the *Unimeter*™, a self-contained 'pay and display' device (Figure 4.6) which is placed behind a vehicle's windscreen. The Unimeter includes a display panel for the driver, a slot for the pre-paid charge card and a display panel clearly visible from outside the vehicle, for inspection and enforcement. Charges can be levied either as fixed tolls (on passage through tolling points), or by time of travel through controlled zones, or as a combination of both.

The Unimeter can be activated either automatically, by roadside beacons, or manually, by the drivers themselves. For toll point charging the toll transaction is acknowledged and validated by means of a coded symbol which changes unexpectedly at random intervals. Scanning cameras can be programmed to photograph vehicles not showing the correct current symbol. For time-based charging the drivers are responsible for switching on their units, and time delays can be built-in, to prevent would-be evaders from switching off their Unimeters after passing check points. Road users would pay the charges by buying or 'topping up' the special plastic cards, or, eventually, by using their credit or debit cards.

According to the system suppliers (Unipass Ltd. of London) the cost of in-vehicle units could be £40, and the cost of the plastic cards less than £1 each. Infrastructure costs would be mainly the costs of the scanning cameras. Unipass calculate that total equipment costs for a medium-sized city could be £6 million, and for a city as large as London £250 million. Annual revenues could be two or three times the first year's equipment costs, so such systems can quickly become huge revenue generators — a matter of concern to some, which is dealt with in the next chapter.

This is not the place to go further into technical details of automatic toll collection. Suffice it to say that the collection of payment for road use without toll plazas is today as technically feasible as paying for telephone use without coin-operated call-boxes.

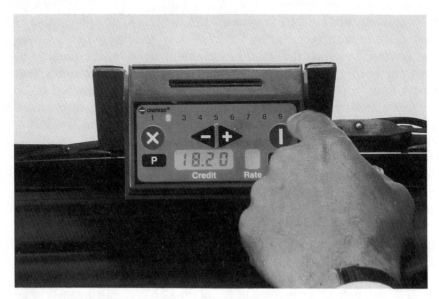

Figure 4.6 The *Unimeter*™ in-vehicle road pricing unit
Source: Unipass Ltd.

4.4 Recommendations for appropriate charging methods

In the course of time electronic charging methods will be developed which will enable road users' accounts to be automatically debited as they use roads, in the same way that customers' telephone accounts are now debited. As with telephone charges, road use charges could be made to vary by time of day and by location, in accordance with schedules determined either by competition or, where there is no competition, between representatives of road suppliers (from the public or the private sector), and road users. Charges should also include appropriate amounts to compensate for pollution and accident costs not covered by insurance.

A variety of electronic road pricing methods are already available, some with substantial track records, and more will doubtless be developed. The features to choose in particular situations will depend on the specific local requirements and on the relevant costs. Until electronic charging methods can be introduced other methods will have to be used. The ones that offer the best combination of efficiency and simplicity appear to be:

To cover road maintenance and operating costs, and pollution costs that vary in proportion to distance traveled For vehicles with heavy axles, either the New Zealand style 'Distance Licence', or the Oregon style weight-distance charge, both of which vary with axle weight and configuration, to reflect the damage caused. For vehicles with light axles, a fuel charge can often meet these costs. A fuel charge is particularly suitable to cover pollution costs that vary in proportion to fuel consumption.

To cover road construction costs, and maintenance and operating costs that do not vary with distance traveled On congested roads, congestion charges are the appropriate way to meet these costs, for reasons given in Chapter 5 below. In their absence, a fuel charge is probably the least unsuitable, because its burden increases as congestion gets more intense. On uncongested roads the advice of Dupuit should be followed: combinations of fuel charges and annual licence fees should be sought that raise the required funds with minimal loss of benefit.

To cover pollution costs associated with certain types of engine As mentioned in section 3.4.4 above, costs due to engines that emit more than 'floor' pollution levels could be charged by means of annual licence fees specific to the type of vehicles concerned. Gross-polluters, responsible for illegal levels of pollution, should be discouraged by fines high enough to deter illegality.

To cover accident costs not already covered by insurance As the risks of accidents vary with distance traveled, a surcharge on fuel would seem to be the most appropriate way to cover accident costs not already covered by insurance premiums. Such payments might be combined with rebates to road owners who have low accident rates.

Destination of revenues from road use charges Under regimes of efficient electronic road pricing, road owners could collect directly the charges payable for the use of their roads.

Until the introduction of road pricing, monies paid by road users in the form of fuel surcharges and annual licence fees could be paid into road funds outside government, for distribution to road providers in direct proportion to traffic flows, having regard to ratios of 'heavies' and other relevant factors. As mentioned in Chapter 2, this would require sophisticated traffic counting arrangements.

More difficult is the question of how to deal with revenues paid by road users to compensate victims of pollution and of accidents. Common sense would indicate that they be routed to appropriate compensation funds,[4] but in a manner that would give incentives to road owners to minimize pollution and accidents on their road systems. One way of doing this might be for the compensation funds to make refunds to road systems that have low accident and pollution counts. If revenues from pollution charges and insurance premiums were paid indiscriminately into compensation funds, or into general revenues, those road providers who operated their facilities less healthily and less safely would be subject to the 'moral hazard' of being able to shift some of the costs of their failures on other road providers, including those who were more successful in maintaining high standards of health and safety on their facilities.

4.5 Is congestion pricing always beneficial?

While prices set freely by interactions of buyers and sellers are usually beneficial, congestion pricing would generally be set by governments. The experience of Singapore, at least in the early phase of its Area Licence Scheme (ALS), indicates that such prices may not always promote the best use of scarce road space.

Traffic studies were carried out in Singapore both before and after the introduction of the ALS in June 1975. From those studies it is possible to calculate the distances traveled in the area by motorized modes by members of different income groups (Zahavi and Roth, 1980). The results are summarized in Table 4.5. They show that all of the vehicle-owning income groups traveled less by car, and in total, after the introduction of the ALS than before. The effects on the non-vehicle-owning households were mixed, with three income groups showing increases and four decreases in total travel. An intriguing finding was that members of non-vehicle-owning households showed a significant increase in travel by car. This was probably due to a shift from bus to car-pooling, as cars carrying four or more people were exempted from paying the ALS fee. Buses lost passengers overall, though the *percentage* of bus travelers in the reduced travel circumstance actually increased.

Road pricing is advocated by economists to make the best use of the road system affected. But the authorities in Singapore seem to have had other objectives. According to a World Bank report on the ALS (Watson and Holland, 1978, p. 12), it was unlikely to have met the criterion of econom-

Table 4.5
Singapore: Daily travel before and after the ALS

Daily travel distance per household by motorized mode.
Household income (thousands of Singapore dollars).

Time Period	Mode	0 - 2	2 - 4	4 - 7	7 - 10	10 - 15	15 - 20	20 - 25	25+	Avg.
Vehicle-owning households										
Before	Car	—	4.36	11.21	18.14	29.69	43.33	47.72	66.76	32.45
	Motorcycle	—	11.32	8.66	7.60	5.80	5.12	4.42	2.18	6.12
	Bus	—	12.56	21.08	28.70	33.40	27.86	27.53	26.81	26.93
	Total		28.24	40.95	54.44	68.89	76.31	79.67	95.75	65.50
After	Car	—	2.35	9.33	12.60	25.22	36.32	38.53	51.57	26.17
	Motorcycle	—	8.35	6.43	4.86	5.91	4.59	3.67	1.86	4.96
	Bus	—	11.75	17.80	29.34	27.66	31.94	30.25	25.89	26.49
	Total		22.45	33.56	46.80	58.79	72.85	72.45	79.32	57.62
Non-vehicle-owning household										
Before	Car	—	0.28	2.11	1.48	1.25	11.18	15.64	—	1.91
	Motorcycle	—	0.08	0.27	—	—	—	—	—	0.12
	Bus	14.47	20.37	34.43	41.45	65.40	58.04	59.19	—	36.42
	Total	14.47	20.73	36.81	42.93	66.65	69.22	74.83	—	38.45
After	Car	0.28	0.45	1.54	5.36	6.49	9.71	2.85	—	3.20
	Motorcycle	—	—	1.09	0.10	1.36	—	—	—	0.59
	Bus	16.15	17.20	30.63	39.80	58.35	56.23	78.43	—	35.39
	Total	16.43	17.65	33.26	45.26	66.20	65.94	81.28	—	39.18

Source: Zahavi and Roth (1980)

ic efficiency, at least in the early days:

> In fact, it [the ALS] was more successful than planners and observers had expected, achieving a reduction in the number of cars of over 70 percent, and a reduction in total traffic volumes of over 40 percent. The achievement of a reduction in excess of the target has resulted in a high degree of underutilization of roads inside the zone, and observers have concluded that the price was set too high. The transport planners in Singapore, however, have not reduced the fee, believing that achieving their long-run objective of modifying attitudes is more important than achieving short-run economic efficiency. In short, having got people out of their cars, they have no intention of inducing them back again in the name of economic efficiency.

The reason that this can be considered important is that, as governments go, Singapore's is one of the best. Those of us who are interested in good road management might ask whether, if even officials as dedicated and intelligent as those serving in Singapore could not introduce a beneficial road congestion pricing system, is any other government likely to do so? Do we want our own government to price some of us off our roads, not to increase the usefulness of roads, but because an elected or unelected official wishes to 'modify our attitude' and 'get us out of our cars'?

Or does the Singapore experience warn us of the danger of giving a monopolist the arbitrary power to charge what it wishes for the use of an important scarce resource? Can it be that the pricing and financing of roads is too difficult a job for governments, and more suitable for commercial organizations subject to competition or regulation?

Annex to Chapter 4
Brief history of road congestion pricing

As car populations and traffic congestion grew rapidly after the Second World War, economists started to apply the tools of their trade to roads. In 1952 James Buchanan wrote that while 'an over-all system of toll charges would seem impracticable ... an appropriate system of tolls might well make rush hour travel on urban routes by commercial carriers almost prohibitive while making travel during night hours almost free of tolls' (Buchanan, 1952). Buchanan suggested that differently-priced annual licences be sold to give holders the right to use roads in congested areas at times of peak traffic. Working independently, Alan Walters made a similar suggestion two years later (Walters, 1954).

Also in the early 1950s, Milton Friedman (of *Free to Choose* fame) and Daniel Boorstin (historian and author, who later served as Librarian of Congress), wrote a paper on the management and pricing of roads, raising many of the issues discussed in this volume. They emphasized the importance of an appropriate pricing system and, to illustrate what was required, mentioned the possibility of impregnating roads with radio-active stripes and equipping vehicles with geiger counters to record the amount of road use. Their pioneering paper was submitted for a competition, failed to win a prize, and was never published. It was re-discovered in 1988, and is reproduced as an epilogue to this book.

The first specific proposal for electronic road pricing was made in 1959 by Professor William Vickrey of Columbia University, in his statement to a Joint Committee of the US Congress (Vickrey, 1959). Prepared in conjunction with the Link Aviation corporation, the proposal required vehicles using the streets of Washington DC in hours of peak congestion to be equipped with 'a self-contained, passive response block which will provide a unique signal identifying any object moving on the ground to which it is attached'. The 'response blocks' were to be identified by electronic interrogators, and the data transmitted to an electronic computer which would sort the charges and send out bills to vehicle owners. The peak period charges envisioned by Vickrey appear to have been of the order of $1 to $2 per trip, and the total cost of the equipment was calculated to be less than $60 million.

Vickrey's proposal was not implemented, but news of it reached England, where the problems caused by traffic congestion were being studied by a Ministry of Transport panel led by Colin Buchanan. Buchanan, a distinguished town planner and civil servant, did not feel that road pricing merited major consideration in his 1962 report *Traffic in Towns*, but ministry staff were interested and the minister, Ernest Marples, set up the Smeed Committee, which prepared the report *Road Pricing: The economic and technical possibilities* (Ministry of Transport, 1964).

Both Vickrey and the Smeed Committee examined road pricing as a way of making the best use of existing road space, rather than as a source of funding for road improvement. Economists who linked the two included Herbert Mohring, Mitchell Harwitz and Robert Strotz, who were all in the Transportation Center at Northwestern University in 1962, and whose work is drawn upon for Chapter 5. Herbert Mohring appears to have been the first to apply these economic principles to actual conditions in a specific place. He calculated the optimal tolls and the implications for highway capacity in the Twin Cities Metropolitan Area (Mohring 1965), and concluded that prices in the range of 0.9 to 1.5 cents per mile could be appropriate under congested conditions and that the urban road network was substantially under-developed.

The Smeed report was followed by other studies in the 1960s and 1970s in England and elsewhere, including an in-depth investigation at the Urban Institute in Washington DC, funded by the US Urban Mass Transportation Administration. The World Bank offered to assist the governments of Malaysia and Thailand to introduce congestion pricing in Kuala Lumpur and Bangkok, but no action followed in those cities. In 1983–85 a detailed study of the possibilities of congestion pricing was carried out in Hong Kong (Hau, 1992b), also without implementation.

In 1971, the Government of Venezuela, assisted by a loan from the World Bank, embarked on a study to provide it with information

> to formulate and implement a policy of road user charges for Caracas capable of provoking an efficient use of the road system, of contributing significantly to the cost-effectiveness of highway-expansion schemes, and at the same time generating fiscal revenue at a scale sufficient to enable the road sector to go much of the way to becoming self-sufficient financially (Voorhees, 1973).

The study team looked at a variety of charging methods and recommended that

> a uniform daily license charge according to vehicle type for the use of road space in a single area of the Caracas Metropolitan Area, would be the best initially (Voorhees, p. 64).

The team's recommendations were not accepted by the government of Venezuela, but its report reached Singapore, where it came to the attention of staff of the inter-ministerial Road Transport Action Committee which, in early 1974, was considering the problems caused by growing traffic congestion in its central area.

On June 2, 1975, Singapore inaugurated its 'Area Licence Scheme' ('ALS'), the first use of road pricing to reduce traffic congestion. World Bank urban transport staff (including the author of this book) were working at the time in Singapore on another study, but had no formal role in the decision to introduce the ALS. The system adopted there was the daily licence charge, which had been rejected for Caracas. Singapore was followed by Bergen where, in 1986, a differential charge was established with little dissent, the revenues being dedicated to road improvement.

Notes

1. Not so high as to ruin the industry producing the vehicles being taxed, which was the result of the 1990 US tax on luxury boats.

2. Information about the Intercommunales was obtained from the Belgian Road Research Centre and the Economists Advisory Group (1972).

3. It is related that when toll collectors at a river crossing in England went on strike, the amounts placed voluntarily by motorists in collection boxes exceeded the amounts normally handed in by the toll collectors.

4. Some experts hold that compensation should not be paid in full to victims because, if it were, they would be discouraged from taking steps to avoid the situations that could trigger the compensation. For example, full compensation for the effects of air pollution would encourage people to live in polluted areas, and compensation for road accidents would encourage careless behaviour on the roads. This issue, which is peripheral to the question of the magnitude of negative externalities resulting from road use, cannot be explored here.

5 Commercial investment in roads

When high roads, bridges, canals, &c. are in this manner made and supported by the commerce which is carried on by means of them, they can be made only where that commerce requires them, and consequently where it is proper to make them. Their expence too, their grandeur and magnificence, must be suited to what that commerce can afford to pay. They must be made consequently as it is proper to make them. A magnificent high road cannot be made through a desart country where there is little or no commerce, or merely because it happens to lead to the country villa of the intendant of the province, or to that of some great lord to whom the intendant finds it convenient to make his court. A great bridge cannot be thrown over a river at a place where nobody passes, or merely to embellish the view from the windows of a neighbouring palace: things which sometimes happen, in countries where works of this kind are carried on by any other revenue than that which they themselves are capable of affording (Smith, 1776, p. ii, 246).

Chapter 4 has shown that it is possible to design charging systems for roads which would enable road users to pay the costs caused by their journeys. Elements of such systems should include: Charges related to pavement damage to ensure that roads are protected from excessive axle weights; surcharges on fuel to pay for accident costs that are not covered by insurance; pollution charges to protect the community from excessive pollution; and congestion charges to prevent excessive overcrowding. Such charges, if correctly designed and applied, would optimize the utilization of existing road systems: no one would use roads unless the benefits to

them exceeded the costs they imposed; and no one would be denied the use of the road if they were prepared to pay the costs arising out of such use.

It is also possible to impose charges that would cover the total costs of building, operating and maintaining all roads carrying substantial traffic.

But how should society go about expanding its road systems? Who would decide where to provide more road capacity, and how much more? Where would funds for expansion come from?

Broadly speaking, there are two possibilities. One is to use the market criterion of profitability, and rely on the voluntary participation of private investors, who hope to benefit financially or otherwise from their participation. This is the method employed to finance the US telecommunications sector which, as proposed in section 2.2, is used in this book to model road systems. The other possibility is to rely on the mechanisms of government to identify the 'public good', and to expand road systems in the light of advice from its experts, using resources raised by taxation. This is the method that was used in the Soviet Union for all investments, and which is still employed by all governments for most road development.

Few will dispute the superiority of the market criterion for commercial investments. The question that has to be addressed in this chapter is whether it can be used for roads.

5.1 Profitability as an investment criterion

In market economies investment resources tend to flow to those uses where their expected earnings are above normal, and to flow out of uses where the expected earnings are below normal. Thus, market forces tend to move the economy to the point at which all investments earn normal returns, 'normal returns' being those received by investors, in cash or in kind, after paying all the expenses that have to be incurred, including wages, material costs, rent for the use of land, and the interest on borrowed funds.

The qualification that returns to investors may be 'in cash or in kind' is made to cover the situations (common in the toll road era) in which investors agreed to accept low returns for the provision of roads serving their neighbourhoods. For the purpose of this chapter, a road is deemed to be 'profitable' if willing buyers are prepared to pay sufficient to induce willing suppliers to provide it.

In the short run, application of the profitability criterion may allow successful investors to earn 'abnormal' profits, i.e. revenues that greatly exceed the costs to them of the monies that they invest.[1] But, in the long run, the effect of successful investments is to attract competition, to relieve shortages and so reduce profits to the 'normal' levels available elsewhere.

It has been shown by many authorities that these principles apply to roads also, subject to certain conditions. One of the earliest statements was by Herbert Mohring:

> To maximize the benefits derived from an existing road network, the highway authority must levy tolls equal to the difference between short-run marginal and average congestion costs. If the resulting toll collections are greater than the total costs of the system (including, it should be emphasized, an interest charge equal to the market rate of return on capital invested in the system), expanding the system, thereby lowering both average and marginal vehicle operating costs and hence optimum tolls, is in order. A long-run equilibrium highway network results if this process of system expansion and toll reduction is continued to the point where network costs (again, including the market return on invested capital) equal toll collections ... Strictly speaking, a long-run optimum highway system requires that tolls equal capital costs only if the production of highway services involves constant returns to scale. Some evidence is available that substantial scale economies exist in the provision of these services. If an activity involves increasing returns to scale, economic theory suggests the desirability of subsidizing this activity. That is, in the case at hand, theory dictates that the highway network ought to be expanded beyond the point at which congestion tolls just cover highway network costs (Mohring, 1965, p. 2).

Mohring's statement might be summarized as follows. To get the most benefit from an existing road network, users should be charged the additional costs resulting from their journeys. If the revenues from these benefit-maximizing charges exceed the total costs of the road system, expansion of the system would be indicated, so long as such expansion involves 'constant returns to scale' in road construction, maintenance and use.

The 'constant returns to scale' condition means that, when a road network is expanded, the unit costs of building and maintaining additional capacity are not changed, and that the unit costs of road users are not changed. For example, if a one-lane road is expanded to become a two-lane road, the condition means that the additional costs of building and maintaining the second lane are the same as the costs incurred on the first, and that the costs to road users would remain the same when the volume of traffic increases in proportion to the increase in road capacity.

The implications of 'constant returns to scale' are discussed later in this chapter, but a further point needs to be made here about the use of profitability as an investment criterion.

Investment criteria are the yardsticks used by investors to help them decide where to place investment funds. Such criteria should not be used only to decide whether complete projects are, or are not, desirable. They should also enable investors to assess specific project features, such as length of road, number of lanes on different segments, optimal sequence of construction, etc., so these criteria govern the main features of potential projects. In the design of an optimal road system, for example, it is not sufficient that total revenues cover total costs; ideally, each element of a road system — each link, each climbing lane, each traffic light, each rest stop — should meet the criterion of additional costs being covered by additional benefits. The condition of costs being covered by revenues 'should be satisfied not simply for the entire network but separately for each and every inch of highway construction' (Strotz, 1965).

The idea that 'each and every inch of highway construction' in an optimal road network should have its costs covered by revenues, and thus be its own profit centre, is an immensely powerful one. Not because it can be applied literally; obviously Robert Strotz knew as well as anyone that viable road systems are measured in miles, not inches. The importance of this statement lies in the corollary that, if a road network is regarded as being made up from component parts, there is no inconsistency between the profitability of each of the components and the profitability of the whole, and that an agglomeration of road components, each financially profitable, can result in an efficient network. This result is typical of market systems in general, which can run efficiently even without overall supervision, so long as each component — each firm — operates at a profit. The exceptions to this generality — situations of 'market failure' in which financial profitability on its own does not ensure optimal results — are described in Chapter 6.

Profitability has two important advantages for the assessment of road projects:

1. investments made on the basis of this criterion can be compared with other revenue-earning investments, including especially railways, and

2. such investments can be carried out by either the public or the private sector.

5.1.1 Comparability of investments

The first point might seem esoteric, but it is of great practical significance. Transport planners in government ministries, and in the international funding agencies such as the World Bank, do not use the same criterion to assess roads and railways. When Sir Peter Lazarus was the senior civil servant in Britain's Department of Transport he visited the World Bank and was asked by its transport economists to explain the principles used in his ministry to allocate funds for different transport modes. Decisions of that kind, he said, were determined by his government on political grounds. Because roads and railways were treated differently, direct comparisons between them were rarely made. After their total budgets were determined by the political processes, the rail investments were assessed, as one group, on the basis of financial profitability, and road investments, as another group, on the basis of benefit-cost analyses, of the kind described in section 5.3 below.

The process described by Sir Peter is, in essence, still followed. It is convenient because it enables planners to avoid the politically sensitive comparisons of roads versus railways and, in the absence of such comparisons, politicians find it is easier to vote monies for loss-making services.

This difficulty is well known,[2] and the most common approach to remedy it is to attempt to apply benefit-cost analysis to railways and other revenue-earning sectors. Although the British Department of Transport uses benefit-cost analysis in the evaluation of non-commercial services, the difficulties of using it for commercial services have not been resolved (Foster, 1975). The approach suggested here, in contrast, is to assess all transport infrastructure projects with the yardstick of profitability. This could become even more logical and practicable to the extent that the use of roads is charged for on a market basis.

Use of a single criterion common to both modes would, for example, shed light on the advantages of converting roads to railways — or vice versa. In the US, the 1991 Intermodal Surface Transportation Efficiency Act (popularly referred to as the ISTEA, as in 'iced tea') allows the states to use federal funds for investment in either roads or in public transport by rail or bus. Use of a common investment criterion would help state legislators and officials to make more informed decisions on the merits of these investment alternatives.

5.1.2 Private funding

The second advantage, that the profitability criterion for investment would enable roads to be privately funded is, like the first, not widely appreciated. 'What difference does it make' it is often said 'whether public or private funds are used to finance needed infrastructure?' There is a vast difference, arising from differences in defining 'needs'.

In the first place, as pointed out by Adam Smith in the quotation at the opening of this chapter, where costs are not required to be covered by revenues (in Smith's words, by 'commerce') there are temptations to provide roads and bridges for reasons of politics rather than user demand. For example, a disproportionate number of highway 'demonstration projects' financed by the US Congress happen to be located in the districts of the members of the appropriation committees concerned (Anderson and Binstein, 1994).

Second, there are numerous cases of public funds being unavailable even for high-priority road projects. For example, according to a World Bank study of China's Guangdong province,

> [I]t is significant that over 2,300 km of existing gravel roads have traffic loadings in excess of 2,300 vehicles per day [which] is at least four times the threshold at which paving becomes economic (Harral, Cook and Holland, 1992).

Another example is the M25 ring road round London, which has been running at full capacity ever since its opening in the 1980s. There are good reasons for believing that road users, if given the opportunity, would have been willing to fund road paving in Guangdong, and a ring road round London, out of their own pockets much earlier, because of the big savings that they themselves would have received from these improvements. It is well established in the US that voters are more likely to support projects which benefit them directly, such as schools or sewers, than increased taxes paid into general revenues.

5.2 Needs assessment as an alternative to profitability

One alternative to profitability as an investment criterion is the 'needs assessment' used in the US. It is described as follows by the Federal Highway Administration (FHWA):

> Estimates of future highway investment requirements are derived through application of the Highway Performance Monitoring System (HPMS) database and analytical modeling procedure. The HPMS data base contains information about current physical conditions and usage for over 100,000 non-local highway segments. The HPMS analytical

procedure uses this data to simulate highway investment decisions and predict system performance. ...

Highway deficiencies are identified when physical or operating conditions deteriorate below prescribed minimum condition standards. ... In general, condition deficiencies will occasion resurfacing or pavement reconstruction while performance deficiencies result in the need for additional capacity on the existing roadway. Each improvement type has an associated cost per lane mile that varies by state.

The HPMS investment/performance procedure prioritizes improvements based on the amounts of funds available and their relative cost-effectiveness levels (FHWA, 1993).

What this means is that the authorities review the physical conditions of all the road segments in their jurisdiction, and the degree of congestion on them. Signals for investment are triggered when physical or traffic conditions fall below the designated standards. If the funds available are insufficient to meet the expenditures thus identified, a rationing process is used to ensure that the most 'cost-effective' works get priority.

This methodology has significant defects:

1. It assumes that all existing road segments have to be retained for ever in good condition and to have the capacity to meet the 'needs' of forecast traffic.

2. It encourages state officials to exaggerate deficiencies; those who succeed in keeping their roads in good condition within their budgets get no increases in funding.

3. The process does not even ask whether users would be prepared to pay the costs of improvements to be made for their benefit.

That a system that generates higher and higher expenditures survives in the US is a reflection of the gross waste that pervades the public sector there, probably because it is politically easier to pay everyone (with taxpayers' money) than to make the hard choices involved in approving some projects and rejecting others. This easy-going attitude is encouraged by the fact (mentioned in sections 1.4 and 2.5.2) that the road financing system does not enable any of the chief players — neither road users, nor state officials, nor federal officials — to reduce costs. As one of the keenest observers of the US road scene pointed out:

In a process not guided by economic criteria, the role of financial aid
from other levels of government can be very seductive and deleterious,
reducing the effective costs of money and, thereby, distorting expenditure decisions (Pisarski, 1987).

5.3 Benefit-cost analysis as an alternative to profitability

Those of us who are transport economists and planners trained in Western
institutions may not take kindly to the idea that our methods are akin to
those used with so little success in the Soviet Union and the 'Third World'.
'Do we not have' the planners will respond 'sophisticated benefit-cost
analysis methodologies developed in Western universities, applied by
experts in the World Bank, and recently recommended for use even in the
Clinton administration?' 'Are these methodologies not used by the British
and other governments?' 'Can they all be misguided?'

It would be wrong to belittle benefit-cost analyses, on which enormous
efforts have been expended by many first-rate minds. And certainly, there
are situations — such as the evaluation of government regulations, or of
multi-use water projects — where there may be no better way. And
benefit-cost analysis is certainly superior to the FHWA's 'needs analysis'
because (unlike the latter) it does attempt to assess benefits as well as
costs. But what benefit-cost analysis has in common with the Soviet and
Third World planning methods is the idea that investment decisions should
be made not by profit-seeking entities responding to demands of consumers, but by political entities guided by expert advisors. It is not easy to
bridge these different approaches.

When comparing the investment criteria *profitability* and *benefit-cost
analysis* it is important to realize that they are entirely different animals.
Profitability is concerned only with the profits — the net benefits —
accruing to those who provide the service being assessed. Benefit-cost
analysis, on the other hand, attempts to bring into the comparison not only
the benefits to the producers, but also the benefits to be enjoyed by those
who would gain from the proposed project. This is why it is not possible to
compare two projects with one another, if one is assessed by its profitability and the other by benefit-cost analysis. For example, a road project
offering *total* annual benefits of 20 per cent of project costs might be
inferior to a railway project offering a financial profit of 12 per cent *to the
railway providers*, because the annual benefits to railway consumers
(which are excluded from the calculations of the railway's profitability)
might be well above the 8 per cent difference. This point was put by

Semmens in another way: benefit-cost analysis adds to the benefit side the benefits of those who gain from the project, but the cost side is not loaded with the value of the benefits lost to the taxpayers forced to subsidize the project in question.

Benefit-cost analysis was first applied to roads in Oregon in the 1930s, to help the State Highway Commission select routes for roads between given origins and destinations. The costs of the different alternatives were estimated and compared with the benefits that each would bring, having regard to the dates of the expected costs and benefits.[3] However, for complicated projects, neither the costs nor the benefits are easy to predict.

The cost estimates carried out in a benefit-cost calculation are comparatively straightforward, and have to be used in profitability calculations also. But even costs can be erroneously estimated: The Humber Bridge in England was estimated to cost £28 million when it was approved in 1971 but, when it was completed in 1981, the bill came to £151 million. The costs of the Channel Tunnel rose from £7.5 billion to £15 billion during its construction, and the estimates of the cost of the Anglo-French Concorde aircraft project rose from £170 million in 1962 to £1,065 million in 1973 before levelling-off at £2,000 million in 1978 (Hall, 1980). Despite many such examples, the problems of cost estimation pale into insignificance beside the difficulties of estimating project benefits.

Some of the benefit components are readily quantifiable. When the project involves paving a gravel road, for example, it is quite straightforward to forecast savings in vehicle operating costs, and in road maintenance costs. This is because there is a good deal of information about the costs of operating vehicles, and of maintaining roads. But road improvements also result in time savings, and in changes in the numbers and severity of accidents (which can go up or down, depending on the circumstances) and these consequences are much more difficult to quantify. Some practitioners of benefit-cost analysis also attempt to quantify benefits resulting from new traffic generated by road improvements, and some even 'the wider effects on the economic development of the region' (Transport and Road Research Laboratory, 1988).

Benefit assessment requires accurate forecasts of traffic. Traffic forecasting is not yet an exact science, and therefore lends itself to manipulation to justify 'political' projects that lack economic justification.

As the benefit-cost criterion takes into account much more than profitability to the supplier, is it not a superior measure? Not necessarily, because of the difficulty of assessing these additional benefits. Many would consider the profitability criterion superior for the reasons mentioned earlier, namely that projects assessed by profitability can be compared to others in the market economy and that they can be financed privately. But there are additional reasons:

1. Under benefit-cost analysis it is much easier to hide errors, and there is no automatic mechanism to weed out those who make them. On the other hand, the errors of those who are over-optimistic in their profit forecasts are quickly found out, and those who make them tend to move to other activities.

2. Some of the factors used in benefit-cost analysis — such as the value of time and accident savings — are difficult to measure, and even to define. Their inclusion offers endless opportunities to 'stretch' benefits to justify poor projects.

3. The assumption that benefit-cost practitioners can properly take into account 'indirect' project benefits, assumes that the practitioners possess super-human qualities and thus assigns to the benefit-cost process powers that it cannot possibly have. Ordinary mortals can guess at indirect effects of projects but generally cannot get close to predicting or assessing them. When Steve Jobs and Steve Wozniak invented the Apple microcomputer they regarded it as little more than a tool for computer hobbyists, and did not see that it would revolution- ize work practices all over the world.

Hans Adler, one of the leading authorities on benefit-cost analysis, put the point as follows:

> The reading of many feasibility studies leaves one with the clear impression that, when a project is not justified, indirect benefits suddenly become important. It is probably not unfair to conclude that indirect benefits are the last refuge of doubtful projects (Adler, 1969).

Where there are no profits (as, for example, in the case of lightly-used facilities in remote areas, or of 'non commercial' railways) there might be a useful role for benefit-cost analysis in project evaluation. But, in situa- tions where roads can be profitable, it is difficult to see why they should not be subject to market criteria and disciplines.

5.4 Using the profitability criterion: dealing with profits

Any discussion of market pricing for roads leads to the question of what should be done with profits. Profits could not arise from payments to compensate for road damage (which should be spent on maintenance and repair), nor on surcharges to cover accident costs (which should be used to make good accident losses), nor on revenues from pollution charges which, (one would expect) should be used to compensate those who suffer from pollution. However, profits could arise from the congestion charges, or rents, paid by those who use scarce road space.

The amounts involved could be substantial: Gross revenues in one city — Los Angeles — could exceed US$3 billion a year (Small, 1992). According to Douglass Lee (1982, quoted by Small and others in *Road Works*, 1989), congestion pricing throughout the US would yield annual revenues of the order of $54 billion (1981 dollars!) under the conditions prevailing in 1981. Benefits in the 1990s would be substantially higher, because of increased congestion and higher valuations of saved time. David Newbery (1990) calculated that congestion costs in Great Britain in 1990 were such that appropriate charges could have raised £12.75 billion a year, and the UK Department of Transport data shown in Table 3.4 (Chapter 3) indicate that revenues from congestion charges in London in 1991 could have been in the range £150 to £400 million a year. These figures are all gross, in the sense that nothing appears to have been deducted from them to allow for rents payable by road authorities to local authorities for the use of land. Nevertheless, they suggest that the surpluses to road providers who impose congestion charges could be considerable. Who should get them?

The short and simple answer is that, in a market economy, profits accrue to those who succeed in making them. In general, roads need to be no exception to this rule, but this matter is so important, and so contentious, that it merits discussion in more detail.

5.4.1 Critical importance of revenue disposition

When economists discussed the pricing of congested roads in the 1960s little attention was paid to the disposal of the revenues. The improved efficiency resulting from better pricing would, we said, bring about more productive use of roads, and the benefits thus generated would be net gains to society. As for the payments made by road users, they would be merely 'transfer payments' from one set of people to another, and they would not affect the magnitude of the benefits. In those days some of us actually believed that there would be no costs to society from transferring money from road users to governments, because governments, always seeking the public good, would use the funds as beneficially as those who paid them.

It is now evident that we were mistaken, and for three reasons:

First, those of us who have seen at close hand how governments work, or who have followed the literature on Public Choice (Buchanan and Tullock, 1962) and the economics of bureaucracy (Niskanen, 1971) can no longer rely on the proposition that governments use funds as beneficially as those who earn them. On the contrary, we are reminded of the words of Adam Smith that 'Kings and Ministers ... are themselves always, and without any exception, the greatest spendthrifts in the society' (Smith, 1776, p. i, 367) and expect such transfers to result in significant loss.

Second, even when governments spend revenues usefully (as most frequently do) there are costs to raising revenues. According to Timothy Hau (1992b), the costs of collecting congestion charges from road users can range from 6 per cent to 30 per cent of revenues.

Third, even if such transfers were beneficial and costless, there is no doubt that many road users would become worse off as a result. Mohring and Anderson (1994) studied the likely effects of congestion pricing on a major US conurbation and wrote that '... in the Twin Cities and most of North America and Europe ... congestion tolls would significantly speed traffic flow, but, for most travelers, not by enough to offset the cost of the tolls they pay'. Timothy Hau (1992a) demonstrated that such losses are to be expected from economic theory, and suggests that much of the political opposition to congestion charges, in Hong Kong and elsewhere, arises from them.

It is therefore now accepted by workers in this field that the disposition of surpluses from congestion pricing — 'surpluses' being those funds in excess of the costs payable by the road pricing entity, including market rents payable for land occupied by the roads — is an important factor in determining the economic benefits from efficient road pricing and a critical factor in its political acceptability. What are the alternatives?

5.4.2 Alternatives for the disposition of surplus revenues

The Smeed Committee devoted just one paragraph (Ministry of Transport, 1964, Para. 8.2.2) to this subject. Before declaring that 'it is clearly outside our terms of reference to suggest how the revenue should be used' it listed the following alternatives without discussing them:

1. as a transfer to general revenues;

2. to compensate residents in areas of high road prices;

3. to subsidize public transport; and

4. to reduce existing taxes on road use.

Since the publication of the Smeed Report many further suggestions have been made, including:

5. to improve the environment, and

6. to strengthen the road network.

These alternatives to having the profits go to the road providers will now be briefly considered:

Transfer to general revenues In principle, this option would make no sense economically and would be politically disastrous, because of the inevitable opposition from road users. However, to the extent that local authorities and other government agencies are the owners of land used for roads, the rents payable to them for the use of their land by commercial road operators would provide the public sector significant new revenues, and indeed would transform roads from financial losers to major money-makers.

Compensation for residents in areas of high road prices It would not be easy to justify compensation to people who, under the changes proposed, may well get improved mobility, a better environment and improved public transport. However, if it turns out that these advantages do not materialize, and that there are significant drops in property values as a result of congestion pricing, there might be a political case — and even an ethical one — for compensation for losses in property values.

Subsidies for public transport These would not appear to be justified, despite the claims that this would be a just way to compensate travelers forced by commercial road pricing to switch from private to public transport. The following considerations apply:

1. The experience of Singapore suggests that those 'priced out' of their private vehicles are more likely to join car-pools than to switch to

public transport. This suggests that subsidies to public transport may do little to help displaced car users.

2. The commercialization of roads and the introduction of congestion pricing would substantially increase bus speeds, thus increasing the quality of their service and substantially reducing their operating costs, even with no increased subsidies.

3. One of the main reasons given for subsidizing public transport is that private transport is subsidized by being under-priced in congested areas; but commercial pricing would eliminate the under-pricing of private transport, and to that extent weaken the case for subsidizing public transport.

4. Public transport, at least in Western cities, is generally unable to recover its costs because of regulations that prohibit the public getting services (such as those that can be provided by shared taxis and high-frequency minibuses) that travelers want and are prepared to pay for (Webber, 1994). Subsidies to conventional public transport services would be unlikely to improve their responsiveness to public needs. Evidence from the US (Lave, 1994) indicates that their main effect would generally be to increase the costs and emoluments of the nice people who provide the current unsatisfactory services.

Reducing taxes on road use This would certainly be an appropriate way to compensate road users who are priced off congested roads, and it would encourage the use of roads outside the hours of high congestion. The main tax candidates for reduction would be taxes on fuel, the annual licence fees paid for passenger vehicles and, for commercial vehicles, licence fees in cases where current licence fees exceed the damage they inflict on the road system. Of these, the annual licence fees appear to be the most suitable for reduction, as they generally bear no relation to the costs of roads.

Improving the environment This would be a 'politically correct' way to use some of the profits earned by road providers, but it is difficult to see any other merit in this proposal if, as suggested in Chapter 3, road users were required to pay directly for environmental damage caused by them.

Strengthening road networks This could be another appropriate way to compensate road users, particularly in those parts of Africa, Asia and Europe where the demand for road improvement is particularly acute.

Conclusion It would seem then that there are economic and political reasons for using surpluses from congestion charges (a) to reduce licence fees and fuel taxes paid by road users, and (b) to strengthen road networks.

5.4.3 Implications of allowing surpluses to remain with road providers

Private enterprise unaided But what would be the implications of leaving such profits with those road providers who succeed in earning them? If these providers are in the public sector, even if they are public sector entities operating (as recommended here) on a commercial basis, the use of surpluses for purposes unconnected with roads would, in the absence of specific legislation, seem to be unacceptable on general grounds: because it would be an abuse of power for a government entity set up for one purpose (providing roads) to use its surpluses for other purposes.

But what if the road provider is a private entity, such as the Toll Road Corporation of Virginia? Should limits be imposed on the powers of private road providers to deal with their profits as they please? So long as the private companies operate at their own risk and expense, and get no monopoly protection from government, it is difficult to see why they should be in any way constrained in the use of their profits. As telecommunications are proposed in this book as a model for roads, readers can consider the telecommunications industry. While a public sector company formed to improve telecommunications would be expected to use its profits for this purpose, few would question the right of private providers such as AT&T to invest their profits in any way they please or to return them to shareholders as increased dividends. Similarly, where an entrepreneur, such as Gordon Wu in South China, provides a new facility entirely at his own risk and expense, it is difficult to see the case for governmental interference in the disposition of the profits.

When government lends a hand Because of the monopoly element that could be involved, and because the commercialization of government services is widely regarded as a means of transferring public assets to the undeserving rich at knock-down prices, it cannot always be right to allow road providers to retain all of their profits. Where profits are earned on roads for which monopoly concessions were obtained, and where prices are not regulated (see section 3.6 above), there can be a case for government to limit the size or the disposition of profits. The key consideration should be the extent to which the road provider benefitted from government assistance. Where assistance is given, there is case for limiting profits, if only to obviate corruption or the appearance of corruption.

However, where concessions are obtained as a result of transparent bidding processes, any profits obtained should generally be at the disposal of those who earn them.

5.5 Using the profitability criterion: dealing with losses

Much more difficult is the question of losses, as commercial markets cannot operate without profits. On some roads, traffic might not be heavy enough to generate sufficient revenue to cover even their operating and maintenance costs. Lightly-used roads in rural areas are most likely to come into this category. This is not necessarily an 'equity' issue — under-utilized roads could be those serving the remote estates of the rich. A commercial road provider would have a number of options:

Seek a general increase in the road mileage fees On the assumption that the commercialized road providers are paid by means of 'shadow tolls' — an agreed amount for each vehicle-mile of travel — the higher the unit charge, the larger the road system that could be covered, as an increase in the charge would turn border-line cases from loss to profit. This would boil down to the fuel surcharge being increased to make additional roads viable. This solution, which would generally make all roads more profit-able, is not to be confused with *cross-subsidization* — using the profits from some roads to meet the losses of others. Cross-subsidization increases the demand for loss-making roads without increasing payments from those who use them, and simultaneously deprives the owners of the profitable roads of opportunities for more productive investments. Cross subsidies inevitably reduce society's capacity to meet its more urgent needs.

Seek additional payments from landowners or other beneficiaries A more focussed solution would be to seek additional funding from the people directly concerned, who would generally be the local landowners. This approach would have to overcome the 'free rider' hurdle: some landlords might be content to have others bear the burden. This difficulty can be overcome by the landowners forming an association which would bind members by legal covenants to pay the road charges. Associations and covenants of this kind are common in St Louis (Mo), and many home-owners there actually own the roads (Gage, 1981).

Sell the road As an alternative to getting support from a landowners' association, the road could be sold to them outright, following the St Louis example. There are numerous cases of services (e.g. US regional railways) that have been made profitable after being transferred to local ownership and management.

Cut costs by downgrading road standards In some situations under-utilized roads can be kept in permanent health but at lower standards.

Abandonment In other cases abandonment might be the only commercial option, and the best social option also. Not all assets are worth preserving for ever, and the abandonment of some allows resources to be concentrated on assets that produce more benefit.

Road commercialization would inevitably result in losers as well as in gainers, and ways would generally have to be found to enable the latter to compensate the former. This matter is discussed in the next chapter.

5.6 What if 'returns to scale' are not 'constant'?

Herbert Mohring's proposition, quoted above, that congested road systems should be expanded to the point at which revenues from congestion tolls just equal highway network costs, is subject to the assumption of 'constant returns to scale'. What if they are not?

To pick up from the point made in section 3.5.1, economic assets are used to the best advantage when the cost of producing an additional unit of output just equals the price that users are prepared to pay for it. This is clear from the consideration that, if the cost of producing an additional unit is less than the amount that a user is prepared to pay, production and sale of this unit can bring immediate benefits to both producer and consumer. If, however, an additional unit can be produced at a cost that is so low that it does not cover total production costs, charging that amount will result in an overall loss to the enterprise in the long run.

> [A] benefit-maximizing level of output could be produced in such circumstances only if the business firm in question operated at a loss. It would presumably be willing to do so only if paid a subsidy (Mohring and Harwitz, 1962, p. 86).

A similar argument holds in the reverse case. The production of an additional unit by an enterprise subject to decreasing returns would cost more than the average cost of production, and a firm being paid a price to cover that incremental cost would make a profit. This is actually the case of the congested road.

One reason that these situations arise is that factors of production cannot always be supplied in small quantities, to fit demand at a particular time. Some factors — such as a machine, or a manager — can only be provided in relatively large 'lumps' which, once in place, offer 'unexploited scale economies' which only become effective when production increases.

In the case of roads, the items that can cause 'lumpiness' include the need for a minimum-width lane to accommodate traffic (a single-lane road, running at half capacity, cannot be narrowed down to half-width lane running at full capacity with traffic squeezed through it), the need for two shoulders, for drainage, for signalling and for management.

There is evidence that investment in roads can be subject to increasing or decreasing returns. In the passage quoted earlier in section 5.1, Mohring referred to evidence that 'substantial scale economies' exist in the provision of roads. But instances of both kinds can probably be found. If, for example, a single-lane road is widened, we would not expect it to accommodate significantly more traffic until it were wide enough for two lanes. We also know that three-lane roads are extremely dangerous, which is why planners try to expand two-lane roads to four-lane ones, skipping the three-lane stage. In an unpublished study of the London to Birmingham M1 motorway, Michael Beesley is reported to have found that the cost of a six-lane limited access road is less than 50 per cent more than the cost of a similar four-lane road. The US Highway Capacity Manual indicates that the capacity of a four-lane road is more than twice the capacity of a comparable two-lane one (Mohring and Harwitz, 1962, p. 87) and that, while an increase from four lanes to six leaves capacity per lane the same, an increase from six lanes to eight can actually reduce lane capacity.

How do these considerations affect the commercial criteria for investment in roads? In some cases road providers might alter the scale of their operations or the prices they charge to allow for increasing or decreasing returns to scale. In others, as seen in section 3.5.1, they would have to charge more than the benefit-maximizing price in order to stay in business. But is there a case here for governmental intervention?

Increasing and decreasing returns occur in many industries and services, including railways, telecommunications and others relevant to roads. Proposals to subsidize increasing return enterprises and to tax decreasing return ones have been made by distinguished economists (Pigou, 1920), but they did not catch on. The costs to government of subsidizing all increasing return enterprises, such as uncongested roads, would probably be prohibitive, even if ways were found to tax decreasing return ones.

In the absence of specific government policies in this area, it seems that the best principle to follow is to allow road providers to expand, contract or abandon their facilities in accordance with their own interests and with the willingness of road users and other beneficiaries to pay for them.

In cases where it is claimed that special economic benefits can be generated by subsidies to particular roads, monies can always be voted by the authorities concerned from general funds. Such subsidies should not, in general, be a burden on other road users.

Notes

1. The search for profitability can also result in substantial losses.

2. *The Economist*, in its issue of August 27, 1988 (p. 46) referred to 'the weakness of all British transport policy that ... fails to compare the merits of investment in road and rail'.

3. Costs and benefits incurred early are valued more highly than costs and benefits deferred.

6 Objections to the commercial provision of roads

More roads will get us nowhere!
Campaign for better public transport
Friends of the Earth
(Poster displayed on a car in Cambridge)

Although it is generally accepted — outside Cuba, North Korea, and some Western universities — that economic systems based on free markets are the most successful in producing wealth and raising living standards, it is by no means accepted that they should be relied on for the provision of public services. Objections of two kinds are raised. First, that there is a conflict between the operation of free markets and 'equity' and, second, that even if free markets are generally acceptable, there are special situations of 'market failure', which require governmental intervention, and that these preclude the commercial provision of public services such as roads. It is also still suggested, in all seriousness, that only government-employed planners, backed by public funds, can provide road networks consistent with national interests and aspirations.

These are big issues, too big to be fully explored here. Before discussing them, however, it is necessary to make the preliminary point that this volume does not pretend that market-type solutions can 'solve' all problems in all circumstances, or even that the market approach will 'solve' all or any road problems. Its purpose is merely to suggest that, by applying to roads the rules of market economies, we could get roads to function better than they function in most countries today, and that they might even function as well as other public services in a market economy, a specific example being the US telecommunications system.

6.1 Would it be 'equitable' for roads to operate commercially?

This is a particularly difficult point to deal with, as those who raise objections in the name of 'equity' seldom explain what they mean by the term. Even the US Congress which, in Section 210 of the 1956 Highway Revenue Act, legislated for the burden of road finance to be allocated with 'equity', omitted to define the term.

In some discussions about roads, 'equity' seems to mean that all vehicle-users, irrespective of income, are entitled to use all roads at all times, without being required to pay for such use when it occurs. The proposal that roads should be treated as commercial resources would clearly conflict with this view of equity. Before dealing with specific gainers and losers, some preliminary points can be made.

6.1.1 Efficient markets do not discriminate between rich and poor

To those who believe that commercialization would hurt the poor, one can point out that markets are, by their nature, indifferent to the incomes of those who participate in them, as they are to colour, race and gender. Markets, if they are free, treat all buyers and sellers equally. It is undeniable that markets offer more opportunities, and more choices, to those with more money, but market economies can deal with this problem by providing 'safety nets' to low-income people. Those who object to market allocations in principle should not be reading this book, which is concerned with bringing roads into the market economy.

Nor should it be assumed that low-income people do not gain from commercialization. Although the reduction of urban traffic congestion, for example, would benefit those who value their time highly (who tend to be in the upper income ranges), it would also help public transport users (who are, except in the poorest countries, in the lower income ranges). Commercialization would also enable all but the poorest to move quickly along the road system when they had to — to catch a train or to get to hospital, for example — by paying the market price. In contrast, under present circumstances, speedy journeys on city streets are not available to anyone, rich or poor, at any price, except to those, (such as heads of state or visiting World Bank delegations), who are important enough to get the police to clear the traffic ahead of them. The fact that traffic congestion offers everyone the same poor service level does not make it equitable, as those whose needs are urgent suffer more than those whose needs are trivial.

This point can be illustrated by the telecommunications service in Sri Lanka. Those fortunate enough to have the use of telephone lines in that beautiful country enjoy the lowest local phone charges in Asia, but those who do not have access to the system have to wait six years to be connected to Sri Lanka Telecom, the government monopoly. This is not necessarily an equitable situation: a rise in local phone charges could enable the authorities to reduce the waiting lists more speedily. Would this make the existing users worse off? In the short run it would but, if the higher charges enabled the service to be expanded, it would offer many more connections and thus be more useful, and the expansion of the service might even bring the charges down again, as it has done other countries.

The same situation exists on congested roads, not only in Sri Lanka but in almost all countries, where below-market prices prevent expansion and ensure bad service. Incidentally, Sri Lanka Telecom licenses private companies to supply cellular service, and this booming business goes some way to relieve the shortage of telephone lines. Similarly, in many countries private companies could, if allowed, provide additional roads.

6.1.2 Disposal of congestion revenues

The analogy with telecommunications in Sri Lanka brings out the point made in the previous chapter (section 5.4.1), about the importance of the disposition of the revenues from the higher charges. A rise in telephone charges in Sri Lanka can only help telephone users if the additional revenues thus generated are allowed to attract more investment, or better management, to the sector. The same applies to roads and, in the discussion that follows, it is assumed that any increased profits resulting from road commercialization are used to attract more investment to roads, and to relieve the shortages that enabled the profits to be earned, especially in congested areas. Clearly, the disposition of such revenues would have major consequences to equity.

6.1.3 Roads should be paid for by beneficiaries, not by all taxpayers

A reasonable person could also assert that it is not necessarily 'inequitable' to require individuals to pay the costs that arise out of their own choices. On the contrary, as these costs have to be paid by someone, it can well be argued that it is inequitable to require others to pay them. What kind of 'equity' is it that does not require individuals to pay for the direct consequences of their actions?

The point that payments should be made at the point at which 'customers' decide to use roads is put by Mohring and Harwitz, (1962, p. 88), who suggest that charges paid directly by road users, in proportion to their use of the roads, are more equitable than 'indirect' payments made by general tax payers.

> If primary reliance is placed on fuel taxes or tolls to finance highway improvements, an individual user is able to decide whether to buy highway services each time the possibility of a trip arises. If such levies as annual license fees are relied upon, a decision is allowed on an all-or-nothing basis. Having reached an affirmative decision, a user's annual payment is in no way affected by the amount he uses the highway system. Finally, with primary reliance on indirect taxes, no decision is left to the individual consumer at all. At no point is he allowed to express a choice as to whether the direct highway benefits he receives are warranted by their direct cost to him.

Mohring and Harwitz proceed to identify the inequity that arises when landowners gain as a result of road improvements and recommend 'carefully chosen' property taxes as a way of dealing with it:

> ...[T]hose who live, do business, or own property near major highway improvements would likely receive greater net benefits or benefit/tax ratios than those at some distance from these improvements. Such benefit disparities are often associated with windfall gains in land values. For this reason, applying carefully chosen non-user levies such as real estate taxes might well provide a more uniform distribution of highway improvement levies.

It would seem then, that, on general grounds, it would be difficult to attack the commercialization of roads as being inherently inequitable. On the contrary, it can well be argued that the commercial approach of having roads financed by users and other direct beneficiaries (such as landowners) is more equitable than payments out of general revenues.

Nevertheless, commercialization is bound to make some people better off and some worse off. Those required to pay more than they paid before would certainly feel that they were being badly treated, and would expect to be compensated. Is it possible to predict who would be the gainers and who the losers?

As a class, road users would stand to gain if the management and financing of roads became more responsive to their wishes. Users of inter-urban roads carrying the traffic they were designed for would be least affected by commercialization. The biggest changes would be most likely to occur at the extremes — on the congested sections, where there would be both gainers and losers, and on the least congested sections, where losers could predominate.

6.1.4 Likely gainers from commercialization

Those who value their time highly If road space were offered on a commercial basis, road users who value their time highly would be likely to benefit more than those who value their time less. It is not only the existing road users who value their time highly who would be likely to gain. The availability of road space on a market basis, particularly in congested urban centres, would in all probability attract back to the roads many of those who abandoned them in the past because they could not afford to waste their time in traffic jams.

Those who value their time highly tend to be the better off, but as was mentioned earlier, others would benefit directly also. For example, the return of better off people to live and work in run-down urban areas would be beneficial to many of those — of all income levels — who already live there.

Users of public transport   Public transport would benefit from a more efficient use of road space, because it uses it more economically than do private cars, especially in peak periods, when a bus with a pcu value of 3 might carry fifty people, while a car with a pcu value of 1 typically carries one or two. Reduced congestion would be likely to increase bus speeds, lowering costs substantially, which could result in reduced bus fares or lower taxes or both. Many of the poor rely on public transport for much of their travel, and would stand to gain from public transport improvement, as would the very old, the very young and the disabled. Reduced fares would enable some of those currently unable to afford to travel by bus (a significant proportion of travelers, especially in developing countries) to enjoy motorized transport. So the beneficiaries of road commercialization would not be confined to those earning high incomes.

Residents in city centres People of all income classes who work or live in city centres would stand to gain from increases in urban mobility and accessibility. Faster traffic would make cities more accessible and less polluting, and therefore more attractive, not only to the people already there, but also to those whose investments create new job opportunities.

Benefits to local authorities Finally, under a rational system of commercial operation, the owners of the land used for roads — generally the local authorities — would receive rents and property taxes from those who own or operate the roads, thus transforming roads from loss-making liabilities to revenue producers. Those revenues would allow local governments to increase services, to lower taxes, or to compensate those likely to lose from commercialization.

6.1.5 Likely losers from commercialization

There are three groups who could become worse off as a result of commercializing roads:

1. Users of congested roads who are forced off them by higher prices, or who have to pay more to keep on using them;

2. Users of lightly-traveled roads which would not generate sufficient revenues to justify commercial operation; and

3. Those who currently receive, or lobby for, official favours, which they could lose under a commercialized system.

Users of congested roads The imposition of commercial pricing on congested roads could result in users of those roads being faced with higher prices at peak periods. As some users would be 'priced off', speeds would rise, so there would be time savings to those remaining on the higher-priced roads, and to those attracted to them by the time savings. But, to some of those remaining, the higher price would be worth less than the savings in time, so they could become worse off.

Those forced off by the higher prices would choose what, to them, would be a less desirable way of making their journeys. Some would travel at a different time, some by a different mode (e.g. public transport), some would join car pools, and some might abandon their trips altogether, possibly choosing to travel instead to other places. All those 'priced off' could well become worse off, at least in the short run, because of being forced to do something they were not voluntarily doing before. The fact that they were benefitting before from a wasteful use of road space does not reduce the loss they suffer on having to give it up. To the extent that their life-styles and habits depended on their uneconomic use of road space, the changes forced upon them might even be regarded as 'inequitable'. For example, those who bought houses in areas served by 'freeways', whose travel costs were to rise as a result of the 'freeways' becoming 'tollways', may well consider themselves not only worse off but also to have been unfairly treated.

Of those remaining on the congested road, some would become better off — those whose time-savings were worth more than the additional price they were forced to pay. But those placing a lower value on the time saved than on the increased price would find themselves worse off.

Users of lightly-traveled roads The situation of those who use lightly-traveled roads — such as are to be found in many rural areas — is much more difficult because, under a commercialized road system, there may not be sufficient funds to pay for their roads even in cases where road users were paying all the applicable direct costs. For example, even if users of lightly-traveled roads paid for all the road maintenance costs, there might not be the funds to cover all construction costs. This problem is, of course, not peculiar to roads, but to all services in remote areas. Those who, by choice or otherwise, live far from others, do not have the access to low-cost services enjoyed by those who live in more crowded areas.

Those who enjoy official privileges The 'advantages' enumerated above would not commend themselves to all road users. Those who depend on political clout, and who enjoy the use of roads financed by other taxpayers, might not benefit directly by having roads provided in response to consumer demand.

Importance of compensation Not many hold that people have a right to receive indefinitely services at prices that do not cover even direct costs, but there is no question that reforms are eased by compensation to those who lose from them, and even to those who only appear to lose from them.

Conclusion on 'equity' On balance, it is difficult to see how the commercial provision of roads can be considered 'inequitable' when compared to the disorderly non-commercial operations which characterize many of today's road systems. Some groups would certainly become worse off if roads were provided on a commercial basis. The main losers would probably be those, especially in rural areas, who depend on underused roads — they would have to find additional funding sources (e.g. from property owners) to maintain their accessibility. But it should not be impossible to compensate those people, as the savings made in public highway budgets would, in most cases, be more than sufficient to pay for their losses. As a practical matter, existing rural roads would, in all probability, be 'grandfathered' for a period to facilitate reform.

Those priced off congested roads could be compensated by reductions in other road use charges, such as licensing fees or fuel taxes.

6.2 Coping with 'market failure'

Commercial markets, served by the voluntary transactions of participants seeking only their own advantage, work well in many circumstances. But the economic literature describes five situations of 'market failure' — situations in which commercial markets cannot be relied upon to provide appropriate services. These are where:

1. *'returns to scale'* in investment are *increasing* or *decreasing;*

2. there are *natural monopolies*;

3. there are substantial *externalities*;

4. *pure public goods* are provided;

5. *merit goods* are involved.

The issue of increasing or decreasing returns to scale has already been discussed in the previous chapter, in section 5.6. The other cases can now be considered in turn, reserving judgement on the question of whether the government alternative to commercial markets can always be relied upon to make things better.

6.2.1 Roads as 'natural monopolies'

A 'natural monopoly' is said to exist where a factor of production cannot be duplicated. In that situation, competition is not possible and a single owner would be in a position to exploit a 'captive' population. Is this a valid objection to the commercial provision of roads?

Before dealing with this issue a preliminary point should be made: monopolies are not new to road users; we confront them everywhere. When we have to wait an hour to enter New York through the Lincoln Tunnel, or when a shock-absorber is broken by a pot-hole in Bombay, there is no option of choosing another road supplier. So the issue is not one of monopoly versus competition, but whether the commercialized road system proposed in this book, which would give no unrestrained monopoly power to any road supplier, could improve the workings of systems dominated by government monopolies.

There are clearly monopoly elements in access roads, as most premises can be accessed from one road only. Roads that do not offer access have less monopoly power, and the further the distance the more likely there are to be competitive routes. So when considering the 'natural monopoly' aspect of commercialized roads it is useful to distinguish between *access roads* offering monopoly access to premises; *main roads* serving residential and other streets and *arterial roads* that link different communities.

Local streets Many access roads are already commercially provided. Private ownership of streets is common in St Louis (Missouri) and in commercial and residential new developments. Streets in shopping centres in the US and in other countries (e.g. the Philippines) are often owned by their (private) developers. Many rural access roads in Sweden are privately owned, typically by property owners' associations (Bergfalk, 1994).

For most people, the main issue with local streets is maintenance rather than new construction. Maintenance by private contractors is common in the US, and does not result in significant problems. Dissatisfaction with maintenance on privately-owned streets probably occurs from time to time, as with maintenance of publicly-owned ones, but no cases have been reported of homeowners or businesses being denied access to their premises by street owners. A local authority or property owners' association wishing to get a better deal on street maintenance is more likely to contract out maintenance to a private contractor than to sell the ownership of its streets but, in the event of such a sale, there would usually be covenants to ensure access rights. World-wide experience so far does not point to any adverse consequences arising out of the commercial ownership of local streets.

Main roads To the extent that main roads are congested, commercial ownership could result in congestion charges being imposed; if congestion charges were considered to be desirable and practicable, they could be imposed directly by a local authority, or by an association of property owners, or by a commercial owner. The question is, then, how would congestion charges affect people on a busy shopping street? Whether the charges were imposed by a commercial owner or by a local authority could be a matter of secondary importance to the people directly concerned.

On the assumption that the objective of the pricing system would be to increase the number of vehicles flowing on the street system, a price for road use would be sought which would result in traffic moving-speeds (i.e. between stops at traffic lights) in the range 20 to 30 miles per hour.[1] Speeds on heavily congested roads would rise. Rationing of road space by price would displace rationing by congestion. Motorists placing a high value on their time would displace those who have time to spare for traffic jams. Pollution levels would fall. Vehicle occupancy would increase, and public transport would be stimulated. A commercial owner of a road would, presumably, pay property tax on its land and, if it made a profit, additional taxes to local and/or national authorities. Thus a loss-making road could be converted into a profitable, commercially-owned income generator. Additionally, people living and working in congested areas, whether users of public or private transport, would stand to benefit from improved mobility. By and large, these activities are likely to bring more good than harm to their communities.

What of the danger of a monopolist 'cornering the market' in road space? The most likely monopolist to attempt to do such a thing would be a local government, which could discover a 'cash cow' in traffic congestion. The remedy is obvious: so long as private investors are permitted to add competitive links to the urban network, and to charge competitive prices, road users would have some protection from exploitation by monopolists. Commercialization that allows competitive entry would be the best method of protecting road users against monopoly.

Arterials The same argument applies in the case of the arterial roads that connect centres of activity with one another. In general, users could be protected from excessive charges by competition or even by the threat of competition. Should consumers be given additional protection by a regulatory body with powers to control the prices charged for highway use? As discussed in section 3.6, this could be appropriate in some circumstances.

It may therefore be concluded that the possibility of natural monopolies occurring in the supply of roads is not an objection to their commercialization, but rather a reason for encouraging commercialization and free entry as the best way to protect the interests of road users.

6.2.2 Roads produce 'externalities'

Buyers and sellers exchanging goods and services can create *externalities*, namely, costs and benefits for people not directly involved in the exchange. For example, factories and cars may produce noxious fumes (negative externalities) harmful to others, while trees provide shade and pleasure, which may be considered positive externalities. Some economists used to urge that transactions involving negative externalities should be discouraged by taxation, while those involving positive externalities should be encouraged by subsidies. This view has come under attack as being too simplistic, for a number of reasons.

First, there are so many activities that produce externalities that it is impracticable to subject them all to assessment for tax or subsidy. Even in these times of political correctness, many men enjoy the sight of good-looking women. Should then male-dominated parliaments vote to subsidize cosmetics? Books and newspapers produce enormous external effects: should we subsidize printing because it increases knowledge? Or should we tax books which the authorities consider to be harmful? One need only ask a few such questions to conclude that it would not be practicable to deal with all externalities in this fashion.

Second, as was pointed out by Ronald Coase (Coase, 1960), externalities involve reciprocal relationships, and cannot be regarded simply as 'baddies' to be taxed or 'goodies' to be subsidized. The sound of a child playing the violin could be a positive externality to its parents, but a negative one to the neighbours. Is the child to be taxed by the neighbours and subsidized by the parents? Clearly not. If the parties can negotiate with one another, agreements acceptable to all concerned can sometimes be reached: for example, sound-proof walls could be installed, by the neighbours or by the parents. Similarly, in the more familiar case of the smoke-emitting factory, it has to be accepted that the elimination of the smoke would not be costless. New equipment might have to be installed, or the factory relocated or even closed down. Workers could lose their jobs, as happened to wood-workers in Los Angeles when the glues used in the furniture industry were declared environmentally unacceptable. Depending on the circumstances of particular cases, it may or may not be possible for the parties concerned to negotiate cost-minimizing solutions. Where solutions cannot be reached by negotiation (because, for example, too many parties are involved) government may have to impose a solution by regulation.

It has to be concluded that not all externalities have to be dealt with by government, but only those which produce significant effects and which cannot be dealt with by the parties themselves. When government has to intervene, it should take into account the costs and benefits to all concerned.

How do these considerations apply to the use of motorized vehicles? There is no doubt that cars, lorries and buses are associated with many important externalities, some positive and some negative. Some of the positive externalities were mentioned in the introductory chapter, but no attempt is made in this book to value them. The most important negative externalities are *accidents*, which were discussed in section 3.3, *atmospheric pollution*, which was discussed in section 3.4 and *noise*, which is usually dealt with by regulation.

6.2.3 Roads are not 'pure public goods'

Some goods and services have to be provided for the benefit of all members of a group, and cannot be provided only for particular individuals. Typical examples are national defence, radio and television broadcasting, and street lighting, which are available to all, irrespective of need. Economists have named these 'pure public goods'. Once the level of (for example) street-lighting is determined for a particular area, all users get the same service, and none can be excluded from it — the blind are entitled to street lighting and are required to pay as much for it as those who can see. Indeed, one of the characteristics of 'pure public goods' is the impossibility of charging those who use them and excusing from payment those who do not. Because of the impossibility of charging, or of excluding non-payers, private markets would not (it is said) supply such goods, and therefore their provision is regarded as one of the functions of government.

Whether the provision of 'pure public goods' is a function of government is an issue that need not be discussed here, as roads for motor vehicles clearly are not in that category. Road users can be required to pay for the use of roads (by one of the many methods described in Chapter 4), and those who do not pay can be — and frequently are — excluded from them. So the concept of 'pure public goods' is not an obstacle to the commercialization of roads.

6.2.4 Roads are not 'merit goods'

In the economic literature, 'merit goods' describe goods or services which are of special merit but which, because of the ignorance of the beneficiaries, not enough would be produced if left to commercial markets. Education for children, pre-natal care, school lunches and water fluoridization are activities for which government intervention is called for under this heading.

There may be cases when it is desirable to provide roads on a non-commercial basis, but it cannot be argued that this is due to the ignorance of road users, who are generally well aware of the benefits to them from better roads. So roads cannot generally be justified as 'merit goods' for provision on a non-commercial basis.

6.3 National interests

The proposition, sometimes heard in Washington DC and other capital cities, that only governments have the information and the resources to plan and provide major road networks, is difficult to accept. Those of us who have seen these activities being carried out in practice know that the officials concerned have neither the information nor the methodologies nor the time required for such undertakings.

In contrast, as will be shown in Chapter 7, it is known that commercial organizations provided road and other transport networks in the UK and the US in the eighteenth and nineteenth centuries, under conditions far more difficult than those prevailing today.

This is not to say that commercial provision would preclude governments from having roads, railways or ports built in accordance with what they perceive to be the national interest. There is no inconsistency between roads for road users being supplied commercially at the expense of road users, and roads for, say, national defence or national unity being supplied by government at the expense of taxpayers. The purpose of this book is to explain how roads could be provided commercially, not to prevent governments providing them for other reasons.

6.4 Conclusions

It may be concluded that it is difficult to sustain any of the conventional objections to the commercial provision of roads. The concept of commercially provided roads might be difficult to implement in practice, but there do not seem to be convincing reasons (other than understandable reluctance to give up power) for governments to prevent roads being financed, planned, built, maintained and operated by commercial entities on the same terms that apply to those provided by governments themselves. The commercial provision of roads is more likely to reduce, than to increase, the likelihood of road users being exploited by monopoly suppliers.

Note

1. As speeds increase above 30 miles/hour, vehicle flows (the numbers going past a point per unit time) tend to decline.

7 Private provision of public roads

A peasant named Yuan Hudang invested 1.6 million yuan [about US$200,000] into the construction of a twenty-km village road. The county government left him in charge of the road management for several years. The road was transferred to the county after his investment was recovered (Guangdong Provincial Communications Department and others, 1992).

In the same way that most telephone users in countries such as China and India have great difficulty in appreciating that telephone service can be provided by private companies, so road users in all countries may have difficulty in envisioning the private provision of public roads. The advantages and disadvantages of commercial provision have been discussed in the previous chapters. Would there be advantages in roads being provided not only commercially but also privately, i.e. under conditions in which private capital is at risk?

7.1 Forms of private sector participation in road provision

The private sector is flexible and can serve in a variety of ways to improve highway services, for example:

1. *Unencumbered ownership* In this role the private sector takes full responsibility for the project and all financial risks, and is entitled to all the rewards. While common in the competitive sectors of the

economy, unencumbered ownership is rare in the provision of roads because of the public sector insistence on regulating tolls and other aspects of highway projects.

2. *Franchises* In this role the public sector contracts with a private entity to provide and operate a highway for a limited period. Under 'Build-Operate-Transfer' (B-O-T) agreements, private investors finance and build roads at their own risk, operate them for an agreed period, and then transfer ownership to the public sector.

3. *Management contracts* In these cases the public sector undertakes the initial investment and contracts for the private sector to manage the operation of its roads.

Management contracts are common in the US for the maintenance of local authority roads. Unencumbered ownership is much less common; most privately-provided roads, bridges and tunnels are operated nowadays under franchise, reflecting the unwillingness of governments to allow private interests to own roads for indefinite periods.

7.1.1 B-O-T projects

B-O-T projects are currently fashionable, especially in the electric power sector. There are many variants including B-O-O-T (Build-Own-Operate-Transfer) and B-T-O (Build-Transfer-Operate). The latter is used in California, to reduce the risk to private operators of public liability claims. Under B-T-O, the state takes formal title to the privately-built facility and then leases it back for private sector operation.

The kernel of a typical B-O-T arrangement is a 'Project Agreement' under which the project promoters have a contract that assures them of a stream of revenues sufficient to meet their costs and allow them a profit. In the case of a power project, the Project Agreement could be a contract with a power authority guaranteeing to buy a minimum quantity of power from the privately-provided power plant, at an agreed rate, adjustable for inflation.

Matters are more difficult in the case of toll roads because, first, there is no one 'buyer' of the roads' 'outputs' and, second, because the paucity of experience with toll roads makes it more difficult to predict future revenues. Promoters often seek Project Agreements that include government guarantees of traffic projections. Governments providing such guarantees retain the financial burden of the long-term liabilities for the roads and, furthermore, two of the main advantages of private provision : the assumption by the private sector of the traffic risk and the private sector incentives to make their services attractive so as to get more customers. If revenues are not guaranteed by governments, national or local, it becomes even more difficult to raise the funds for them. 'It is clear that most commercial lenders remain uncomfortable with the revenue risk of a highway project' (Ornitz, 1994)

B-O-T projects tend to be complicated. Although electricity generation is the leading sector for them, the Hub power project in Pakistan took over nine years to negotiate. The main elements of a typical B-O-T agreement are shown in Figure 7.1

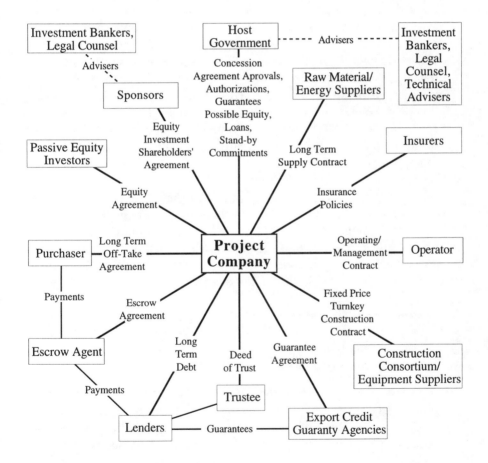

Figure 7.1 B-O-T project structure
Source: Augenblick and Custer (1990)

7.2 Advantages of private provision

Although workers in the private sector are not necessarily wiser nor more industrious than those in the public sector, private provision has some clear and distinct advantages:

Enhanced performance In many situations, private ownership may be expected to produce better performance than the public ownership of a commercialized entity, such as the New Jersey Turnpike.

> In particular, private ownership would be likely to provide more effective monitoring and commercial incentives for the firm's management than public ownership. Private investors would be placing their own wealth at risk by investing in the firm, and would therefore have more incentive to monitor and take an active interest in the commercial performance of the firm and its management. Furthermore, the management of a private firm would have greater incentive to heed the interests of its shareholders, given that it would face the threat of a hostile takeover otherwise, and would possibly face the threat of redundancies if a takeover occurred. This same constraint does not exist in the case of public ownership of a firm (Meads and Wilkinson, 1993, p. 75).

Less concern with politics Privately provided roads are more likely to be provided in response to users' needs than are government programmes which often respond more to political than to economic priorities. For example, California's AB 680 legislation (described in section 7.6.2 below), stipulated that at least one of the projects it permitted had to be in the north, and at least one in the south, irrespective of merit.

Lower costs According to Gómez-Ibáñez and Meyer (1993, p. 142), the costs per km of roads in France built by the private company Cofiroute, were 23 per cent below the comparable figures for the government-controlled Sociétés d'Économie Mixte (SEMs).

> Ten percentage points of the difference was reportedly because of more cost-sensitive roadway design, including a slightly narrower median and the use of swale drainage systems where possible. The remaining 13 percentage points were from higher productivity of labor and equipment.

Better information Private providers on the look-out for profit are likely to be better and more quickly informed about opportunities for road improvement in their areas, than are government agencies concerned with operating existing systems. Furthermore,

> [a]s well as the personal incentives that private investors would have to monitor the performance of their firm directly, share analysts would have incentives to monitor the commercial performance of the firm on behalf of large groups of private or institutional investors, and to distribute the results of this research. Investors would be able to respond to this information by changing the level of their shareholding in the firm. Any resulting adjustment in the firm's share price would provide information to the firm's management on financial markets' assessment of their commercial performance (Meads and Wilkinson, 1993, p. 75).

Speed of response If allowed to by the local planning processes, private providers can get roads financed and built more quickly than public institutions. This is not because the private sector employs better people, but because it is not constrained, as are public agencies, by purchasing rules designed to protect the public interest. Private operators, on the other hand, can strike quick deals when speed is to their advantage.

Ability to finance expansion Private providers have access to sources of funds seeking profitable investments, and can use them to improve and extend road networks. Publicly-owned firms, on the other hand, can be subjected to political constraints on expansion for a variety of reasons.

Competition One of the most important advantages associated with private provision is competition. In the seventy years prior to 1984, telecommunications in the US were run on a commercial basis by AT&T. The service was probably the best in world, and the cheapest. The system's Bell Laboratories, where the transistor was one of many devices invented and developed, had few rivals in excellence and innovation. Despite the significant results obtained by this private sector monopoly, most observers agree that its abolition in 1984 introduced significant product innovation and cost-cutting as a result of the newly permitted competition.

These results are to be seen not only in the US. Countries as diverse as Argentina, Britain, Jamaica and Mexico all privatized their telephone systems, leaving most services in the hands of governmentally-protected monopolies. After the event, consumers in all four countries demanded competition to spur the development of even better services and lower prices. In contrast, Sri Lanka allowed three companies to provide cellular telephone services, and the resulting competition has driven down rates and improved service quality.

Similar results are likely from competition in the provision of roads. A commercialized city road authority, working to financial targets and responsive to its customers, may be far superior to urban road systems today. But competition — or the threat of competition — in the form of private firms being allowed to provide additional road links, could bring even better results. This is likely to be illustrated by the completion of the Dulles Greenway and the SR-91 improvements (see section 7.6) — privately-provided road links offering enhanced accessibility to road users in Northern Virginia and Southern California.

7.3 Examples of privately provided roads

The following examples are given to illustrate the accomplishments and the difficulties facing private providers of public roads.

7.3.1 Some early roads, privately provided

Privately provided roads preceded the motor car. In the beginning of the nineteenth century, hundreds of turnpike companies operated in the UK and US. In 1830 there were in Great Britain 1,116 turnpike trusts maintaining 22,000 miles of toll roads, which accounted for about one-fifth of the total road system (Rees Jeffreys, 1949). These companies were financed almost entirely by private capital and received tolls from road users.

The British example was followed by toll road companies in the US. The first turnpike road to operate in the US, connecting Philadelphia and Lancaster, was chartered by Pennsylvania in 1792 and opened in 1794. Other roads quickly followed and, by 1800, 69 companies had been chartered (Klein and Fielding, 1992). The number of turnpike companies chartered in the US eastern states between 1792 and 1845 were tabulated by Klein and Fielding and are shown in Table 7.1. The total length of these roads exceeded 10,000 miles. Relative to the size of the economy at that time, such investments in roads were very large. In the US, their comparative magnitude exceeded the public sector investments in the Interstate Highway System after the Second World War (Gunderson, 1989).

Table 7.1
Turnpike incorporation, 1792–1845

State	1792-1800	1801-10	1811-20	1821-30	1831-40	1841-45	Total
NH	4	45	5	1	4	0	59
VT	9	19	15	7	4	3	57
MA	9	80	8	16	1	1	115
RI	3	13	8	13	3	1	41
CT	23	37	16	24	13	0	113
NY	13	126	133	75	83	27	457
PA	5	39	101	59	101	37	342
NJ	0	22	22	3	3	0	50
VA	0	6	7	8	25	0	46
MD	3	9	33	12	14	7	78
OH	0	2	14	12	114	62	204
Total	**69**	**398**	**362**	**230**	**365**	**138**	**1562**

Note:

CT:	Connecticut	MA:	Massachusetts	MD: Maryland
NH:	New Hampshire	NJ:	New Jersey	NY: New York
OH:	Ohio	PA:	Pennsylvania	RI: Rhode Island
VA:	Virginia	VT:	Vermont	

Source: Fielding and Klein (1992)

However, road development in the US, as in the UK, was interrupted by the rise of the railways, which put most of the eastern turnpikes out of business. California, however, was a late developer, and 150 toll roads were put into operation there by private interests between 1850 and 1902 (Klein, 1994).

There was some development of private toll roads in the US in the twentieth century but they, in their turn, were superseded by the public sector 'freeways'. However, even as late as 1933 there were, in the US alone, over 200 private companies operating toll bridges.

The demise of the turnpikes is often used to illustrate the weakness of the private provision of public services, but it actually shows one of its main strengths: private sector provision, unlike public sector operations, ceases when the demand for it becomes inadequate.

Table 7.2
Private toll road projects, 1993

Toll Road	Length (miles)	Cost ($ million)	Status
ARGENTINA			
Buenos Aires, northern link	59	$470	A
Buenos Aires, western access	35	220	A
Buenos Aires, airport access	36	160	A
Cordoba state highways	N/A	110	S
Chile-Argentina tunnel	N/A	500	S
River Plate bridge	31	1,000	S
S. America Super Highway	1,429	2,500	S
19 operating concessions	6,215	1,200	O'91
AUSTRALIA			
Sydney Harbor Tunnel	1.4	$550	O '92
F4 Freeway, Sydney	6.2	180	O '92
F5 Freeway, Sydney	8.7	216	O '92
Melbourne Bypass	N/A	770	S
Sydney-Brisbane Tollway	N/A	3,100	S
Newcastle-Queensland Freeway	217	720	S
M2 Freeway, Sydney	12	776	S
Eastern Distributor, Sydney	N/A	540	S
NW Transport Link, Sydney	13	340	S
Swan River Tunnel, Perth	N/A	98	S
AUSTRIA			
Trans-European Motorway	N/A	N/A	S
Semmering Motorway	N/A	N/A	F
BALTICS			
The Hansaway (Berlin-St. Petersburg)	N/A	N/A	S
Via Baltica (Warsaw-Tallinn)	N/A	N/A	S
BRAZIL			
Sao Paulo Beltway	108	$2,200	S
Anhanguero-Bandeirantes tollway	46	580	S
Castello Branco tollway-Sao Paulo	7	240	S
Dutra-Trabalhadores Caroalho	300	860	S
Pinto tollway			
BULGARIA			
Kelotina-Svilengrad Road	186	$330	S
CANADA			
Northumberland Strait Crossing	8.2	$1,200	C
Highway 407, Toronto	75	900	F
2nd St. Clair River Bridge	N/A	75	S
CHILE			
El Melon Tunnel	N/A	$25	C
Algarroba-Cartagena	16	17	F
La Dormida route & tunnel	55	88	F
Santiago Airport Access	1	5	F
Santiago-Farellones	22	7.5	F
Santiago-San Antonio	63	67	F
South Access-Conception	70	15	F
Mirador del Valle-Santiago	32	50	S
North Access-Conception	63	60	S
North Riverside-Santiago	9	80	S
Puchuncavi-Nogales	17	5	S
Santiago-Valparaiso	79	85	S
CHINA			
Hong Kong-Guangzhou Super Highway	180	$1,500	C
Guangzhou Ring Road	14	363	C
Yangpu Bridge	0.4	250	C
Zuhai-Hainan Highway	56	N/A	F
Shunde Tollway	N/A	186	S
Boca Tigris Bridge	2.5	300	S
Zuhai Tunnel & Bridge Link	26.7	910	S
Wuhan Highway	11	58	S
Liaoning Toll Highway	47	166	S
Hangzhou Bridge	6.2	45	S
Beijing-Hong Kong Highway	1,492	8,000	S
Huizhou-Heynan Highway	N/A	250	S
Harbin Ring Road	40	N/A	S
Taiwan-Fujian Bridge	2.5	100	S

Toll Road	Length (miles)	Cost ($ million)	Status
Shenzhen-Shentou Highway	177	$555	S
Panyu-Guangdong Bridge	1.7	139	S
Guangzhou-Shaoguen Highway	224	868	S
Yautian-Huizhou Highway	40	104	S
Foshan-Sanshai Highway	20	729	S
Guangzhou-Zhuhai Highway	47	591	S
Foshan-Kai Ping Highway	50	278	S
Huizhou-Heynan Highway	42	139	S
COLOMBIA			
Bogota-Puerto Salgar Highway	45	$119	F
Bogota-Villavicencia Highway	35	47	S
Bogota-Caqueza Highway	19	80	S
North Bogota Tollway	28	54	S
Barranquilla-Cienega	37	17	F
DENMARK			
Femer Belt Crossing	12	$3,460	S
FRANCE			
Lyon N. Ring Road/Tunnels	5.3	$470	C
Marseilles Road Tunnel	1.5	221	C
M.U.S.E.	29	5,400	A
Paris Peripherique Extensions	14.3	260	S
GERMANY			
Bad Kreuznach Bridge	N/A	$9	A
Hamburg River Elbe Tunnel	2	300	F
Dortmund-Muhlheim Tunnel	22	5,900	S
Freiburg East Tunnel	N/A	N/A	S
GREECE			
Athens-Attica Highway	36	$920	F
Gulf of Corinth Bridge	1.6	450	F
Aktion-Preveza Tunnel	0.6	48	F
Rion-Antirion Bridge	2.2	480	F
Western Peripheral Motorway	9	120	F
Athens Beltway	31	1,000	F
Perama-Salaminas Tunnel	0.6	40	F
Thessaloniki Tunnel	0.9	190	F
GUATEMALA			
Motorway upgrades	466	$69	S
HONDURAS			
Tegucigalpa-Palerola Freeway	50	$50	S
HONG KONG			
Eastern Harbor Crossing	5.3	$565	O '89
Tate's Cairn Tunnel	2.5	282	O '91
Western Harbor Crossing	1.2	900	F
Rt 3, Tai Lam Tunnel/Road	5	1,250	F
Tsing Ma Bridge	0.9	930	F
Rt 3, Country Park Road	6.2	1,300	S
HUNGARY			
M1/M15 Motorway	35	$220	C
M5 Motorway	81	460	F
M3/M30 Motorway	159	1,000	F
M7 Motorway	88	2,500	F
Szekszard Bridge	12	100	C
Dunanguaros Bridge	N/A	N/A	S
ICELAND			
Hvalfjordur Tunnel	N/A	$36	S
INDONESIA			
Wiyoti: Wiyono North-South Tollroad	11	$175	O '90
Jakarta-Bandung Toll Highway	29	360	S
Cikampek-Padalarang Road	37	500	F
Jakarta Outer Ring Road/RAN	23	500	F
IRAN			
Qeshm Island Gulf Bridge	1.6	$100	S
IRELAND			
Dublin Ring Road	N/A	$250	F
Dublin Bridges (2)	N/A	62	C
West Link	2	40	O'90

Table 7.2 continued on next page

Table 7.2 continued from previous page

Toll Road	Length (miles)	Cost ($ million)	Status
ISRAEL			
Haifa Tunnel	2.8	$120	F
Cross-Israel Highway	174	2,000	S
ITALY			
Pordenone-Conegliano	9.3	N/A	C
Sarre-Traforo Del Monte Bianco	12.1	N/A	C
Aosta Est-Aosta Ovest	6.8	N/A	C
Livorno-Civitavecchia	23	N/A	C
MALAYSIA			
North-South Toll Road + Connectors	577	$2,300	C
Serebam-Port Dickinson Road	18	50	C
Kuala Lumpur-Karak Toll Road	N/A	185	S
Johor-Singapore 2nd Causeway	30	370	A
Penang Toll Bridge	N/A	215	F
Sham Alam Urban Expressway	N/A	510	F
Kuala Lumpur-Sepang Tollway	31	500	S
MEXICO			
Guadalajara-Colima Highway	92	$125	O '89
Cuernavaca-Acapulco Toll Road	163	780	O '90
Monterrey-Nuevo Laredo Toll Road	106	127	O '91
Zapotlanejo-Logos	94	250	O '91
Cordoba-Veracruz	61	180	O '91
Merida-Cancun	155	180	O '91
Tecate-Mexicali	94	300	C
La Tinaja-Cosoleaque	143	615	O '92
Mexico City-Guadalajara	200	1,200	C
Mazatlan-Culiacon & Los Mochis-Estacion Don	181	377	C
Leon-Logos-Aguascalientes Toll Rd.	70	231	C
Cadereyta-Reynosa	109	270	C
Santa Ana-Sonoyta	134	N/A	S
NETHERLANDS			
Wijker Road Tunnel	N/A	$250	A
Rotterdam Tunnel	N/A	300	S
Scheldt Tunnel	N/A	525	S
PAKISTAN			
Karachi Expressway	11	$400	S
PANAMA			
Corredor Norte	N/A	$75	S
POLAND			
A1	N/A	N/A	S
A2	N/A	N/A	S
A4	N/A	N/A	S
A34/A12	N/A	N/A	S
PORTUGAL			
Tagus River Bridge	6	$450	F
ROMANIA			
Via Vita	800	$3,000	F
RUSSIA			
Moscow-Minsk-Brest	675	$1,500	S
SOUTH AFRICA			
Two new toll roads + upgrades of existing roads	248	$170	O
Orange Free State tollways	N/A	94	A
THAILAND			
Second Stage Expressway	20	$1,060	O '93
Bangkok Elevated Transport System	35	3,140	C
UNITED KINGDOM			
Dartford Crossing	1.7	$146	O '91
Severn Estuary Bridge	3	915	C
Birmingham Northern Relief Road	30	850	A
Birmingham Western Orbital Route	44	835	F
River Tamar Crossing	N/A	185	S
M74-M8 Road	N/A	170	S
Skye Bridge (Scotland)	N/A	38	A
River Forth Bridge (Scotland)	N/A	820	F
Glasgow Bypass	30	N/A	S

Toll Road	Length (miles)	Cost ($ million)	Status
UNITED STATES			
Dulles Extension (VA)	14.7	$330	C
SR 91 Express Lanes (CA)	10	126	C
Santa Ana Viaduct Express (CA)	11.2	700	A
San Diego Expressway (CA)	10	400	A
Mid-State Tollway (CA)	85	700	A
Fargo/Moorhead Toll Bridge (ND-MN)	0.1	1.6	O '88
Tampa Bay Toll Road (FL)	N/A	N/A	F
San Jose Lagoon Bridge (PR)	2.1	124	C
PR66 (PR)	15	500	A
Ponce Beltway (PR)	N/A	200	A
Camino Falcon (Laredo-Corpus Christi, TX)	200	N/A	S
Camino Columbia (Laredo, TX)	22	80	S
Southwest (Houston, TX)	40	N/A	S
Dallas Toll Roads-NTA (TX)	120	N/A	S
Southern Beltway (Houston, TX)	21	250	S
Dallas and San Antonio toll roads (TX)	N/A	N/A	S
Austin-San Antonio (TX)	120	N/A	S
Rt. 3, Mass. upgrade	20	N/A	S
Chicago Skyway	7.5	N/A	S
Orlando Western beltway	10	225	S
Minneapolis beltway	N/A	2,500	S
Phoenix priced HOV lanes	N/A	440	S
Phoenix VUE 2000	160	2,800	S
URAGUAY			
Montevideo-Punta del Este	80	N/A	F
VENEZUELA			
Caracas-La Guaira Expressway (upgrade)	9.4	$92	S
YUGOSLAVIA			
E75 Highway upgrade	110	$330	F

KEY:
S = under study
F = franchise competition under way
A = awarded franchise
C = under construction
O = in operation (year)

Source: Reason Foundation (1994)

7.3.2 More recent roads, privately provided

The extent of private sector involvement in roads in recent years can be seen in Table 7.2. One of its most striking features is the contrast between the number of roads planned by the private sector and the number actually under construction or in service. The private provision of public roads is difficult and time-consuming. Some of what has been accomplished is described below, and the chapter will conclude with a discussion of the impediments that constrain private sector participation in the roads sector, and how they might be removed or reduced.

7.4 United Kingdom

As part of the Thatcher revolution, the British government encouraged the private sector to invest in Britain's road network. In 1991 the *New Roads and Street Works Act* was passed to enable major infrastructure projects to be approved without the need for individual parliamentary bills for each project.

7.4.1 The Dartford river crossing

In 1986 the government awarded a contract to Dartford River Crossing Ltd. (a company jointly owned by Trafalgar House PLC and three financial institutions) to construct a £210 million toll river crossing to be built across the Thames at Dartford. The 1.7 mile crossing includes a 1,476-foot cable-stayed centre span bridge, the longest in Europe. The crossing was built as a Build-Own-Transfer (B-O-T) project, and is to be transferred to the government free of debt as soon as sufficient tolls are collected. The financing problems were eased by allowing excess revenues from the existing Dartford toll tunnel to support the new project.

7.4.2 The Birmingham Northern Relief Road

In 1989 the government invited proposals to finance, construct and operate the Birmingham Northern Relief Road, which is to go northwards for about fifteen miles from the M6 motorway, close to the M42 junction, and then twelve miles west to rejoin the M6 near Cannock. This twenty-seven-mile expressway, which is expected to relieve congestion in one of England's busiest urban areas, is to be operated as a toll road for fifty years, after which it is to be transferred to the government free of debt. The contract price is likely to be about £350 million.

The right to build and operate the BNRR was won in August 1991 by Midland Express Ltd., a company jointly owned by Trafalgar House (the successful operator of the Dartford Crossing) and the Italian conglomerate Iritecna. The project is now going through the public enquiry process which is required for all major road improvements in the UK.

7.5 Continental Europe

Because public funds were scarcer in twentieth-century Europe than in America, governments there were more eager than in the US to rely on toll roads, many of which had significant private sector inputs. However, because some toll roads became more profitable than others, governments tended to amalgamate them into unitary financial systems, with the stronger ones cross-subsidizing the weaker brethren, and consequential weakening of financial management.

7.5.1 France

Since the Middle Ages, the main roads in France were the responsibility of the central government, and Adam Smith remarked (Smith, 1776, p. ii, 251) that

> [T]he great post roads [there] ... are in general kept in good order; and in some provinces are even a good deal superior to the greater part of the turnpike roads of England.

After the Second World War there was an urgent need to upgrade the main road network but funds were not available, so a law was passed in 1955 allowing high-capacity expressways (*autoroutes*) to be provided on a concession basis, with tolls being allowed under 'exceptional circumstances'. In 1960 a national plan for the creation of 3,500 km of *autoroutes* was adopted. Responsibility for implementation was given to five p ublic–private undertakings known as *Sociétés d'Économie Mixte* or, more familiarly, SEMs. In practice the SEMs were more 'public' than 'private' undertakings and were described by a minister at the time as the 'false nose of the state' (Fayard, 1994).

Progress was not satisfactory and in 1970 the law was changed to allow the participation of purely private entities. The administrative arrangements, as modified, required the transfer of the roads to the public domain after thirty-five years or less; the payment of fees by concessionaires to the government; government guarantees of 75 per cent of approved borrowings; the provision of short-term loans to meet revenue shortfalls; public ownership of the rights-of-way, with the concessionaires having the powers of compulsory purchase of land; and government control of design standards (Button, 1989). Four private companies were formed in the early 1970s, to build the roads and operate the concessions, and all included participants from the major French public works construction companies. Although nominally private, the new companies enjoyed governmental guarantees for a high proportion of their loans, and other privileges.

All the concessionaires, including both the SEMs and the new private companies, faced increasing financial problems in the 1970s. The 1973 oil crisis resulted in increased costs and lower traffic flows; the government reneged on its obligation to allow tolls to be raised to meet cost increases, and the private companies do not appear to have taken the most stringent measures to control the costs of the building contractors who formed part of their consortia. In 1981 the new Mitterrand government took over three of the four private concessionaires, leaving only Cofiroute in private hands (Gómez-Ibáñez and Meyer, 1993, pp. 109-122). In 1982 the government 'harmonized' the toll rates in an organization designed to combine uniform toll rates with cross-subsidies to ensure that the financially stronger concessions supported the weaker ones. In 1989 and 1990 the government further weakened its road financing system (as Britain had done sixty years earlier) by transferring surpluses of toll revenues to non-road purposes. It also refused to allow tolls to rise in step with inflation.

Of all the French toll road operators, only Cofiroute managed to stay out of the cross-subsidy network and went on to turn from loss to profit in 1987, seventeen years after its establishment. Employing over 1,300 people, it also has interests in road provision outside France. It claims to be the largest toll road operator in the world, and to have raised over US$20 billion for roads from private sources. Cofiroute is a key participant in California's SR-91, described in section 7.6.2 below (*Public Works Financing*, July/August 1993).

7.5.2 Italy

The Italian toll expressway network was established in 1924 with the commissioning of the thirty-mile Milan-Lake route, probably the first toll expressway in the world. By 1990 the Italian expressway network was more than 6,000 km long, almost all of it tolled. These toll roads are operated by twenty-two concessionaires, the largest of which is the Autostrade Company, in which the state has a holding, and which is responsible for the management of over 1,600 miles of toll expressways. The Italian concession companies work closely with the government; they benefit from government guarantees and, in return, are obligated to operate loss-making parts of the system and to return all roads to the government at the end of the concession periods.

7.5.3 Spain

Public/private partnerships for the provision of toll roads were also important in Spain, where over 2,000 km of '*autopistas*' (toll expressways) have been built by private concessionaires, the majority in the 1970s (Gómez-Ibáñez and Meyer, 1993, pp. 122-144).

The need for improved roads became evident in the 1960s, but the use of public funds for expressways was felt to be unjustified because, it was said, most of the benefits would go to the more prosperous regions, especially those benefiting from the boom in tourism. In 1967 the 'National Spanish Motorway Plan' was published, which called for the construction of 4,800 km of '*autopistas*' by 1985.[1] The first concessions, for roads totaling about 1,000 km in length, were granted in 1967, on the basis of specific ordinances for each of them. In 1973 a decree was issued implementing the law of October 5, 1972, on the construction, preservation and operation of *autopistas*, in concession. This legislation established general standards, applicable to all *autopistas*, which

> ... allow the State to decide on the construction of motorways, the route, their technical characteristics, the conditions of financing and exploitation, etc. Once these decisions have been taken, the State entrusts the construction of the projected motorways to the private sector, allowing it in return the exploitation of the motorway on a toll basis. The concession period may not exceed fifty years, including the period of construction (OECD, 1987, p. 99).

This decree shows clearly that the private sector was invited to implement the national road programme, not to make its own. To avoid placing excessive burdens on Spain's own financial resources, the authorities required that at least 45 per cent of funding for the *autopistas* had to come from overseas. Concessionaires had to invest at least 10 per cent of the costs from their own resources. As the concessionaires were not able to absorb the currency risk to the foreign investors, this was guaranteed by the government, which also guaranteed 75 per cent of the investments made by foreigners in the *autopista* programme.

The Spanish programme started well, and eleven companies were granted concessions. However, the oil crisis of 1973 raised costs and reduced traffic, forcing the government to take over three of the eleven concession companies, and to use its own funding (in the form of interest-free loans) to complete their projects. The exchange rate guarantee also cost the government dearly; by 1990 it had paid over 300 billion pesetas to fulfil its obligation to foreign investors.

In 1982 Spain elected a new government, led by the Socialist Felipe Gonzales, which halted the *autopista* programme and substituted *autovias,* expressway-type roads that were toll-free. The new government complained that its predecessor's guarantee policy encouraged the concessionaires to take unnecessary risks and that, in particular, the foreign exchange guarantees encouraged them to seek foreign loans at the lowest interest rates, without regard to the exchange risks.

The reasons for preferring *autovias* to *autopistas* are instructive. First, many sections of the *autopistas* were under-utilized, because traffic was diverted by the tolls, and because the restricted number of tolled entrances made them unattractive for short journeys. Second, the *autopistas* were much more expensive to construct than the *autovias*, because the requirement that travelers should have the option of an un-tolled route required them to be built on new rights-of-way. *Autovias*, on the other hand, could be improved (as was much of the A1 'Great North Road' in England) by adding new lanes to the existing ones. The use of 'shadow tolls', as discussed in sections 4.2.5 and 8.1.1, would have overcome both problems.

7.5.4 Hungary

Eastern Europe's first privately financed road became a possibility in 1991 when the government of Hungary, acting on the advice of the European Bank for Reconstruction and Development (EBRD) passed a road concession law (Reina, 1994). The government had earlier created a fund, largely fed by fuel tax revenues, to finance road expansion, but the fund did not generate sufficient funds to finance Hungary's road expansion programme.

The M1-M15 motorway, when completed, will connect Budapest with the main roads to Vienna and Prague. The Hungarian segments comprise a 26.7-mile (42.4 km) extension of the existing M1 motorway to the Austrian border, to complete the 162-mile Vienna–Budapest motorway, and a nine-mile (14.5 km) branch to the Czech border, to complete the link with Prague. The proposed toll is 350 florint (about US$3 at 1992 prices) for cars, and four times as much for trucks. Unlike in France, Mexico, Spain, and most other countries, restrictions will be imposed on the use of the alternative 'free' routes, so all foreign trucks, and some local ones, will be forced to use the tolled motorway. US$380 million were raised to cover construction and financing costs and a reserve account for maintenance.

Most of the road will have four lanes, but the M15 spur will start with only two, and will be widened when traffic volumes increase sufficiently to justify four lanes. The government prequalified four consortia and eventually awarded the concession to HEEC, which is comprised of French and Hungarian entities, and Hungarian and Austrian subsidiaries of the German contractor Strabag.

Financial support was obtained from the EBRD, which had earlier recommended the concession route, from the Banque Nationale de Paris, the Hungarian Savings and Commercial Bank, and from French and German commercial banks. There is no government guarantee — unlike most of the road financing arrangements in Europe, in Hungary there is real private capital at risk. To reduce currency risks, 40 per cent of the debt was provided by local banks (Ornitz, 1994).

The main construction contract, at a fixed price, was awarded to Strabag Osterreich, who are working to designs carried out by Hungarian government engineers. All concerned are under pressure to complete the road by the end of 1995, in time for the 1996 Budapest World Fair.

7.6 United States

The federal Intermodal Surface Transportation Efficiency Act of 1991 (ISTEA, as in 'iced tea') included provisions to encourage the flow of private finance to the US roads sector. Privately provided new toll roads, bridges and tunnels, as long as they were not part of the Interstate Highway System, became eligible for 50 per cent grants from the federal Highway Trust Fund (Poole, 1992). By lending these funds to commercial road operators, the states can use the repayments to create revolving funds to finance other toll road projects. To take advantage of this facility, states have to pass their own legislation to allow the private provision of public roads. Until 1995, only Arizona, California, Florida, Minnesota, South Carolina, Texas, Virginia and Washington have done so.

California and Virginia are the states in which privately-financed projects are most advanced. Two projects — one in each state — are completely financed and under construction: the Dulles 'Greenway' in Northern Virginia, close to Washington DC, and the SR (State Road) 91, in California's Orange County, adjacent to Los Angeles. Both were designed to relieve congestion in rapidly growing suburban areas, both are to be toll roads incorporating state-of-the-art toll collection technology; and both reached the construction stage as a result of enormous efforts of dedicated individuals. Because of their importance as models for future development, they are described below in some detail.

Although government funds available under the ISTEA provisions have been used to assist in the financing of some toll roads, neither the Greenway nor the SR-91 projects took advantage of them, presumably because the complications involved with government funding made it unsuitable. However, had the proposals in this book been in force, both of the companies operating these roads would have received 'shadow tolls' based on their traffic, with no conditions attached. The projected revenue streams from this source would have surely helped them to raise investment funds.

7.6.1 Virginia's Dulles Greenway

The entrepreneur who conceived the idea of a privately provided extension to the Dulles Toll Road was Ralph Stanley. A graduate of Princeton University and Georgetown University Law Center, and an investment analyst, Stanley cut his teeth in the politics of transport (or 'transportation', as it is called in the US) as an assistant to US Department of Transportation Secretaries Drew Lewis and Elizabeth Dole. From 1984 to 1987 he served the Reagan government by running UMTA — the Urban Mass Transportation Administration, now the Federal Transit Administration — where he did much to encourage the private provision of public transport services. Stanley achieved national fame when, in responding to UMTA being awarded the Order of the Golden Fleece (an 'honour' created by Senator William Proxmire to highlight government waste), he assured the Democratic senator that 'we got this prize the old-fashioned way — we earned it!'

In 1987 Stanley left UMTA committed to promoting projects, such as roads, usually undertaken by governments. He looked all over the US for an opportunity to supply a road, and chose the Dulles Toll Road extension because he believed it met the five conditions he stipulated:

1. Good prospects for adequate traffic;

2. A small number of landowners occupying his proposed right-of-way;

3. The ability to provide the road by the time it was needed;
4. Prospects for good authorizing legislation at the state level; and

5. The expectation that transport would remain a top issue in the locality.

Development in the area of the proposed road was triggered by the Dulles International Airport which was constructed in the 1960s, together with its own Dulles Airport Access Road (DAAR) dedicated for airport use only. This road established what came to be known as the Dulles Corridor which, like many other airport access roads, stimulated extensive development. But this could not be served directly by the DAAR, which was reserved for airport travel.

To serve local needs a new toll road was built by the Virginia Department of Transportation alongside the DAAR. This road, which extended from the Washington Beltway almost to the Dulles Airport, was opened in 1983, as the Dulles Toll Road. It was so successful that its twenty-year traffic forecasts were actually achieved eighteen months after opening. The Dulles Toll Road stimulated further development in the Dulles Corridor, and substantial queues developed at its toll booths, which had two consequences relevant to this book. First, as mentioned in section 4.3.2, the Virginia DOT decided to introduce electronic non-stop toll collection to reduce the queues at the toll booths. Second, as development extended beyond Dulles Airport, Stanley identified the proposed Dulles Toll Road Extension — a fourteen-mile road from the airport to the town of Leesburg — as the best candidate to become the first modern privately provided toll road in the US.

Stanley established the Toll Road Corporation of Virginia (TRCV) to implement the project. On July 20, 1989, Virginia's Commonwealth Transportation Board authorized the project, the first private toll road to be authorized in Virginia since 1816. The Italian toll road operator Autostrade agreed to operate the road and to assist with the financing. The estimated cost was $155 million. Stanley than had to get the land for the right-of-way, raise the funds, and obtain further authorizations from Virginia, e.g. permission to levy a toll. Under his leadership, most of this work was done: the main players in the project were put in place, forty-nine out of fifty required land parcels were assembled, environmental permits were obtained, and the project was successfully promoted in Northern Virginia and Washington DC (Reinhardt, 1994).

But Stanley was unable to raise the funds for the project he launched, and left it in 1993 to pursue other ventures. Michael Crane assumed the leadership of the project as Chief Executive Officer and succeeded in assembling the financing package. Northern Virginia investor Magalen Bryant, whose family committed over $50 million to the project, then engaged Charles E. Williams — a retired Major–General in the US Army Corps of Engineers — to complete the development phase of the project and take it through the construction phase.

Construction started on September 29, 1993 and is due to be completed by the contractor — Brown & Root of Texas — within two years, six months ahead of schedule. The Dulles Greenway will thus be the first of the new generation of toll roads to open in the US, beating California's SR-91 (see next section) which, despite its four months' head–start, is taking longer to build because of the heavy traffic on the existing lanes (*PublicWorks Financing* July-August 1994).

A salient point about the land acquisition is that all the land required for the Dulles Greenway was obtained voluntarily. Some landowners donated land at no charge, others required payment, but no land was acquired by compulsion, though the county had the necessary powers, and was report-ed to be prepared to use them.

Toll rates had to be agreed with the Virginia State Corporation Commis-sion (SCC). They are set to start at $2.75 for the fourteen-mile road, about twenty cents per mile. Equity returns are capped by the SCC at 30 per cent after tax during construction, and dropping to 17 per cent in later years (*Public Works Financing*, September, 1993).

The financing was obtained with great difficulty. Goldman, Sachs and Co. (one of Wall Street's leading financing firms) brought the road to the financial markets as early as 1990, but without success.

> [A]t that time, few lenders in the taxable markets were willing or able to assess project risks for a purely private toll road with no state credit support. Lenders who did take the time to understand the traffic studies were intrigued. But they found plenty of other reasons not to be a leader in a first-of-a-kind, real-estate driven infrastructure project during a recession ... The lack of legal or political precedents made the financial closing process extraordinarily — almost overwhelmingly — complex (Reinhardt, 1994).

The $155 million estimate for the total cost proved over-optimistic. By the time the financing was arranged in September 1993 the total commit-ment was $139 million in equity, and $279 million in debt at a weighted average rate of 10.18 per cent per year. In accordance with toll road tradition, much of the equity was obtained from local investors. Barclays, NationsBank and Deutsche Bank participated in the short-term debt financing, while insurance companies led by CIGNA Investments, Pruden-tial and John Hancock provided long-term finance.

7.6.2 California's SR-91

In the summer of 1989 the California legislature passed Assembly Bill 680 (AB 680) which enabled the California Department of Transportation (Caltrans) to develop partnerships with private entities to design, build and operate toll highways under thirty-five-year leases on state-owned rights-of-way. Caltrans promptly established a Department of Privatization charged with the task of arranging four demonstration projects, of which at least one had to be in northern California and at least one in the south. Road developers worldwide were invited to submit proposals and ten were received. Four of these were selected,[2] and the winning teams invited to negotiate development agreements. The winning projects were:

1. State Route 91 express lanes, ten miles, in Orange County;

2. The State Route 57 extension, eleven miles, in Orange County;

3. The San Diego Expressway, ten miles, near the Mexican border; and

4. The Mid-State Tollway, eighty-five miles, near San Francisco.

Summary information about these projects is given in Table 7.3. All have to satisfy local planning and environmental regulations and are subject to delays by lawsuits and other obstacles.

The SR-91 project is the most advanced of the four. It is described as a 'congestion reliever' and consists of four new travel lanes in the median of the existing State Route 91, which carries 200,000 commuter vehicles in and out of Los Angeles every weekday. The sponsoring company, California Private Transportation Company (CPTC), is owned by Kiewit Diversified Group, the Cofiroute Corporation, and the main builders of the road, Granite Construction Corporation. The sponsors raised $126 million for the project and enabled work on it to commence in July 1993. It is expected to be open for traffic in 1996 (Reinhardt, 1993).

SR-91 is the first modern US toll road to be financed and launched (but the Dulles Greenway may be the first to open for traffic); the first toll road to have no toll booths; and the first in the US to employ congestion pricing (Poole, 1993). The absence of toll booths means that all vehicles using the new lanes will have to be equipped for electronic road pricing, which is to be designed by a Kiewit subsidiary, MFS Network Technologies Inc.

Table 7.3
Proposed ('AB 680') private road concessions in California

Subject	State Rt. 91	Rt. 15 extension	State Rt. 125	Mid-state
Operator	Cal. Private Transportation Corporation.	National Tollroad Authority Corporation	California Transportation Ventures.	California Toll Road Company.
Length	10 miles, with possible extensions.	11 miles	10 miles	85 miles.
Counties and Terminations	In Orange County, connecting Riverside County and Rt. 55.	In Orange County, linking Rt. 57 with Rt. 73.	In San Diego County connecting San Diego and the Mexican border.	Alignment undecided; the Franchise Zone includes portions of Alameda, Contra Costa, Solano, Yolo & Sacramento Counties.
Estimated Costs	$88 million	$700 million.	$400 million	$1.2 billion.
Description	New lanes on the median of an existing highway.	Elevated ('viaduct') highway running down a seasonal riverbed.	New route through undeveloped private lands.	New route through various developed and undeveloped lands.
Franchise Term	35 years.	35 years.	35 years (lease).	Two overlapping 35-year leases.
Base Rate of Return	17%.	20.25%	18.5%	21.25%
Toll Rates	Rates unregulated, congestion pricing planned.	Rates unregulated, congestion pricing planned.	Rates unregulated, congestion pricing planned.	Rates unregulated, congestion pricing unlikely.
Environmental Obstacles	Few, since no new highway corridor.	Likely problems; wildlife, wetlands, and growth issues.	Likely problems; wildlife, wetlands, and growth issues.	Sierra Club has filed an environmental suit, problems likely
Local Public Agency Receptiveness	Orange County supportive, Riverside County raising objections	Receptive, so far.	Cities of Chula Vista and San Diego suing for concessions.	Too soon to know.

Source: Klein and Fielding (1992)

One of the complications with the SR-91's electronic road pricing system is that, for reasons that make little economic sense,[3] vehicles carrying three or more people are to be exempt from the toll. The vehicles will still have to carry transponders and drive past a 'spotter booth' where they will be visually inspected to make sure they carry at least three persons. So much for 'high tech'! Pictures of vehicles that do not meet requirements will be taken to aid the enforcement of traffic laws (Boie, 1993).

7.7 Mexico

In 1989, following the election of Carlos Salinas as president, the Mexican government embarked on a vigorous highway construction programme, which required the equivalent of US$6.5 billion to be provided by the private sector for 5,400 km of new toll roads and eight bridges. They were to be completed or under construction before 1995 as B-O-T (Build-Operate-Transfer) concessions. By 1993, concessions were granted for 4,000 km of highways, of which 1,500 km were open for traffic, representing an investment equivalent to US$4.1 billion. But some of the new roads carried little traffic. As a result, the funding (which came mainly from Mexican banks) dried up and the programme has slowed down. What went wrong?

The Mexican road programme succeeded in putting idle road-building resources to work quickly. However, probably as a result of haste, possibly as a result of political pressures, it contained fundamental flaws:

1. The road segments for which concessions were offered were all taken from the planned national network of the Secretariate of Communications and Transport. This network, which may or may not have included the most urgently needed improvements, specifically excluded links in Mexico City and other urban areas (which come under different jurisdictions) where needs for additional road space are most acute.

2. The toll levels were determined by the government, which also guaranteed the traffic flows on the new roads. The flows were 'guaranteed' in the sense that the concessionaires were promised payments corresponding to the governmental traffic forecasts, and the additional payments were provided by extensions to the concession periods.

3. The bids for these B-O-T concessions were awarded not on the basis of lowest cost or lowest toll, but on the shortness of the concession

period. In other words, to get a concession one had to undertake to transfer the completed road to the government, free of debt, as early as possible. As a result, concessions were awarded for periods of as low as eight years.

4. In keeping with the short concession periods, tolls had to be high, typically 500 pesos a km, corresponding to 24 US cents per mile.[4] This compares to 4 cents a mile on some US toll roads, payable by road users much wealthier than Mexico's.

5. Toll concessions were only offered in corridors already served by un-tolled roads.

6. Toll collection, at conventional toll booths, is costly and slows down traffic.

Would the Mexican authorities have done better to adopt some of the approaches suggested in this book? Let readers judge this, in the light of the following considerations.

Bids should have been on the toll levels Assuming that the authorities were right to require the roads designated in their own plan to be built first, the government could have specified the concession periods and invited bids for the lowest toll levels. This is how many cities in France contract with private sector firms for the supply of water, and is the essence of the UK's DBFO schemes described in section 8.1.1 below.

A non-discriminating road fund would have allowed tolls to be lower and reduced the diversion to 'free' roads The high tolls were due in part to users of the toll roads being required to pay the toll in addition to the road user charges paid for the use of the 'free' roads. A road fund into which all paid, and which would finance some of the costs of the new expressways, would have enabled the new roads to be built with lower toll levels.

A properly managed road fund might have enabled the concession periods to be lengthened A basic reason for the short concession was the financial insecurity in Mexico which made it difficult to borrow for more than ten or twelve years. A well-managed road fund could provide a particularly secure source of funds. The main risk to a road fund is not lack of traffic, but fear that the monies would be diverted to other purposes, particularly by government. Guarantees against political risks are obtainable (Watkins, 1994). One can envisage confidence being increased by getting the EBRD, the Inter-American Development Bank or the World Bank to advise on how such funds should be managed, and guaranteeing the 'political' risks, and thus enabling concession periods to be lengthened to twenty or twenty-five years.

Finally, *allowing the market to choose the road sectors to invest in* could have resulted in the most urgent schemes being implemented first. Even if they were reluctant to allow complete freedom of choice, the Mexicans might have adopted the California AB 680 approach, and encouraged private operators to seek and finance profitable investments in roads of their own choosing, at their own risk.

7.8 Far East

7.8.1 China

In early 1978, following the fall of the 'Gang of Four' and the rehabilitation of Deng Xiaoping, the authorities in Beijing announced a series of measures to put China on the road to modernization. Instead of relying on the mass mobilization of the past, the new arrangements were based upon 'innovative incentive devices and a system of personal responsibility that would relay individual energies into a collective economy, not through coercion, but enlightened self-interest' (Oborne, 1986). In 1979 the biggest privatization measure in history was introduced — peasants were allowed to sell agricultural produce in free markets. 1979 also saw the establishment of four 'Special Economic Zones' (in Shantouo, Shenzhen, Xiamen and Zhuhai) in which foreign direct investment was permitted for the first time in thirty years.

The private provision of roads by the private sector was also sought as part of these reforms. The preferred mechanism was the conventional toll road supplied on a B-O-T (Build-Operate-Transfer) basis. For example, a foreign businessman invested in the construction and management of the Taiyuan-Yangquan highway in the north of central China, total length 170.9 km. The total planned investment is 3 billion yuang (Guangdong Provincial Communications Department and others, 1992).

One of the best-known B-O-T road projects is the Guangzhou–Shenzen 'Superhighway', conceived and developed by the Hong Kong entrepreneur Gordon Wu. Wu's grandfather came from the mainland to Hong Kong, where Gordon Wu's father built up a thriving taxi company and sent eight of his nine children to study in the US. While a student at Princeton, the young Wu got to know the New Jersey Turnpike, and developed the ambition to build a similar road from Guangzhou (Canton) to Shenzen, at the edge of Hong Kong.

The Guangzhou–Shenzen superhighway is being built in three phases. The first is a 122.8 km dual three-lane tollway accommodating vehicles up to 120 tons in weight, traveling at speeds of up to 120 km per hour. With fifteen interchanges, the road runs along the eastern corridor of the Pearl River delta, and thence to Guangzhou, where it is to connect with a ring road now under construction. The total cost of this phase is US$1.2 billion. Phase two is to extend the road over the Pearl River to Zhuhai, and phase three will extend it northward to Hengyang, in Hunan.

The project is organized as a joint venture between Hopewell Holdings (Wu's investment company) and the Guangdong Provincial Highway Construction Company, a subsidiary of the Guangdong provincial government. Hopewell is responsible for the road's design, construction and maintenance, and in return is entitled to receive 40 per cent of the project's profits over its thirty-year concession period (Pyle, February, 1994).

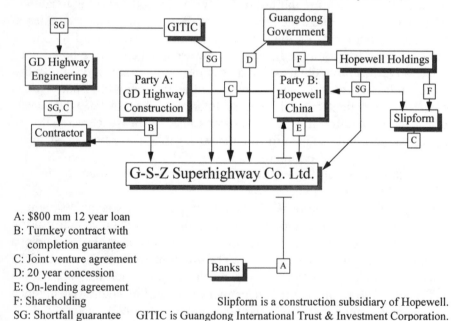

A: $800 mm 12 year loan
B: Turnkey contract with
    completion guarantee
C: Joint venture agreement
D: 20 year concession
E: On-lending agreement
F: Shareholding   Slipform is a construction subsidiary of Hopewell.
SG: Shortfall guarantee   GITIC is Guangdong International Trust & Investment Corporation.

PRINCETON PACIFIC GROUP

Figure 7.2 Structure of the Guangzhou–Shenzen project
Source: Pyle (January, 1994)

7.8.2 Japan

Although toll roads were known in Japan as early as 1871 (OECD, 1987, p. 93), they were not introduced on a large scale until after the Second World War, when Japan's roads, like those of France, needed drastic upgrading. Indeed the situation in Japan was much worse than in France; in 1956 three-quarters of Japan's primary roads were unpaved, there were fewer than 800,000 motor vehicles, and policy-makers were debating whether, with Japan's good railway and water transport systems, it was even necessary for it to develop motorized road transport (Owen, 1994).

A mission from the US in 1956 reported that Japan's rail and water modes would fail to meet its transport needs and recommended that they be upgraded, and that a modern road network be developed also. The World Bank supported this view and lent US$100 million for the initial phase of the expressway programme, while advising the Japanese to shop for funds in world markets. As further loans followed, the President of the World Bank, Mr Eugene Black, insisted that all World Bank loans be matched dollar for dollar by borrowings from commercial markets.

In that period, the government appointed the Japan Road Public Corporation (JRPC) to coordinate the road development programme. The roads were carefully built, with bridges — and even tunnels — used extensively to minimize damage to the country's traditional environment.

Within thirty-five years there were 60 million motor vehicles in Japan and it became 'the most toll-road oriented nation in the world' (Takeda, 1989) with some seventy different toll expressways totaling over 6,600 km in length. The JRPC has grown to be a major corporation with a staff of 8,600 and annual revenues equivalent to US$10 billion. It is directly responsible for over 5,000 km of expressway and is orchestrating the construction of about 7,000 km more.

Did the private sector have anything to do with this massive road programme? It had a supportive role, helping the government to carry it out. Considerable sums were raised on financial markets, but only under the protection of government guarantees. About two-thirds of JRPC's work load — including research and surveys, construction management, maintenance and new construction — is now contracted out to private sector firms. But, to this day, the private sector has few significant entrepreneurial activities relating to the provision of road links that are not part of the JRPC's programme.

As in France, the financing of the different expressways is co-mingled, with those in surplus supporting the ones in deficit. Japan also follows a policy of uniform toll rates for the same vehicle-type throughout the nation, except that in the large conurbations rates are 20 per cent higher than normal in recognition of congestion costs. However, the 20 per cent surcharge is not high enough to reduce congestion to acceptable levels, and critics complain that urban congestion and urban charges are both too high!

7.8.3 Thailand

The private sector has been less successful in providing roads in Thailand, where Bangkok's Second Stage Expressway project, a planned 35-km elevated expressway, is the focus of a major dispute between the government and the project's financial backers, which include the Asian Development Bank.

Bangkok's 16.8-mile First Stage Expressway, recommended by a team of German consultants in the 1970s, consisted of three legs of elevated highway radiating from the city centre, northwards towards the airport and southward to east and west suburbs. It was completed by the state-owned Expressway and Rapid Transit Authority (the ETA) in 1990 (Reina, 1992).

The second stage, contracted to cost US$1.04 billion, was awarded as a thirty-year B-O-T contract by the ETA to the Bangkok Expressway Company Ltd. (BECL), a consortium of private companies headed by the Japanese giant contracting firm Kumagai Gumi, which was to be allowed to charge a toll of 30 baht (about 80 pence or US$1.20). The BECL was expected to operate the expressway and to retain 18 baht of the toll (60 per cent), passing 12 baht to the ETA, which needed the funds for land purchase and other expenses.

Even at the 30 baht toll, the Second Stage Expressway was not expected to cover its costs, and was to be funded in part by the revenues from the first stage. One of the mysteries in the affair is how it was possible to identify, and then select for construction, an unprofitable urban expressway in Bangkok; but that is another matter.

Equity for the second stage, in the amount of US$220 million, was supplied by Kumagai Gumi and other sponsors, but the bulk of the funding — US$796 million — came in the form of senior debt provided by a consortium of eleven Thai banks and thirty-one foreign ones. These funds were made available without guarantee from either the government or the sponsors. In making their commitments, the banks relied on the favourable investment climate existing in Thailand at the time, and on the projected earnings to the BECL from both the First and Second Stage Expressways.

The arrangements started to unravel when the ETA was unable to make the necessary land available to the contractor in time to meet the agreed construction schedule, which had to be renegotiated. In March 1993, just prior to the completion of the 19-km first sector of the second stage, the government sought to re-negotiate the 30 baht toll that had been previously agreed. It proposed a 20 baht toll, 18 baht of which would go, as agreed, to the contractor BECL, and 2 baht to ETA, which, as a result, was threatened with bankruptcy and would be unable to purchase more land. In consequence, the ETA stopped paying BECL the 60 per cent of the revenues from both expressways, as it was obliged to do under its contract. These developments caused the banking consortium to stop funding the operations of BECL, which found itself without the funds to continue work, and in possession of a completed expressway section for which it was not allowed to charge the toll rate previously agreed (Tam, June, 1993).

BECL refused to open the expressway to traffic despite warnings from the police that a riot would break out should it fail to do so. On August 30, 1993 BECL was served a court order and told to instruct the independent engineer to certify the road as safe and complete. The independent engineer refused to do so, and thereupon the ETA took over the road, opened it for traffic, and started to collect the tolls by itself, in flagrant violation of its agreement with BECL. To add insult to injury, the ETA charged the 30 baht toll originally agreed — not the 20 baht which BECL was required to charge earlier in the year (Tam, September, 1993).

Early in 1994 Kumagai Gumi signed a memorandum of understanding to sell its stake in BECL at a bargain price to a consortium of sixty Thai investors. Meanwhile the lending banks demanded reimbursement from the government of the amounts lent to BECL, plus interest (*Public Works Financing*, February 1994). The episode is understood to have weakened international confidence in B-O-T projects, and to have severely damaged Thailand's credit standing.

7.9 Objections to the private provision of roads

In view of the failure of many governments to meet the needs of road users why are not more roads provided by the private sector? The previous chapter (section 6.2) has shown that the provision of roads is not prevented by the types of 'market failure' generally cited by economists, and this chapter has shown that roads were privately provided on a massive scale as early as two hundred years ago.

Seven obstacles to the private provision of roads are often cited, and some of them have been illustrated in the previous examples:

1. Difficulty of getting necessary rights-of-way;

2. Difficulty of road providers getting paid;

3. Competition from public-sector 'free' roads;

4. Uncertainty about legal liability;

5. Fear of exploitation by private road monopolies;

6. Difficulties of interaction with public road authorities; and

7. Difficulty of raising funds in capital markets.

7.9.1 Getting the rights-of-way

The private provision of roads is often dismissed as a serious possibility on the ground that only by the use of 'eminent domain' — the power of government to employ compulsory purchase to appropriate private property for public use — can the required right-of-way be assembled (Goldstein, 1987). This problem, which is of special concern to those sensitive to the importance of property rights, can be dealt with in at least three ways:

Existing corridors can be used There are numerous cases in which rights-of-way suitable for roads are readily available in existing transportation corridors. The Dulles Toll Road in the Washington DC area, for example, was built in the right-of-way of the existing Dulles Airport Access Road. Underutilized rail 'ways' can also provide opportunities for new roads: A major US toll road — the Pennsylvania Turnpike — was built on the base of an uncompleted railway, and a railway in Port-of-Spain, Trinidad, was converted into a reserved route for buses. Substantial areas are occupied by underutilized railway track in London and in many other cities.

The private sector can make quick deals The options available to the private sector to purchase land are often underestimated. For one thing, the private sector — unlike many governments — can carry out quick deals with landowners without having to go through time-consuming statutory procedures which, inter alia, limit the amounts payable.

The private sector is not constrained by rules which limit the compensation payable to assessed market value, and developers have been able to consolidate land covering large areas and a variety of interests (Starkie, 1990).

Furthermore, private entrepreneurs often have the choice of more than one route. Pipeline builders, for example, routinely consider alternative routes, negotiate with different groups of owners, and settle with the first group that comes up with an acceptable arrangement. Where buyers compete with competing groups of sellers, there is extra pressure on the sellers to agree to reasonable deals. It is instructive that in the case of the first modern privately-provided roads in the US — the Dulles Greenway and the SR-91, discussed earlier in this chapter — the rights-of-way were either already on the existing corridor or were obtained by negotiation with the landowners, without the use of government compulsory purchase powers. Of course, many landowners stand to gain substantially from improved accessibility to their land, and there are many recorded cases of land being donated at no charge for improved access. In the turnpike era, 'turnpike companies frequently convinced landowners to accept turnpike stock as compensation' (Klein and Fielding, p. 334).

Compulsory purchase can be invoked Finally, there remains the possibility of government using its powers of compulsory acquisition ('eminent domain') to obtain land for privately provided transport infrastructure. This was frequently done in the turnpike age to facilitate land acquisition without the private sector giving up the rewards of successful investment nor the risks of unsuccessful ones. This solution will not please libertarians, and others opposed in principle to compulsory purchase, but its application to privately-provided roads will not make them worse off, because these powers exist and are nowadays frequently used when roads are provided by the public sector.

7.9.2 Getting paid

In well-ordered societies, there would be nothing to prevent private providers from getting paid as easily as public ones. The importance of not discriminating against private providers was emphasized in Chapter 2, and section 4.2.5 in Chapter 4 described how 'shadow tolls' can achieve this objective, and allocate, on the basis of traffic counts or any other agreed criterion, amounts payable to any owner.

Furthermore, the development of electronic road pricing and other modern methods of payment enables highway providers to levy appropriate charges where costs are particularly high, as on congested roads.

Unfortunately, not all societies are well-ordered, and the Bangkok example given in section 7.8.3 above shows that investors can never be assured of payment. However, risks can be compensated for by budgeting for higher returns, or they can be minimized by insurance. For example, the World Bank group can guarantee private investors against political risks, such as expropriation, while leaving the private sector to handle the commercial risks, such as cost over-runs (Watkins, 1994).

7.9.3 Competition from 'free' roads

Even a brief review of the history of toll roads indicate that competition from 'free' roads (literally 'freeways') is a major obstacle to the private provision of roads. To expect private investors to risk their funds on a road that requires payments from users, when alternative routes do not require additional payments, is to expect a great deal. However, as mentioned earlier, the use of 'shadow tolls' could mitigate this difficulty.

In some situations, the funds generated by shadow tolls on a privately provided road might be sufficient to cover all its costs but, even where they were not, earnings from shadow tolls would enable a lower toll to be charged by the private road providers than would be the case if they were deprived of the revenues from road user charges 'earned' on their roads. As a result of the lower toll, less traffic would be diverted to the parallel 'freeway'.

7.9.4 Uncertainty about legal liability

This has to be regarded as a serious problem in the current US legal climate. It has forced some of the private firms which are negotiating to receive franchises in California to lease, rather than own, the roads which they are to operate in that state.

A key element in the litigation problem in the US is its product liability system, under which any person can claim injury, sue and claim large damages at practically no risk. This is made possible by the system of 'contingency fees', under which lawyers agree to be paid a percentage (typically 25 to 30 per cent) of damages they obtain, earning nothing if they lose. As those who lose in US courts do not have to pay the legal costs of those who win, litigants pay negligible costs if they lose, and stand to gain substantially if they win. Juries in 1992 sided with 52 per cent of cases that went to trial in the US (*Wall Street Journal*, July 12, 1994) but, under the US system, litigants do not even have to sue in order to be paid:

they can get money through intimidation, by threatening a lawsuit.

Another factor that discourages enterprise in the US is that the system haphazardly damages wealthy corporations ('deep pockets') not because of negligence or misconduct, but because of the perception that they can afford to pay. Thus, a New Mexico jury, wishing to proclaim that 'the coffee's too hot out there' awarded Stella Liebeck $2.7 million (later reduced by a judge to $480,000) at the expense of the McDonald's hamburger chain because she burned herself in 1992 by spilling hot coffee on her lap while traveling in a car. Even those who do not spill drinks on their laps are now forced to buy cooler coffee. And an Alabama doctor, Ira Gore, was awarded $4,000 in compensatory damages and $4 million in punitive damages because the paint on a car he bought had been damaged and then re-finished.

This legal system is reported to cost US businesses $132 billion a year, most of which is passed on to consumers in the form of higher prices, or to shareholders in the form of lower dividends and stock prices. Some businesses, such as Cessna aircraft, were forced to cease operating in the US for fear of lawsuits. Legal reform is high on the agenda of the new US Congress and, one would hope, in other places also.

However, some insurance experts still do not see this as a serious problem. Private owners of local roads associated with shopping centres have lived with this issue for years, and have no difficulty in obtaining insurance. Toll roads, such as the New Jersey Turnpike, obtain insurance without difficulty and the claims experience is wide enough to enable the insurance industry to set rates. However, the need to insure against claims would certainly raise toll rates, possibly by as much as 5 per cent.

7.9.5 Fear of exploitation by road monopolies

A major objection to the private provision of public roads is that road owners would be monopolists and thus in a position to exploit their customers. Would householders living alongside a privately-owned street, for example, have to pay a toll each time they approach their homes? Would main street traders lose customers as a result of urban congestion charges? Would a company owning a private arterial expressway increase the highway charges to the detriment of the communities that depend on it?

The monopoly issue has already been addressed in the previous chapter (section 6.2.1), where it was concluded that commercialization, with open entry to new providers, would reduce, rather than increase the potential danger to the public of exploitation by monopolists. The same points apply

to the private provision of roads, subject to government having the power
to intervene in cases of exploitation by a monopolist. Furthermore, while
there are no known examples of monopolistic private road owners denying
residents access to their premises, there are numerous examples of private
road providers being exploited by toll-evading road users and by governments denying them the powers to collect tolls due to them (Klein and
Fielding, 1992, p. 338).

A more troubling aspect of the monopoly issue is the reluctance of
officials in existing roads departments to tolerate the loss of *their* monopoly. This difficulty, which is discussed in the following section, was evident
in Virginia, where the main opposition to Ralph Stanley's bid to provide
the Dulles Greenway came from within the Virginia Department of
Transportation. Some of its officials argued that, if the project was a good
one, it should have been provided by the VDOT.

7.9.6 Difficulties of interaction with public road authorities

Private entities wishing to provide roads on a commercial basis do not
operate in a vacuum. They have to interact with powerful governmental
organizations whose interests and procedures could often conflict with the
interests of private road providers. Problems of two kinds can arise:

1. The private providers may be in direct competition with the activities of
    the governmental agencies they are required to deal with.

2. Governmental procedures often require competitive bidding for the
    delivery of services. Potential suppliers of roads or road services may
    be inhibited in presenting their proposals to the authorities by the fear
    that others may be invited to bid to supply the suggested facilities.

The first difficulty, which was illustrated by the reluctance of Virginia's
Department of Transportation to allow a private firm to build and operate
the Dulles Greenway, shows the conflict of interest that arises when a
public road agency is required to allow an outside entity to do the kind of
work already being done by its staff. David Starkie (1990) pointed to this
conflict of interest within the UK Department of Transport:

> Central government is itself a promoter of roads. Department officials
> who will be advising Ministers on a private road proposal will also be
> advising Ministers on the Department's road programme. There will
> be, therefore, two road promoters, the private sector and the public
> sector but with the unusual ... circumstance that the public sector

promoter is advising Ministers on possibly competing road schemes. The fact that the Department appears to be both judge and jury with respect to road schemes has long been contentious, but the prospect of private road schemes possibly competing with public road schemes brings the conflict into sharper relief.

Starkie proposes to deal with this conflict by ensuring that those who are in the group 'advising Ministers' should not be in the same entity as those 'promoting' public sector roads. This kind of separation is, of course, desirable, but may not be achievable in practice. The proposals in this book go much further; they would separate the road corporations (or other road suppliers) from the funding agencies which, in their turn, would be prohibited from discriminating against private sector road suppliers. Additionally, to protect the interests of road users, officials would have no powers to prevent private entities improving road networks at their own risk and expense, so long as local planning and environmental rules are complied with.

The problem of whether to require competitive bidding is more difficult, and may be illustrated by the examples given earlier in this chapter. When Ralph Stanley offered to provide the Dulles Greenway, the Virginia Department of Transportation considered implementing the project itself, but it did not see the need to seek other bidders to compete against Ralph Stanley's Toll Road Corporation of Virginia. But when the British and Mexican authorities wanted private concessionaires to implement specific road projects in their countries, they did seek bids. The reason is clear, and offers a principle of distinguishing between different situations.

In the British and Mexican cases, the projects were already in their respective road programmes and the initiatives to seek private sector implementation came from the governments themselves. But in the Virginia case the initiative came from Stanley, the private operator. This seems to be a useful guide: when a public authority wants a part of its own programme to be implemented by a private concessionaire, a transparent bidding process seems essential, if only to protect officials from accusations that valuable concessions are being given away to their private sector friends.

But when the initiative for a project comes from a private entrepreneur, who offers to implement it at his own risk and expense, and who does not seek governmental assistance, nor assurances that the government would not itself build a competing route, it is difficult to see why others should be invited to bid. Indeed, the possibility that other bids could be invited is likely to put off many such offers, which are not costless to prepare.

Where initiatives are made by the private sector, but governmental help is sought, e.g. for land acquisition, public bids should be required.

7.9.7 Difficulty in raising finance in capital markets

This is certainly a major practical problem. Many financiers, like many other people, feel more comfortable doing what they know than breaking new ground. Privately provided roads are comparative strangers in Wall Street, where investors' representatives are happier funding facilities for electricity, telecommunications and water supply than roads, which have less predictable earnings.

It has proved to be difficult to raise money even for privately provided roads in the US. Raising funds for roads in, say, China, India or Mexico, requires much more effort and higher prospective returns. At the very least, financiers will require protection against political risks (e.g. might the road be nationalized?) and currency risks (e.g. as tolls are paid in local currency, what happens if it is devalued?).

This obstacle can only be overcome by careful project selection and a clear identification and assessment of the risks. Some large private sector banks or international lending agencies are able to guarantee the political risks. Currency risks can be dealt with by guarantees that the tolls would be maintained at agreed levels in terms of the currency to be repaid. Where dedicated road funds exist, their revenues could possibly be used to secure loans. Each case has to be dealt with on its merits. Once confidence is established, further financing becomes easier, and if it is lost, as in Bangkok, financing becomes much more difficult.

7.9.8 Conclusions on objections to the private provision of roads

It may be concluded that the objections to the private provision of roads, though substantial, are not insuperable.

Rights of way for roads are already available in many places, and can be obtained in many others.

Even where conventional tolls are impractical to collect, 'shadow tolls' and electronic road pricing offer new ways of getting paid. Shadow tolls also eliminate the problem of the competing 'free' roads.

Fear of the monopoly power of private road providers is not uppermost in the minds of road users, who have more to fear from the inadequacies of the governmental road monopolies. The reluctance of some government officials to countenance the loss of their monopoly is likely to pose a bigger obstacle to private road provision.

The absence of a clear legal framework to guide and protect investors poses a major problem for the private financing of roads in the US, in the Russian Federation, and in many other countries. It has already led investors in California roads to prefer leasing operations to the legal risks inherent in ownership there.

When private entities are invited to implement projects in government programmes, concessionaires should be selected on the basis of transparent bidding procedures. But when entrepreneurs initiate project proposals to be carried out at their own risk and expense, and when these involve no help from governmental powers, others should not generally be invited to bid in competition.

The difficulties of raising finance are formidable, but may be expected to ease as borrowers and lenders learn to understand each other's problems and to seek solutions to further mutual interests in financially-sound road projects.

The application of at least some of the concepts described in this book — private ownership, dedicated road funds, 'shadow tolls', and electronic road pricing — could make roads more attractive to investors.

7.10 Conclusions on the private provision of public roads

This brief review suggests that, for reasons that may have been good at the time, the roads sector was never open to the market economy. In the nineteenth century land transport was dominated by the railways, cars were scarce, and the difficulties of collecting payments for road use reduced the capacity of the private sector to provide them. Those who did provide roads for horsedrawn vehicles — governments (as in France) or turnpike companies (as in the UK and US) — had to contend with much popular opposition, due to the necessity of collecting the appropriate taxes or tolls.

Things changed in the twentieth century. The advent of motor vehicles by the million, and the ease of collecting from their owners fuel taxes and licence fees, enabled governments to extract payments from road users. However, governmental regulation greatly curtailed the freedom to provide roads, and the private sectors were generally allowed only to implement components of governmental programmes. 'Public–private partnerships' were developed along the lines of partnerships between riders and horses, the private sector taking the role of the horse.

Can we do better in the twenty-first century, now that we have both the demand for roads and the means and techniques to pay for them? The last chapter discusses the prospects and ways for change.

Notes

1. In 1973 the programme was expanded to 6,594 km.

2. Those favouring free markets might ask why it was necessary to choose four, and why all ten could not have been allowed to proceed. But the Assembly Bill 680 allowed for only four projects.

3. In a 'command economy', which prefers regulations to prices to allocate scarce resources, it makes sense to give priorities to car pools on under-priced roads. But, if there is congestion pricing, the price itself encourages car-pooling to an appropriate extent, and exemptions to car pools reduce revenues and add unnecessary complications. Singapore abolished car pool exemptions for these reasons.

4. Some Mexicans claim to be able to fly the 300 miles from Mexico City to Guadalajara more cheaply than the cost of the road tolls.

8 Roads to the market

There is nothing more difficult to take in hand, more perilous to conduct, or more uncertain in its success, than to take the lead in the introduction of a new order of things. For the innovator has for enemies all who have done well under the old conditions, and lukewarm defenders in those who may do well under the new (Machiavelli, 1513).

The main message of this book is that three conditions have to be met before roads can be admitted as members in good standing of the market economy:

1. *Road suppliers should be allowed to provide road space* Those wishing to provide roads have to be allowed to do so, on terms no worse than those enjoyed by governmental providers. It is not enough to allow the provision of privately-financed toll roads subject to unfair competition from governmental 'free' roads.

2. *Road users should be allowed to buy the right to use road space* Reliable payment mechanisms have to be devised to enable road users to pay for roads, payment being made either directly to those who provide roads, or into dedicated road funds out of governmental reach.

3. *Roads should be recognized as economic assets, and their ownership vested in entities established to exercise the powers and responsibilities of ownership* Privately-owned roads already meet this condition, but the vast majority of roads do not.

These conditions would require no budgetary appropriations — no expenditures, nor any loss of funds to general revenues — but they would shift power over roads from the 'command economy' towards the market economy. To what extent are these conditions being met?

None of them are satisfactorily met anywhere but, as shown below, elements of the first are being met in the UK, of the second in the US, and of the third in Sub-Saharan Africa.

8.1 Reports on progress to date

8.1.1 In the United Kingdom

The good news from the UK is the decision of the government to test the concept of 'shadow tolls' (described in section 4.2.5) to enable the private sector to be paid for providing new road capacity without the disadvantages of conventional tolls. In August 1994, the Highways Agency of the Department of Transport, a new entity established in April 1994 to manage, maintain and expand the UK's trunk road network, invited interested parties to compete for selection to negotiate its first 'Design, Build, Finance and Operate' (DBFO) projects (Rickard, 1994).

Four projects, requiring investment of some £380 million in total, were selected for the Department's 'initial tranche' of DBFO projects. Different kinds of projects were selected to test out the method in different local circumstances:

One project is for a motorway link between the M1 and A1 roads near Leeds;

The second an upgrading to motorway standards of the A1 road between Alconbury and Peterborough;

The third an upgrading to a dual-carriageway Class A road of the A 417/A419 connection between Swindon and Gloucester, and

The fourth for improving, maintaining and operating the A69 road near Hadrian's Wall.

Potential contractors were invited to express their interest by September 30, 1994, to design, build, finance and operate one or more of these four projects which were described in detail in the invitation document (Highways Agency, 1994). The Agency received a strong international response and selected eleven consortia (including companies from France, Germany, Italy, Japan and Spain). It plans to receive the bids by mid-April and to let the first contracts in July 1995. Bidders are to be required to indicate the lowest toll they would be prepared to accept for contracts that could last as long as twenty-five years, after which the improved roads would be taken over by the Highways Agency. Although the Agency did not specify that the contracts would be awarded to the lowest bidders, it indicated that the proposed toll levels would be a critical factor in the selection process.

In December, the Highways Agency identified four further projects for which DBFO contracts are to be sought. Their total value was estimated to be £164 million.

The bad news from the UK is that the Treasury is still opposed to relinquishing control of the revenues garnered from road users. It defends its position by repeating its objections to the 'hypothecation' or 'earmarking' of tax revenues. As was pointed out in Chapter 2 (section 2.5.5), enabling road users to pay for road space is no different in principle from allowing water users to pay for water and telephone users for telecommunications. The Treasury may be right to resist 'earmarking' or 'hypothecation' of revenues, but it is not being logical in considering payments for roads as falling under that description, while allowing people to pay their gas bills to gas companies. Until the Treasury can be persuaded or instructed to change its attitude, commercialization of roads in the UK will not be possible and road users there will have to depend on the 'command economy' for their infrastructure.

The situation of road providers in the UK can be appreciated by comparing the position of the holders of DBFO concessions with that of other road suppliers in the UK. The concession holders will have clear property rights, with associated obligations and privileges. The obligations will be spelt out in the contracts with the Highways Agency, and will require the concession holders to provide road services meeting clearly-defined standards. In return, the concession holders will have the privilege of receiving an agreed fee for each vehicle-mile 'produced' on their respective roads. The number of vehicle-miles to be produced will not be stipulated in the contract: it will be in the interest of the concession holders to make their roads as attractive as possible, so as to increase their revenues and profits. The concession holders will have estimated the likely traffic on their roads before making their bids, and may well lose money if their estimates turn out to have been too optimistic.

Other road providers in the UK will have neither the obligations nor the privileges of ownership. Their assets will earn them no returns, and they will expect to receive their revenues from political allocations of central or local government funds. Even the management of the Highways Agency itself will not know the level of funding it is to receive, because road providers in the UK do not have dedicated revenues, such as could be obtained from road users unrestrained by political control.

8.1.2 In the United States

The good news in the US is the strong tradition that road users pay for roads. Indeed, until the 1980s, it was taken for granted in the US that *all* revenues from road user charges should be dedicated to roads.[1] Thirty-three states have highway trust funds, and in thirty-two of them all the revenues collected from road use are dedicated to road maintenance or improvement. As the private provision of public services is also widely accepted, and as the private provision of public roads is being demonstrated in California and Virginia, the prospects for the commercial provision of roads in the US, without discrimination against private provision, might be considered to be reasonable.

Unfortunately, there is, as in the UK, a major obstacle to reform. In the US it is the US Congress, which has a major influence on road provision through the federal 'Highway Trust Fund' (HTF), described in section 2.5.2. The HTF enables officials in Washington DC to determine the proportion of revenues collected from federal road user taxes to be allocated to roads; the formula for allocating the total between the various states; and the burdensome conditions the states have to comply with in order to get their shares of these allocations. For example, it is the HTF mechanisms that enable the federal authorities to withhold 'trust' funds from states that do not meet the demands of the Environmental Protection Administration regarding, say, arrangements for vehicle emissions testing.

More to the issues raised in this book, HTF regulations discriminate against privately provided roads, and even against publicly-owned toll roads. It will meet 90 per cent of the cost of a new state-funded road but only 50 per cent of the cost of a privately-funded road, although users of both roads pay into the HTF equally. Although waivers can be negotiated with the Federal Highways Administration, which is currently supportive of 'public-private partnerships', HTF regulations do not allow roads, bridges or tunnels forming part of the Interstate Highway System to be converted to toll facilities, except that up to three demonstration projects to test congestion pricing are allowed on Interstate facilities.

In November 1994 American voters elected a new Congress dominated by members of the Republican party, committed to major reforms including the devolution of federal power to the states. Roads is a topic worthy of their early attention. The way to reform is technically easy but could be politically difficult. The powers of the HTF expire automatically unless renewed before September 30, 1997. All that is necessary for reform is for Congress to decline to renew the HTF, and to abolish the taxes that support its road financing activities. The responsibility for the collection and disbursement of highway funds would then devolve to lower levels of government — the states and counties — which could make their own road-financing arrangements.

The US federal/state road financing system is so wasteful that most states would be financially better off without it (Roth, 1990). States fully responsible for their own roads could encourage the private sector to assume more of the burden of road provision by legislating to prohibit discrimination against privately-provided public roads. They could also reimburse private providers by means of 'shadow tolls', along the lines of the UK DBFO procedures described in the previous section. Special transition arrangements could be negotiated for hard cases, such as Alaska and Hawaii. Congestion pricing could enable the District of Columbia to finance its own roads, and the rent payable for its road space could help to restore Washington DC to financial solvency.

Defenders of the existing system argue that principal roads have to be 'planned' on a national basis and that federal involvement in road financing is necessary for considerations of defence. The proposition that the federal government can, by taking some sort of comprehensive over-view, improve the processes of planning US highways, might sound plausible to those ignorant of both highway planning and of the ways of Washington DC. But there are no recognized techniques of road planning that can improve on commercial criteria, and no reason to suppose that Washington today would be any better at highway planning than was Moscow in the days of the Soviet Union. On the other hand, the toll road networks constructed in the UK and the USA in the eighteenth and nineteenth centuries were provided without guidance from central planning authorities, and it is unlikely that such guidance would have produced a better network.

As for the defence argument, there is nothing to stop the armed forces using their own budgets to pay for improvements needed to enable (say) heavy weapons to move on US roads. But, when offered this opportunity in the 1960s, the military declined to spend any of their funds for such purposes.

To the extent that national road standards, and liaison between states, are helpful, there are many organizations (such as the American Association of State Highway and Transportation Officials, and the Transportation Research Board) capable of arranging for the necessary studies and recommending appropriate standards. Co-ordination between states is successfully achieved, without formal federal involvement, in other areas, e.g. the licensing of heavy commercial vehicles for inter-state movement. It is difficult to believe that highway officials of neighbouring states could not co-ordinate their road investment plans without federal intervention.

It should be emphasized that the main objection to the HTF arrangements is not to federal road provision as such, but to the damage caused by federal involvement in the financing of *state* roads. The reforms proposed in this book would not, of course, preclude Congress from directly supporting purely federal roads if it so chooses. It does already finance such roads on federally-owned lands.

8.1.3 In Sub-Saharan Africa

The state of the roads in Sub-Saharan Africa (S-SA) was referred to in section 1.5 of the introductory chapter, and poor maintenance was identified as the major problem. To remedy this situation, the United Nations Economic Commission for Africa, and the World Bank, launched the Road Maintenance Initiative (RMI) in 1988. This programme, which is financed by European governments, is administered by the World Bank. The officials managing the RMI quickly realized that the existing systems were not working, and decided that the attitudinal changes needed to bring about improvements could come only from within the countries themselves.

The first phase of the RMI focused on raising awareness of the need for sound maintenance policies and identifying the reasons for past inadequacies. Seminars were held in which representatives from all S-SA countries participated, and which led to new thinking on road provision throughout the region. It was realized that the road maintenance problems were not unique, but were a sub-set of more fundamental problems, namely, weaknesses in the institutional arrangements for managing and financing Africa's roads. Roads in the newly-independent African states were almost invariably managed by governmental roads departments which proved incapable of maintaining the roads for which they were responsible. Participants in the seminars might have derived some comfort from the knowledge that such weaknesses are also to be found outside their region.

In its second phase, the RMI moved from diagnosis to reform. To identify choices for improvement, it organized seminars and workshops in seven target countries: Cameroon, Kenya, Madagascar, Tanzania, Uganda, Zambia and Zimbabwe. In addition to government officials, those taking part also included representatives of chambers of commerce, road transport associations, farmers, and other road users. Important breakthroughs came during workshops in Tanzania, Zambia and Zimbabwe, as the private sector stakeholders — who were suffering enormous losses from the poor road conditions — offered to provide finance for maintenance, over and above the road user taxes they were already paying, provided they were assured that these funds would go to road maintenance and be efficiently spent.

The key concept that emerged from the ensuing debates was one that is not new to readers of this book — *commercialization:* bringing roads into the market place, putting them on a fee-for-service basis, and managing them like other business enterprises. The discussions on commercialization led to consideration of four key factors associated with it, namely:

1. Creating *ownership* by involving road users in road management;

2. The need for secure and stable *funding* sources;

3. The assignment of *responsibility* among government entities;

4. The creation of appropriate *management* structures.

Ownership The issue of road ownership was not properly addressed by the RMI, possibly because it was considered that all existing roads were owned by the respective governments, and that the prospects for privately-provided roads were too remote to be relevant to immediate problems. Instead, by implying that ownership could be vested in the users, the concept was used to achieve the important objective of involving the road users directly in road management. One way of doing this was by appointing representatives of road users' organizations to serve on the boards of the Road Funds (described below) which were established as a result of the RMI. But the road users were also involved directly in road management. For example, as shown in Box 8.1, the Federation of Zambian Road Hauliers voluntarily assists the authorities to combat the overloading on Zambia's roads.

Funding The need for regular and reliable funding sources led to the establishment of dedicated Road Funds (Heggie, 1995). At least nine were functioning in 1994 — in Benin, Central African Republic (CAR), Ghana, Mozambique, Rwanda, Sierra Leone, South Africa (since 1935), Tanzania and Zambia. The ones in Tanzania, Zambia and the Central African

Box 8.1 Private sector in Zambia enforces vehicle weights and dimensions regulations

A recent 24-hour vehicle survey carried out in July 1993 by the Federation of Zambian Road Hauliers (Fedhaul) showed that there was widespread overloading (some vehicles carrying excess loads of 40 to 50 tons), minimal enforcement and that many of the overloaded vehicles passed the weigh bridges when they were closed. The current fine of 500 kwacha ($1.00 equivalent) was too low to act as a deterrent and the road traffic regulations were ambiguous and difficult to enforce. Following the survey, Fedhaul recommended that the legislation be amended to clarify the regulations and that a new penalty system be introduced.

The penalty system should cover incorrectly distributed loads and overloads. Their suggestion was that, when a vehicle exceeded the Gross Vehicle Mass, or axle weight, punitive fines should be imposed, starting at $60 for the first 1,000 kg overload and rising to a maximum fine of $10,000.

All Public Service Vehicles should carry written instructions from the operator detailing the amount of cargo to be loaded. If details on this document exceed legal weight limits, the operator should be liable for the fine. If the shipper or forwarding agent has loaded cargo in excess of what is shown on the shipping document, the shipper or forwarding agent should be liable for the fine. If the vehicle is found to be carrying goods in excess of the manifested cargo and the operator's instructions, the driver should be liable for the fine.

Following the survey, the Ministry of Communications and Transport agreed to appoint *voluntary* road traffic commissioners, nominated by the organizations representing the road transport industry, to help enforce road transport regulations and, in particular, to supervise operation of weighbridges. The voluntary commissioners have powers to stop traffic, impound vehicles, and make arrests.

These arrangements are now in place, and over 400 trucks were impounded during the first month of operation in early 1994. However, since the new penalty structure is not yet in place, the road traffic commissioners can only make vehicles off-load the excess, which must then be collected by another vehicle. This procedure has virtually eliminated the 40 to 50 tons of overload, but is not a sufficient deterrent. Fedhaul is therefore continuing to press for punitive fines.

The road transport organizations have willingly taken on the task of voluntary traffic commissioners because it protects the road pavement and reduces unfair competition, particularly from foreign vehicles using international transit routes.

Source: Heggie (1995)

Republic were reported to be functioning particularly well. The Funds are managed by boards on which road users are represented. In Zambia the majority of the members are from the private sector. Tariffs generally consist of vehicle licence fees and fuel levies. They are collected on top of other taxes and paid directly into the Road Funds. Revenues are expended on road maintenance, but consideration is being given in some countries to enable the funds be used for rehabilitation and even for new investment.

The new African Road Funds received approval even in a report by the World Bank which, in earlier times, tended to discourage them:

> The establishment of new road funds involves more than just earmarking revenues to road maintenance. It also includes reforms to improve the efficiency of road agencies and the establishment of road boards with technical experts and representatives of the user community, who oversee the allocation of revenues and the setting of priorities. Countries in Africa are starting to adopt a promising 'commercialization' approach to making road fund operations more economically based and more user-responsive. Tanzania provides a noteworthy example of best practice. Moreover, the automatic revenue flows have been designed to avoid building up a fund surplus and hence to discourage wasteful spending (*World Development Report 1994*, p. 50).

The parliamentary resolution to open the Tanzania Road Fund is shown, in translation from the Swahili, in Box 8.2.

Responsibility The consideration here was that responsibility for any task on any road would be clearly assigned to a specific agency at the appropriate national, regional or local level, so that all concerned know who is responsible for the tasks that have to be performed for each road section. Such assignments of responsibility require accurate road inventories, classified by functional level.

Management When S-SA roads were managed as government departments, the main duty of the managers was to make sure that funds allocated were properly spent as appropriated. This approach was legitimate, but did little to ensure that available funds were sufficient to achieve their objectives, or that they were spent to best advantage. The commercial approach introduced as a result of the RMI focuses on such questions and, at the behest of local road users, highlighted road maintenance and brought in commercial management methods to improve it.

Box 8.2 Parliamentary Resolution used to open a Special Account to support Road Maintenance in Tanzania

DECLARATION
ON THE OPENING OF SPECIAL ROAD FUND
'THE ROAD FUND'
AS ANNOUNCED BY THE MINISTER OF FINANCE

BECAUSE the government has an intention of strengthening the maintenance of core roads in the country after realizing the importance of roads in the restructuring of the country's economy;

AND BECAUSE in fulfilling this objective it is necessary that funds must be obtained for this purpose;

AND BECAUSE under the present procedure of road maintenance, the internal revenue and development fund is not enough for this purpose;

AND BECAUSE in accordance with Clause 17 (1) of the 'Exchequer and Audit Ordinance' (Cap. 439) whereby the government can open a special fund;

THEREFORE, FOR THOSE SPECIAL PURPOSES,
THIS PARLIAMENT IS SUGGESTING THAT

(a) There should be a special fund called 'The Road Fund.'
(b) The objectives of this fund should cover costs of rehabilitation and maintenance of major and core roads.
(c) Money for this fund should come from:
   (i)   Road tolls as charged from diesel and petrol at an amount to be decided by the Minister of Finance, effective July 1991/92.
   (ii) Various levies and duties from motor vehicles such as licenses, registration and transferring of vehicles, at an amount to be decided by the Minister of Finance effective July 1992/93.

The Ministry of Works will be responsible and will monitor this Special Fund and the Ministry of Works will need to get an authority from the Planning Commission and the Ministry of Finance before embarking upon any project.

Note: Translated from the original in Swahili.
Source: Heggie (1995)

8.1.4 Conclusions on progress-to-date

While in no country has the road sector emerged from the command economy, the acceptance of shadow tolls and dedicated road funds, and the active involvement of road users in the financing and management of Africa's new road funds, provide the basic elements of a mechanism for moving roads in the direction of the market economy. This mechanism can be put in place even without the use of electronic charging devices which, when developed, would make it even easier to manage roads as economic assets.

The principal obstacles in the way of reform are no longer technical, but are now primarily institutional.

8.2 Next steps

8.2.1 Bring about institutional reforms

As the main obstacles to reform are institutional, institutional reforms are the most important steps that can be taken by those who want road users to be able to obtain additional mobility by paying for what it costs. The precise nature of the reforms will vary from country to country.

In the UK, the most urgently needed change is to overcome the Treasury attitude that treats as 'hypothecation' the right of vehicle-owners to pay the costs of the infrastructure they require, and uses this slogan to determine the level and allocation of road expenditure, matters which could be handled better by commercial markets.

In the past, discussion on roads in the UK may have been along wrong lines, such as the 'right' of road users for 'free' use of the 'Queen's Highway'; whether the total amounts paid in road use taxes exceed, or fall short of, the total amounts spent on roads; and the 'right' of environmentalists to oppose motorways. These issues are all peripheral to the main point which is whether, in a free society, road users should be allowed to participate in markets for road space or whether their demands for better road facilities have to be confined to the political arena.

In the US, the most urgent need is to dismantle the federal Highway Trust Fund, which is used by officials 'inside the Beltway' to determine the level and manner of road expenditures in fifty states. The US Congress has an opportunity to deal with this issue by declining to renew this arrangement when it expires in 1997. The abolition of the HTF would allow the different states to develop road funding systems more responsive to the needs arising from their local circumstances. Special transitional arrangements could be made for jurisdictions such as Alaska, the District of Columbia and Hawaii, whose roads are now largely paid for by road users in other areas.

In many other countries the needs for improved motorized mobility are even more urgent, as can be attested by anyone familiar with the traffic of Bangkok, Beijing, Bombay, Lagos, and Mexico City, and with the difficulties of moving agricultural products from rural areas into those cities. The application of economic markets to the roads of those countries could, simultaneously, reduce the worst cases of congestion and generate funding for appropriate expansions of road networks.

But the necessary reforms will not come by themselves. Those who have done well under the old conditions are not easily overcome. Road users wishing to obtain better roads through economic markets will have to mobilize their representatives to apply the necessary political pressure.

8.2.2 Introduce 'shadow tolls'

The introduction of 'shadow tolls' is probably the easiest reform to implement, the most useful, and the least threatening to established interests. It enables new road providers to enter the market and to shoulder some of the major risks (of cost over-runs and of inadequate traffic), and the responsibility for maintaining the value of their investments. Furthermore, the principle of payment in proportion to traffic encourages the development of 'user friendly' roads dedicated to attracting and satisfying travellers.

'Shadow tolls' can be introduced in at least two ways:

1. Limited coverage; and

2. General coverage.

Limited coverage Roads for shadow tolling are determined by government, which invites pre-qualified concessionaires to bid the lowest toll they are prepared to accept, to build, maintain and operate specified types of roads. As mentioned in section 8.1.1, this is the method recently introduced in the UK, where the authorities have invited bids for eight separate schemes. It is likely to result in different shadow tolls being paid for the different schemes. Similar arrangements, for urban water supply, are well-established in France, where private concessionaires bid for the right to supply water in accordance with municipal specifications.

General coverage Government offers to pay the same shadow toll to all entities, including governmental organizations already responsible for roads. The funds for this are obtained from road users, and in consultation with their representatives, preferably in conjunction with a dedicated road fund. This basic payment — corresponding to a standard charge for electricity or telephone use — would be a minimum charge for road use, payable by all road users. It would not preclude higher charges being imposed in special circumstances, corresponding to peak-time or long-distance telephone charges.

Comparison between the two methods The first is the simplest to introduce, but has the disadvantage that it is only applied to a small number of roads, leaving the government with an unlimited commitment for the rest of the network. In contrast, general coverage would enable the whole road network to be commercialized, and improved at the expense of road users to the standards they are willing to pay for.

The recommended approach is to start slowly, with limited coverage, as has been done in the UK, and to expand coverage as appropriate in the light of experience. A major advantage of a limited start is that the bids made by private road providers to build, maintain and operate different kinds of roads will give the authorities — and the road users — good estimates of the costs of providing roads of different kinds. This information would help to determine the suitable level of charge for general coverage. Furthermore, experience in managing and implementing such programmes can be accumulated to keep up with expansion.

8.2.3 Establish dedicated road funds

The new road funds recently established in Africa (described in section 8.1.3) show that institutional changes can be made even under the most difficult conditions. Indeed, it is often the difficulties that spur the changes. To be successful, road funds have to be managed by competent people clearly accountable to those who pay the funds. The best way to achieve this accountability is to have representatives of those who pay, serve on the funds' management boards. Road funds have to get their revenues from convenient sources — such as levies on fuel — and they have to be large enough to achieve their purposes

A major objection to dedicated road funds is that their surpluses are seized by governments as soon as they are accumulated. Ways to establish such funds outside governments need to be explored. They could be placed in commercial banks and even managed by bank personnel, whose honesty could literally be guaranteed by their employers. The advantage of such funds is that they would ensure steady revenue streams to pay for roads, and could even be used as security for loans from local and overseas lenders.

8.2.4 Eliminate discrimination against privately funded roads

Governments wishing to attract private investors to roads should eliminate rules that discriminate against the private sector. Revenues from taxes — such as fuel taxes — dedicated to road improvement should be made available for the building and maintenance of all roads, including those financed privately, by an acceptable allocation system. The 'shadow tolls' described above provide one means of achieving this objective. If governments wish to finance roads that are not financially viable, they should make specific allocations out of general funds; but it is neither equitable nor efficient to require other road users to pay for them.

8.2.5 Develop electronic methods of charging for road use

While electronic road pricing is not essential for the implementation of the institutional reforms described above, it would certainly be helpful to move roads towards the market economy. Indeed, it would be difficult for the market to deal with traffic congestion without electronic road pricing. As was mentioned in Chapter 4, much work has already been done to develop systems that can assess road use charges against vehicle owners without the vehicles having to stop at conventional toll gates. One objective of this work should be to develop national — or even international — standards that would enable vehicles to be charged irrespective of their origins. The systems that enable credit cards to be used world-wide offer useful precedents. Indeed, one approach to the problem might be to enable road use to be charged to credit cards, as are telephone calls on aircraft and in airports.

Additionally, systems should be developed that do not identify users, to meet the common objection that some road users might not wish their movements to be monitored by government agencies. One way of dealing with this objection would be to allow for payments to continue to be made in cash, for those who wish it.

8.2.6 Roles of government

If roads were to become part of the market economy, should governments have roles in them? Of course they should. All levels of government have a legitimate interest in the existence of safe highways, built to standards responsive to the economic demands of users. But it does not follow from this that government has to provide the roads, or even determine their standards. Government has a legitimate interest in a well-fed population, but many — even in the US — would argue that it does not have to tell people what to eat, and most would agree that it does not have to operate food shops. What then would be the legitimate roles of government if roads were part of the market economy? There would be different roles for different levels of government.

Central government It is generally agreed that the highest level of government should be concerned with defending its people and in encouraging their commerce, and for these reasons it has an interest in the provision and maintenance of adequate road networks.

But central government also has an interest in ensuring that its people have the right institutions for their development. *Markets* are institutions of major importance and their supervision has always been regarded as an appropriate government function, e.g. introducing and checking weights and measures. Clearly, the introduction of markets for road space, which would enable buyers and sellers of this commodity to interact to their mutual benefit, is an appropriate task for all central governments, as would be the development of appropriate pricing mechanisms.

Other functions of central government could include ensuring that roads are provided to consistent standards, and that road users are not exploited by monopoly road suppliers, whether of the private or public sectors.

States or provinces would have major roles in the road sector, even if roads were commercially provided. In the US, states are responsible for devising suitable financing systems for roads, and this can include the organization of dedicated highway funds which do not discriminate against privately provided public roads. States are also concerned with safety, which can require intervention both in the design of roads (e.g., to ensure that the geometry, surfacing and signing of roads minimize accident risks) and in their management (e.g., to ensure that motor vehicles are not driven in a manner that poses danger to others).

Local government roles are particularly important in dealing with the extreme conditions of congestion and underutilization of highway facilities. In areas of congestion, city governments are in a position to initiate pricing measures (as described in Chapter 4 above) which would not only relieve congestion but also earn substantial revenues to hard-pressed municipalities and enable them to reduce income and other taxes.

If roads were in the market economy, those underutilized could pose much more difficult problems to local authorities. If their costs were not covered by revenues from road user or landowners, it would be the local authorities which would have to decide which to subsidize and which to abandon.

8.2.7 Need for working examples

The introduction of commercially provided public roads is likely to be most successful if implemented as a result of voluntary arrangements between willing buyers and willing sellers. One way to accomplish this would be for the private sector to build new roads in response to commercial needs, and to operate them on a commercial basis. If new road space is provided as an 'add-on' to an existing system, and if road users find it worthwhile to patronize it and pay the charges, and if the charges cover all costs (including congestion and environmental costs), all concerned benefit, and there would be no obvious losers. Even those who do not use these new roads would benefit from reduced congestion on the old ones.

The need for new road links — such as the Dulles Greenway and the SR-91 roads described in the previous chapter — is enormous, especially outside the US, which is comparatively well-endowed with roads. The biggest deficiencies are in Africa, Asia, Europe and Latin America, and it is in those areas that market reforms could do the most good.

The initiative for such demonstrations should come from the localities concerned — e.g. from Bombay or Shanghai — not from agencies outside them looking for 'guinea pigs' to experiment on. Financing organizations, such as merchant banks, or the international lending agencies, could, once acceptable conditions were negotiated, provide finance against the security of road fund revenues obtained from congestion charges. In this manner traffic congestion, often considered to be a 'disease of civilization', could be made to generate the funds that could help to restore civilization to these stricken cities.

Note

1. This is not the position taken in this book, which recommends only that road user payments dedicated to roads be separated from payments rendered as taxes.

Epilogue:

'How to plan and pay for the safe and adequate highways we need'

by

Milton Friedman and Daniel J. Boorstin

Authors' introductory note

This paper was written in 1951 or 1952 when we were both teaching at the University of Chicago. It was entered, without success, in a contest offering a prize for the best essay on its topic, and was forgotten until discovered by one of the authors (Friedman) in 1988. It is published here as originally written, as a contribution to the on-going discussion on the role of private enterprise in the provision of highway services.

The title of the essay was not of our choosing. The footnote on page 233 is our own. The endnotes were added by Gabriel Roth.

I. The Proposal: A shift to the private enterprise point of view

The building and maintenance of our highways is today almost exclusively a governmental operation. We have become so used to this that whenever the question arises how to solve our highway problems, we take it for granted that we are simply asking how we can improve government planning of roads and government financing of them. The proposals in the present essay are based on an attempt to re-think the problem from the outset and to refresh our imagination on this problem by putting the question in another way. Suppose we ask not how the government can do a better job for us, but how our highways might be provided by free private enterprise.

Like automobiles, shoes and cigarettes, highway service is a product offered to a number of individual consumers. How can this product be most economically provided? How can the type of service be provided for which there is the greatest consumer demand? How can this service best be paid for? For the production and financing of automobiles, shoes, and cigarettes we do not make any collective 'plans' or make collective estimates of 'needs'. Instead we rely on each individual deciding for himself how much he 'needs' and how much he is willing to pay. We rely on the prospect of profit to lead other individuals to meet this "need" by producing the products and selling them on the free market. Producers who satisfy the needs of customers at least cost prosper; those who do not, fail. We test whether a thing is worth producing by whether consumers are freely willing to pay a price at which other individuals are freely willing to produce it. The 'planning' is decentralized, the paying is voluntary, and the 'need' is evaluated by each individual according to his own lights. The problem of 'planning' and that of 'financing' are both solved at the same time. These are the fundamental principles of our free enterprise system; these are the principles that have produced our material prosperity and at the same time enabled us to preserve political freedom — to avoid having politics engulf the whole life as it has come so close to doing not only in Communist countries but in most other parts of the world.

Why should planning and paying for our highways needs be treated differently than planning and paying for other services or commodities? Highway services do have some peculiarities which make it unwise or impossible to leave their provision entirely to free private enterprise. But these peculiarities are not so great as they are generally assumed to be; and they have become less important as a result of the growth of our economy and modern developments in technology. In any event, we should not take it for granted that these peculiarities require that highways be and remain a government monopoly, or that the principles of private enterprise cannot be applied to solve this problem as they have so brilliantly solved others. The accepted approach to this problem is an illustration of the way in which the proponents of our free enterprise system accept the role which is given them by their opponents — a role as fighters of a rear-guard action against socialism. While they devote their energies to preventing further encroachment by government, they take for granted that those areas in which government is at any moment operating must be so operated. Those of us who believe in free enterprise should show as much imagination, intellectual daring, and willingness to experiment in extending the scope of free enterprise as the opponents of free enterprise have shown in seeking to extend the power of the state. If we do, we shall find that much now being done by the state could better be done by free enterprise. We shall discover that the trend of opinion toward collectivism of the past few decades has led us all to accept many kinds of state action as inevitable and desirable that will turn out not to be so if we examine them from a fresh point of view.

Highways are a touchstone of the whole problem. There are exciting prospects of introducing the many benefits of free enterprise into the provision of highway services, and avoiding many of the evils of government operation. The measures proposed in this essay are of three types:

a) Those clearly feasible, desirable, and capable of being introduced promptly; here particular practical proposals are made;

b) Those more speculative, requiring more knowledge and experiment before they can be adequately evaluated; in this class the present essay attempts at least to suggest areas of investigation and experimentation which might be productive of practical proposals in the long run;

c) Other possibilities which must still be regarded as visionary.

We have deliberately included the visionary possibilities along with certain practical proposals in the hope that these may stimulate others. While we recognize that it is not possible to go all the way, that government will have to continue to play an important role in the provision of highway services, our main purpose has led us to walk as little as possible along this well-trodden path and to give our attention primarily to opening or exploring some new paths.

Two important facts should be noted at the outset which may put this suggested change to a private enterprise point of view in its proper perspective.

1. The introduction of private enterprise would be likely to lead to a substantial increase in actual expenditure on highways.

The public now expresses its demand for highway services by paying for them in the form of license fees, gasoline taxes, and tolls on the toll roads that have been mushrooming in recent years. But, strictly speaking, the highway-consumers who have been paying these fees have not been getting their money's worth. This appears from the simple fact that the amount paid in state and federal motor-vehicle fees, motor fuel and motor carrier taxes has year after year been decidedly greater than total current expenditures on roads (for maintenance and administration of state, county, and local roads and city and village streets, debt retirement, and interest on debt). In 1950, for example, receipts were in excess of 3 billion dollars, while expenditures were only about 2.25 billion dollars. In addition, toll roads have in general been extremely profitable, which is of course a major reason why they have been tending to increase in number. By the criteria of private enterprise, therefore, the provision of highway services is already a highly profitable business. The introduction of the profit incentive would thus confer a double benefit on the users of highway services: it would not only lead to greater efficiency in the expenditures now being made; but also to a substantial expansion in the highway system.

2. The provision of highways is neither too expensive nor too large-scale an activity to be conducted by private enterprises.

By comparison with other activities carried on by private enterprise, the provision of highway services is a small industry. As noted above, in 1950, about 2.25 billion dollars were spent in the maintenance and operation of all state, county and local roads, and city and village streets, debt retirement, and interest on debt. The railroads spent more than three times as much on current operations (including interest, rents, and dividends); the automobile, perhaps six times as much. Consumers spent more than this sum on cigarettes, other tobacco products, and smoking supplies, even after subtracting the part of their expenditure on these items that went to taxes; they spent more than this sum on hiring domestic servants; they spent more than twice this sum on alcoholic beverages, again after subtracting taxes; they spent between twenty and twenty-five times this sum on food.

Highways bulk larger in capital outlay than in current expenses, but even here they are by no means exceptional. Total capital outlay on roads in 1950 was about the same as current expenditures, about 2.25 billion dollars. Gross public expenditures by all private enterprises were more than twenty times this amount, net capital expenditures (after deducting depreciation charges and the like) more than ten times as large. More than five times as much was spent by private enterprises on building new houses and dwellings as was spent by governmental units on building roads and streets.

Clearly, sheer size and expense are no justification for government operation of our highways system. If this conclusion and the preceding comparisons seem surprising, it is, we believe, because highways have been provided by governmental activity, therefore requiring collective action for financing and becoming footballs of political discussion, whereas the other activities have been carried on by myriads of separate enterprises through an impersonal market mechanism that attracts little attention. What seems large and difficult for government gets done almost without attention by private enterprise.[1]

II. Economic peculiarities of highways

The correct explanation of why the provision of highways has been so exclusively a governmental function is, we believe, to be found in three real peculiarities of highways that raise obstacles to their operation by private enterprises. Some grasp of these peculiarities is essential if we are to get the benefits of private enterprise in the provision of highway services, and at the same time avoid doing serious damage in the process. These peculiarities are:

1. The technical difficulty of charging for the use of roads

In fairness, the people who drive on a road should be charged for the service received, and in proportion to their use of the service. But from the very nature of the road it is difficult to charge each traveler on the road this kind of price directly. Automobile license fees and the gasoline tax are attempts to charge people for the use of roads indirectly. They are, however, very crude means. The charge does not depend on the particular road used, so the taxes involve the same charge for the use of a super-highway and a dirt road, or for the use of a crowded road on which it would be desirable to discourage traffic, and a little-used road. The tax varies from one kind of vehicle to another in a way that may bear only a rough relation to the difference in the amount of highway service used or cost imposed by use.

The inability to identify the particular highway use for which a particular dollar in tax is paid also makes it almost inevitable that this kind of charge be collected by government. This simple fact has played an important part in keeping the provision of highway service a governmental function. A consequence has been that it is now difficult or impossible to tell which roads are paying their own way and which are not.

A really thoroughgoing and satisfactory solution to the problem of improving our roads will, therefore, require improvement and refinement in the method of charging for their use. Yet it must be emphasized that, however crude may be the present method of charging people by means of gasoline taxes and license fees, it is vastly better than paying for roads and highways out of general tax revenue. For at least it establishes some relation between use and payment, and thereby imposes the cost of highways at least roughly on those who benefit from them. In so doing it creates some incentive for the economical use of highways.[2]

At first glance, it seems hardly possible that this apparently trivial problem of how to charge people for the highway services they use is a key to the whole problem of how to plan and pay for better highways; yet it is just that. This fact cannot be too strongly emphasized. It is a key not only for a system that would involve operation of roads by private enterprise but equally for the present system of public operation. Should a particular road be built? How should it be built? How should it be financed? Should an existing road be maintained, improved, or allowed to deteriorate? If we could charge directly for the service of the road, we could answer those questions — whether under private or public ownership — in the same way that we now decide how many automobiles should be manufactured, what kind of automobiles should be manufactured, how their production should be financed, whether a particular model should be discontinued, and so on.

If there is a price for road services at which traffic on a new road would pay for the cost of constructing it, it should be built; if the extra traffic on a better road or the higher price people would be willing to pay would yield enough revenue to pay for making it better, then it should be made better. If the receipts on an existing road do not cover costs of maintaining it, it should be allowed to deteriorate. This is the test we apply to the bulk of our economic activity. We have never been able to discover a better or more effective test; and every attempt to dispense with this test — such as has occurred in times of governmental price controls or in socialistic experiments — has raised staggering difficulties to which no satisfactory solution has yet been found.

2. A road is in some measure a natural monopoly

Given one road between two places, there is seldom any justification in precisely duplicating the road — even if it were possible; if there is more traffic to be carried, common sense suggests that the desirable thing is to enlarge the road, not build a duplicate road. In this sense a road is a 'natural monopoly'.

With respect to most items, say automobiles, or furniture, if one producer were to try to charge consumers a price considerably higher than the cost of producing automobiles or furniture, consumers have the alternative of buying from another producer — or if there is only one producer at the moment, there is a strong incentive for someone else to go into the business. And there is no technological barrier to prevent other people from going into the business or to prevent the simultaneous existence of a number of firms all producing essentially the same product. In such cases, the consumer is (or can be, provided government avoids the creation of an 'artificial' monopoly) protected against exploitation by the actual or potential competition of other enterprises capable of producing the same product. The maintenance of vigorous and active competition has in this way been a major source of our high standard of living.

With a natural monopoly like a road between 'A' and 'B', such protection cannot be present to the same degree. If a private owner of a road charges a toll, say, that is considerably higher than the cost of providing the highway service, there is little possibility of someone else building a precisely duplicating road. The absence of the competitive check tends to lead to a check via government control. This is how the existence of 'natural monopoly' helps explain the socialization of highways.

But while it is clear that there is an element of natural monopoly in roads, the extent of monopoly power is always limited, and much more sharply limited in some cases than in others. While it may not be feasible to duplicate the precise road between 'A' and 'B', there are almost always other ways of getting from 'A' to 'B'; by roundabout routes, by railroad, by plane. Even more indirectly, it is possible to avoid going from 'A' to 'B' by doing business elsewhere, or by transacting business by writing, wiring, or telephoning. This indirect competition sets limits, and in many cases very narrow limits indeed, on the monopoly power inherent in the ownership, say, of the road between 'A' and 'B'. One drastic and almost unnoticed effect of recent technological change, and of the growth and development of our economy, has been progressively to lessen the element of natural monopoly in roads. That monopoly element today is much smaller than it was, say, one hundred years ago; and every year with the development of our means of transportation and communication it becomes less and less. These changes make it far more feasible today to introduce elements of private enterprise and competition into our highways system without danger of undue exploitation of the consumer, than it would have been at an earlier stage in our economic development.

3. The 'neighborhood effect' of roads

The benefit a person receives from the existence of a road, or from its being in good repair, may not be proportionate to the amount he himself travels on the road. A person living on a road, for example, who traverses it say only twice a day, may be willing to pay much more for the privilege of having a road there than a non-resident who also traverses it twice a day. The resident will want the road to make it easier for his friends to visit him; to improve the appearance of his house; to avoid noise, dirt and congestion, and perhaps for still other reasons. As a result, it is not fair that the cost of road-maintenance should be borne exclusively by the people who travel on it. More important, the amount people are willing to pay directly for the privilege of travelling on a street or road may not be an adequate indication of the amount it is appropriate to spend on that street or road. If one could charge not only for such direct benefits but also ferret out all the indirect benefits and charge each person the amount he would be willing to pay for them, the sum thus obtained would be a better measure of the amount it would be worth spending on the street or road.

Wherever such indirect benefits can be identified and charged for, it is highly desirable that they should be. We should try more than we have in the past to find ways of measuring the economic advantage which private individuals (other than travelers) receive from particular roads, to make them pay fairly for these advantages, and hence to enlist their initiative and concern in the improvement and maintenance of our roads. But we cannot hope for more than modest success in this endeavor. In consequence, the existence of 'neighborhood effects', where they are important, imposes a major obstacle to the introduction of private enterprise in the provision of highways. They are likely to be particularly important in cities, which is why our proposals are least adequate for city roads and streets.

But here again, the importance of 'neighborhood effects' should not be overestimated. In one sense, every economic activity has 'neighborhood effects': the suburban supermarket benefits from people in general having cars, because this enables it to draw on a larger circle of customers. It does not therefore follow that the supermarket should be assessed directly for some part of the costs of the customers' cars, or that too few people will have cars unless this is done. Insofar as the supermarket benefits, it can — and competition will force it to — reduce the price at which it sells its product, and this price reduction gives potential customers just the right additional incentive to buy cars, so that in effect the supermarket is contributing to the cost of the cars. In the same way, the suburban super-market benefits from good roads, but this does not create any 'neighbor-hood effects' that justify building more roads than consumers are willing to pay for in the form of a fee for travelling on the roads. The 'neighbor-hood effects' that are important are those that do not get effectively expressed in some such way in the form of an increase in the direct demand for highway services.

Benefits from highway service may also accrue to the nation as a whole rather than to individuals separately. Perhaps the most important example is the value of roads for national defense. Where such benefits are impor-tant they may justify building roads at government cost that would not otherwise be needed.

These are the three main peculiarities of highways from an economic point of view. How can we overcome them or at least reduce them so as to put the building and maintenance of highways more and more on a common footing with other economic activities in a free-enterprise economy, thereby bringing to our highways the initiative, competition, efficiency and freedom from political manipulation that only free enterprise can provide?

III. Practical proposals

We shall consider separately three classes of highways:

1. turnpikes (express roadways covering extensive distances);

2. ordinary inter-city roads; and

3. intra-city roads (roads within cities).

The problems and the solutions are different in each case.

1. Turnpikes (express roadways covering extensive distances)

In this case, the three peculiarities listed above, while present, are all at a minimum. It is not particularly difficult to charge a toll for an express highway, or to vary the toll appropriately for different kinds of vehicles;

the 'natural monopoly' is at its minimum (the greater the distance traversed by a road, the more likely that there are alternative roads or other
means of transportation) and the 'neighborhood effect' is of negligible
importance (express highways are mainly ways of getting through the
countryside as quickly as possible, not means of access to businesses or
dwellings along the way). But beginning with this case we therefore start
with the simplest of the problems, the one where it should be easiest to
assimilate highway construction and maintenance to other private enterprises.

Our plan for the construction, maintenance and operation of super-
highways is simply the following: turn them over to private enterprise.
There is nothing impossible about this suggestion: toll roads have frequently been privately owned. Indeed, it is no more impossible than that
many other demands of the community should be adequately supplied by
individual enterprises, when they are allowed to make a profit on the
venture. It involves no new administrative trick, no new government
commission or public corporation; all it requires is that we allow to operate
in this field the normal incentives of private business which have built our
factories, our railroads, and our department stores.

Whenever an individual or firm wishes to construct a new turnpike he
will offer to the state highway commission (or that of several states if it is
interstate) a detailed proposal. This proposal would include: the points
between which the turnpike is to be constructed; the route to be taken; the
method of construction. Approval of the state highway commission is
required for two reasons:

1. to assure that the highway meets minimum safety standards — just as a
    building license is frequently required for a new factory building for
    the same reason;

2. because the building of a road may require governmental assistance in
    condemning some of the land required — just as is now the case in the
    construction of a pipe line or railroad.

If the state highway commission finds that the plans meet legally enacted
minimum standards, and that the offer is a bona fide offer (and not a
device say for acquiring a particular piece of land) it shall approve the
proposal, authorize the firm to proceed to build the road, and give the firm
the cooperation (but not the financial assistance) of the state in the legal
process of condemning any land required which cannot be obtained
through direct purchase. When construction is completed, the owning firm

may charge any toll it thinks proper for the use of the road.

If all roads were toll roads, this would be all there would be to the plan. But if there are other roads, and if these other roads are being financed by a charge that does not depend on the particular road travelled — as at present by gasoline taxes and license fees — an additional problem arises. For the toll road would then be operating under an undesirable handicap: the traveler would be paying in two ways for travelling on the toll road — in the form of the toll, and in the form of gasoline taxes — but the owners of the road would be receiving only the toll; in consequence, they might not have an incentive to build a road even though people were willing to pay enough (in both ways) to justify its construction. The proper solution to this problem is for the state which collects the gasoline taxes to pay the owners of the toll road a sum equal to the tax on the gasoline consumed on the road.* In this way, the toll charged will equal the actual price consumers are willing to pay for the *additional* convenience of a turnpike.[3]

Current practice on toll highways suggests another possible, but in our view undesirable, source of income to the owners of toll highways — namely, the sale of franchises for commercial enterprises (restaurants, filling stations, motels, gift-shops, etc.) bordering the highways. It is not likely that this would in fact be a source of income even if the owners had the power to sell such franchises. The owners of the road could charge for a franchise only by limiting the number of concerns and thus enabling them to charge higher prices than they could get elsewhere; but this would make the road less attractive to travelers than otherwise and so diminish the toll receipts from any given toll. In general, gains from the franchises would be more than balanced by losses in tolls. While self-interest alone would therefore generally prevent the use of the power to sell franchises even if the toll-owner had such power, it seems undesirable to give him any exclusive privileges that are not absolutely essential to the construction of the road, in line with the general aim of strengthening competitive forces and eliminating monopoly power.

Though described in terms of new toll roads, there is no reason why this plan could not equally be applied to existing toll roads. These are now generally operated either directly by states, or by public corporations. They could readily be sold to private concerns, by open competitive bidding.

---

* This would, of course, raise a variety of detailed administrative problems — estimation of the amount of taxes due, division of payments between states, and the like. While in practice these problems would doubtless be important and troublesome, none that we have been able to think of seems sufficiently serious to render the proposal impracticable.

Getting the government out of the business of providing service on toll highways in this way, and opening this area of economic activity to private enterprise, is the quickest and most efficient means of meeting the current demand for such highways. Individuals risking their own funds in the search for profits will have a far stronger incentive than government officials spending public funds to build highways that will most effectively serve the public's need and to build them at minimum cost. Political pressures that now tend to play so important a role in determining what roads are built, and who builds them — pressures that even the most public-spirited highway officials cannot fully resist — will be minimized if not entirely eliminated. The incentive to secure the maximum total return will operate to keep the toll on such highways down and will assure that highways are built whenever the price that the community is willing to pay for the service of a toll road will cover its cost.

The only defect of private ownership and operation arises from the natural monopoly element that will necessarily be present. This is a real defect that there seems no way of fully eliminating. However, given the significant indirect competition from alternative routes and alternative means of transport over long distances it seems clearly a tolerable defect, and much less serious than the basic and fundamental defects of alternative solutions to the problem.

2. A policy for ordinary inter-city roads

For the great bulk of inter-city or country roads, the 'neighborhood effect' is little, if at all, more important than for long-distance toll roads. The natural monopoly element, on the other hand, is considerably more important: the available alternatives are frequently fewer because these roads are used to traverse shorter distances, and in some cases a particular road may be the only way of getting to a particular place or city without incurring inordinate expense. This feature alone would require somewhat more governmental intervention than in toll roads. But the most important difference from toll roads, and the most serious obstacle to full-fledged operation of these roads by private enterprise is the greater technical difficulty of charging directly for the use of the roads. A long-distance toll road is very much like a railroad line, with a limited number of 'stops' along the way. On such a road a 'conductor' can collect your ticket and require a ticket for a particular station you want to go to. But on an ordinary inter-city highway with its great number of entrances and exits, any such direct method of selling tickets for particular trips is obviously not feasible.

We have already emphasized that this technical problem of how to charge for the use of roads and how much to charge is a key to planning and paying for better roads. It arises equally under public or private operation of the roads. If it has not been recognized as a key problem, it is not because the problem has been 'solved' under our present system. It is rather because it has generally been ignored. When the state goes into business, nobody worries much whether people are getting what they are willing to pay for; or whether the people who are doing the paying are those who are receiving the service.

We have not been able to devise any simple and satisfactory solution to this problem; and in consequence we see no way to turn the provision of inter-city highway services over to private enterprise in the same thorough-going fashion that we have suggested for toll roads. So far as we can see, the collection of fees for the use of roads will have to continue to be performed by government in some such indirect way as is now used — though it should be possible to improve on the present method in detail. But this does not mean that government must continue to take direct responsibility for constructing, maintaining and operating these roads. The operation of the roads can be separated from the collection of revenues. Accordingly, our proposals for inter-city roads fall under two headings:

a) suggestions for improving present techniques of charging, together with some highly tentative ideas for novel methods of charging;

b) a plan for turning the construction, operation and maintenance of these roads over to private enterprise.

a) How to charge and how much to charge

i) What is an 'ideal' system of prices

We have already indicated some of the crudities of our present system of charging for highway services by license fees and gaso-line taxes. An ideal system of prices would have the property that the price paid for a unit of highway service would be just equal to the extra cost of providing that unit of service. Of course, there is generally more than one way of providing an additional unit of service: improving the road, new construction, reducing congestion, and so on. If one method costs less than another, more highway

service should be provided that way and less in other ways. As this
is done, the cost of providing additional service the first way will
rise, the cost of providing additional service the other ways will fall.
The efficient combination of ways of providing highway service has
been reached only when this process has been carried to the point at
which the extra cost of providing one additional unit of service is the
same no matter how it is provided — which is why we could speak
of 'the' extra cost in describing an ideal system of prices.

These principles require that the price, say, of a mile's travel on a
highway would vary from vehicle to vehicle — the cost of providing
a mile's travel for a passenger car is clearly much less than for a
heavy truck; that the price vary from road to road — the cost of
providing an extra mile's travel on a dirt road may be different than
on a concrete road, on a road through built-up areas than on a road
in the open country, on a road through mountains than on a road in
flat country; and even that the price vary from one time of the day to
another — the cost of providing an extra mile's travel at peak hours
of travel and congestion is clearly different from providing this same
service at slack times. It would also mean that the price would
depend on how much demand there is for highway service at various
prices, for the cost of providing an extra mile's travel may depend
on how much road service in total of various kinds is being provided.

This is the kind of price system free competition and private enterprise tend to produce where they can operate. Individual enterprises
in their ceaseless search for profit try now one price now another,
and in the process tend to approximate to the structure of prices
described, for, if attained, there would be no further opportunities to
profit by departing from it. Of course, in a dynamic world, the ideal
structure of prices is itself always changing, which is why experimentation is always going on and why the relations among prices in
the competitive sector of our economy are in continuous flux.

ii) How to improve the present system

Without the actual test of the market a close approximation to the
ideal system of prices cannot be expected. The difficulties in the
way of achieving the proper system are multiplied manyfold for
highways by the necessity of using a simple system like the gasoline
tax in which payment is for highway services in general rather than
for a particular use of the highways. Nonetheless, it should be

possible to do a good deal better than we are now doing.

In order to improve on present methods of charging for the use of highways, the basic need is for detailed, thorough, and continuous study of the costs of providing additional highway services on each type of road to each type of vehicle. Such studies have, of course, been made, and are doubtless now under way. Their goal should be some simple formula for charging for highway service that, on the one hand, permits collection of the charge without excessive administrative cost, and, on the other, imposes charges that are in proportion to the extra cost of rendering each type of service. For example, if it were a fact that the extra cost of providing services to different types of vehicles is in proportion to the amount of gasoline consumed, and that the extra costs are roughly the same for different types of roads, then the present gasoline tax would be a highly satisfactory formula. Presumably, however, this is not the case: the extra cost for heavy vehicles is apparently much greater than their extra gasoline consumption per mile of travel, which is the justification for the higher annual license fees to which they are subject. In this same class would be taxes on tires or oil or some other expense of automobile operation that varies with the amount of travel; conceivably one of these might vary more nearly than gasoline consumption in proportion with costs of providing highway service.

Somewhat further afield would be a charge per ton-mile of traffic. It seems not at all unlikely that costs of providing highway service vary more nearly with ton-miles than with gasoline, oil or tire consumption. Such a tax would be more difficult to collect than present gasoline taxes, but it does not seem clearly impracticable. Perhaps each vehicle could be required to carry a sealed speedometer that would accumulate the number of miles travelled and on the basis of which a tax would be paid once every three or six months. Or perhaps, the gasoline tax could be relied on for passenger car travel but supplemented by such a ton-mile tax for trucks, buses and the like.[4]

For both such ton-mile taxes, the present gasoline tax, and the other taxes mentioned, a real problem arises, and now exists, of allocating receipts among states. The receipts should go to the state in which the travel occurs, but now it goes to the state in which the tax is paid. This is a problem that requires interstate agreements. In principle, it would not seem impossible to solve it — at least if states charge the same taxes. Sampling studies of traffic should at moderate cost permit estimates of the amount of traffic in each state on the basis of which states could re-imburse one another.

All these methods of charging have the defect that they do not permit variation from one type of road to another, or from one time of day to another. Here we have no experience to guide us except for toll roads. Yet the gains of having such a system are potentially so great that it would be worth devoting a good deal of technical effort to devising some means of making differential charges on different roads possible. For, if this could be achieved, it would not only contribute to more rational planning and development of roads by public authorities, but would also make it far easier to turn the task over to private enterprise.

iii) Atomic age suggestions

One possibility that has occurred to us may be worth outlining, even though it may be completely visionary. Suppose it were possible to incorporate minute traces of radioactive material in the paint used to mark center lines of roads, and that cars could carry sealed geiger counters that would accumulate the impulses received. A charge could be levied of so many cents per so many impulses to be paid periodically. The amount of radioactive material could then be varied from road to road and each road could be posted with signs showing the class in which it fell. On this scheme, the cost would depend on time taken to traverse a road, not on miles, so the prices would be expressed as, say, one cent per ten minutes. And the price charged could vary from vehicle to vehicle, so this system would permit differentiation of charges both from vehicle to vehicle and road to road.

This scheme may well be completely impractical at present or at any foreseeable time in the future, yet it may be worth expanding a bit on its operation for illustrative purposes. One obvious disadvantage is that by making the charge on a per time basis it might stimulate speeding. Offsetting this disadvantage is the incentive it would give to avoid peak hours of travel, since it would take a longer time to travel any given distance at such hours than at times when traffic is light. The effect here would be similar to that of lower charges for electricity consumed during off-peak hours, a practice now fairly common.

Such a scheme would also greatly facilitate experimentation with different rates to see how sensitive traffic is to changes in the rate. Such experimentation is almost ruled out if it has to be done simultaneously for all roads, whereas under such a scheme it could be done on a much smaller basis. The scheme would permit a wider variety of types of roads, since expensive roads for which there is a demand could be financed by high charges on such roads, whereas now, if constructed at all, people who drive over them are in effect paying less than their economic cost and are being subsidized by other travelers. And the reverse of this is, of course, that it would permit low rates for inexpensive roads or poor highway service. Finally, under the plan of private operation to be described below, it might make possible competition among enterprises in price as well as in other ways: each enterprise could establish its own price for its own section of the roads — though this would require not only that the charges be recorded in the vehicles that traveled on the road but also, reciprocally, that there be some method of estimating the charges accumulated in all vehicles that have used the piece of road in question.

b) How to operate the roads, given a method of charging

Let us assume that, at least for the time being, the only feasible method of charging for highway services is similar to existing methods in the sense that the charge is independent of the particular road traveled. For definiteness, we shall assume that the gasoline tax is the only method of charging. The necessity of using this tax means that the state must undertake to fix the price for highway services and to collect the tax. It does not, however, follow that the state must also decide where to build new roads, and take responsibility for constructing them, or for operating, and maintaining, existing roads.

An alternative, and in our view much superior plan is the following. Let the state highway commission divide the roads of a state into convenient sections. Let it then call for bids from private enterprise for the maintenance and operation of these sections. The call for bids will specify that the contractor will receive from the state a sum equal to the taxes collected on gasoline consumed on the highway section in question. The bids will take the form either of an offer to pay a specified sum per year for the franchise of maintaining the section in question, or of the additional sum per year demanded by the contractor from the state. In general, no bids requiring that the state pay an additional sum would be accepted — in these cases the general presumption would be that the road in question should be allowed to deteriorate; but there might be some cases (for example, roads important for national defense) in which an exception to this general rule would be justified. For the rest, the highest positive bid would be accepted. In addition to receiving bids on existing roads, the highway commission would also be ready to entertain bids for permission to construct new highways under similar terms.[5] Again, in general only bids requiring no payment by the state over and above the gasoline taxes would be accepted. In view of the large capital investment required for new highways, contracts for such highways would be for a relatively long period, whereas contracts for maintaining existing roads could be for shorter periods.

The only technical problem this plan would raise would be estimating the amount of gasoline consumed on each section of the road. This might be a troublesome problem in practice but it does not seem impossible to solve it at moderate cost through carefully planned sample studies of volume and kind of traffic.

What advantages would such a plan have over existing practices? On old roads, the plan would mean considerably greater economy in their operation and maintenance. The contractors would have a strong incentive to keep costs to a minimum — an incentive difficult to match when the care and maintenance of roads is the responsibility of a public body subject to political pressure and without any clear-cut test of efficiency. In addition, the contractor would have an incentive to perform the maintenance in a way involving the least interference with traffic, and to make improvements that would make the road most attractive to travelers. For the income of the contractor would depend directly on how much traffic he could attract to his road.

For new roads, the plan would provide a means of making the tastes and preferences of travelers fully effective. it would establish precisely that direct and strong link between the needs of the public and the building of highways, the absence of which is the chief defect of our present system. Highway enterprises would be continually on the lookout for possibilities of building roads that could attract traffic, i.e., for which there is a great need. Of course private enterprises, no less than public ones, would make mistakes. But the costs of the mistakes would be borne by the contractors, not the public, just as gains from good judgement would be received by them. And the contractors would be guided by the right aim, the aim of satisfying the demands and needs of the public for highway services, unmixed by the many irrelevant considerations that are bound to enter public decisions. It need hardly be repeated that this is the technique for meeting the needs of the public that is responsible for our high standard of living.

Even assuming that no more refined method of charging than the present one can be devised, here is a plan that puts the provision of highway services in important respects on the same footing as the provision of most other services in our economy. Competition would take the form of competition in the quality of services offered. The absence of price competition is a serious defect, but it is a defect that is present equally under public operation. Under either public or private operation, if the price per mile of travel (or its equivalent) is set very high, traffic will be reduced, the amount of roads it pays to maintain will be relatively small but it will pay to make them high-quality roads with a light density of traffic — just as when cities fix taxi-cab fares and fix them very high, cabs tend to be relatively few but extremely luxurious and available with a minimum of waiting time. If the price per mile of travel is set very low, traffic will be encouraged but it will not pay to maintain good roads. There will be a very high density of traffic on inferior roads — just as when cities fix taxi-cab fares very low, cabs tend to be small or ancient or battered, and it is difficult to get a cab much of the time. The right fare is some-where between, with enough roads of high enough quality so that conges-tion is relatively infrequent and with few enough roads so that only few are very lightly travelled.

The discovery of some scheme for charging different prices on different roads — such as our fanciful idea of radio-active center lines and geiger counters — would solve this problem in the most satisfactory way. It would then be possible to let individual contractors fix their own prices and to have competition in price as well as in quality. The one problem that would then remain would derive from the natural monopoly element on roads. To avoid exploitation of consumers in cases where this element is important, it might be necessary to give some public authority the power to establish maximum rates.

3. Suggestions for intra-city roads

We come, finally, to roads within cities. These raise by all odds the most difficult problems: the technical difficulty of charging for the use of roads is at a maximum; the natural monopoly may be important; and neighbor-hood effects for the first time are extremely significant. In addition, the parking problem is added to that of transport. For these and other reasons, the plan suggested above for inter-city roads does not seem feasible.

In the light of these difficulties, we have not been able to devise any acceptable general plan fundamentally different in its broad outline from the present system of planning, constructing and operating city streets.

Unfortunately, this does not mean that the present system — judged by its fruits — is anywhere near ideal. Indeed, casual observation suggests that city streets and highways are currently the segment of the nation's highway system most in need of improvement. Even without thoroughgoing reform of existing methods, a number of specific changes might produce significant improvement.

a) Give cities their full share of motor-vehicle taxes

Cities now receive much less than they are entitled to. In line with the general principles outlined above, taxes collected on gasoline consumed on city streets, and that part of other motor-vehicle fees attributable to such traffic, should be made available for maintaining and improving such streets. This should be done city by city, each city receiving its share of total receipts on the basis of appropriate sample studies of traffic. This method of distributing revenues would be a radical departure from current practice. It is estimated that roughly half of the total miles of travel by all vehicles in the United States occurs on city streets, which probably means that not far from half of all gasoline consumed is on city streets (less truck than passenger travel is on city streets which would reduce the percentage of gasoline consumed, but this may well be more than offset by the greater amount of gasoline consumed per mile of city than of country driving).[6] Yet cities apparently receive only about five percent of state receipts from gasoline taxes and motor-vehicle license fees. Cities themselves impose some motor-vehicle taxes. Nonetheless, it seems clear that cities are receiving not much more than one tenth of the amount to which their traffic entitles them — which is a major reason why they are spending too little on roads.

The greater deficiency of city than of other roads — if our casual observation is right — is a striking illustration of the importance of the general principles for which we have been pleading. The preferences of consumers of highway services as expressed in the sums they have paid for such service have not been appropriately translated into expenditures on highway service. A proper allocation of gasoline and motor-vehicle taxes would permit more than a tripling of the annual expenditures currently being made for the maintenance and administration of city and village streets, even if cities devoted to other purposes all of the general revenues they now spend on roads and streets. This in turn would justify vastly higher capital expenditures than are currently being made.

b) Reducing the size of administrative units

In large cities, in particular, administrative units are so large as to make effective participation by the community difficult. Smaller units would enable public spirit and constructive assistance to be mobilized much more effectively. It would also facilitate a more intimate and informed performance of the officials in charge of streets.

c) Privately operated throughways

There may be some possibilities for private throughways or turnpikes to solve the problem of through traffic. The general principles discussed above in connection with turnpikes apply equally to such throughways.[7]

d) Parking should be charged for

Parking meters furnish another striking illustration of the gains from the application of private enterprise principles. Almost uniformly, the results from their introduction have exceeded the expectations even of their supporters. Making people pay *directly* for the space they use has resulted in a vastly more efficient and satisfactory use of space. They are otherwise getting something for nothing, so have no incentive to economize space. The use of parking meters should be extended wherever feasible. In addition, experimentation is highly desirable in methods of charging for parking on city streets under conditions where existing types of parking meters are not justified — in side streets and residential neighborhoods. Perhaps some method of charging by the week or month can be devised and thus give an incentive to greater provision of off-street parking. It goes without saying that expansion of privately constructed and operating parking garages, parking lots, and the like should be encouraged — and certainly should not be inhibited as they now sometimes are by legal limitations on prices they are permitted to charge.

IV. Conclusion

The major theme of this essay is that the deficiencies in our present system of planning and paying for highways are a particular example of the general inferiority of socialistic governmental enterprise to free private enterprise. The provision of highway service is a socialized industry removed from the test of the market. The result has been that total expenditures on highways have been too small, that these expenditures have been improperly distributed among different kinds of roads, and that we have too little highway service per dollar spent.

Unfortunately, special peculiarities attached to the provision of highway services make it impossible to provide such services completely through competitive private enterprise: the industry cannot well be completely desocialized. Yet much can be done in this direction. Substantial improvement in highway services requires that we desocialize as much of the industry as we can, and that we seek to bring private enterprise tests to bear as fully as possible on the rest of the industry.

Long-distance turnpikes can be fully desocialized; and the maintenance and operation of inter-city roads can be largely desocialized, though at present there seems no way of doing so fully because of the technical difficulty of charging directly for highway services. City streets and roads probably will have to continue to be almost entirely provided by governmental bodies, but private enterprise tests suggest that a much larger fraction of total receipts from gasoline and motor-vehicle taxes should be made available for their maintenance and construction. A move in this direction would radically alter the sums available and permit rapid and striking progress in removing some of the worst defects in our highway system.

If our suggestions seem strange, it is at least partly because we have become so accustomed to regarding the provision of highway service as a government function; what seems strange when suggested for highways seems natural when suggested for railroads. But in this and in other areas we must be ready to think about problems afresh, to reexamine our ingrained notions, if we are to succeed in maintaining the vitality of our free enterprise society, protect it from the encroachment of government, and maintain it as a bulwark of personal freedom.

Notes

1. As was noted in Section 7.3, the magnitude of private investment in US roads in the early nineteenth century exceeded in comparative magnitude the twentieth century investment in the Interstate Highway System.

2. This was written before the establishment of the federal Highway Trust Fund, which weakens these incentives.

3. This recommendation for ' shadow tolls' predates by many years the discussion in Sections 4.2.5 and 8.1.1.

4. As mentioned in Section 4.2.3, both New Zealand and Oregon impose such charges, the 'ton' being measured as the axle load.

5. As mentioned in Section 7.6.2, California invited bids on this basis, with the significant difference that the bids had to cover all the costs of the new roads, not just the excess required in addition to the revenues collected from the taxes on gasoline consumed on them.

6. Fuel consumption in 'stop-go' traffic conditions is significantly higher than when traffic flows freely.

7. Recent technological advances in electronic road pricing open many opportunities for the provision of new road links in congested urban areas.

References

Adler, Hans A. (1969), 'Some Thoughts on Feasibility Studies', *Journal of Transport Economics and Policy,* Vol. III, No. 2, p. 236, University of Bath.

Amos, P.F. (1980) 'Black Taxis in Belfast', in Workshop Proceedings *Paratransit: Changing Perceptions of Public Transport.* Bureau of Transport Economics, Director General of Transport, South Australia.

Anderson, Jack and Michael Binstein (1994), 'A Highway of Pork', *The Washington Post*, p. C9, July 31.

Augenblick, Mark, and B. Scott Custer, Jr. (1990), 'The Build, Operate and Transfer ("BOT") Approach to Infrastructure Projects in Developing Countries', Working Paper WPS 498, August, World Bank.

Beesley, M.E, and G.J. Roth (1963), 'Restraint of Traffic in Congested Areas'. *Town Planning Review,* Vol.33, No. 3, pp.184-196, Liverpool University Press.

Bergfalk, Lars E. (1994), 'Policy and Organization for the Management of Minor Rural Roads — an Example from Sweden'. Swedish National Road Administration, Stockholm.

Block, Walter (1979) 'Free Market Transportation: Denationalizing the Roads', *Journal of Libertarian Studies*, Vol III, No. 2, pp. 209-238.

Boie, Patrick (1993), 'HOV Detection', *Public Works Financing*, July/August, p. 19, Westfield, New Jersey.

Brazier, Nona M. (1994), 'Stop Law That Hurts My Minority Business', *The Wall Street Journal*, January 12.

Breedlove, Buzz (1993), 'Motor Vehicle Inspection and Maintenance in California', California Research Bureau, Sacramento. Based on random roadside survey data obtained from the Bureau of Automotive Repair.

Buchanan, J. M. (1952), 'The Pricing of Highway Services'. *National Tax Journal,* Vol. V, No. 2, pp. 97-106, June.

Buchanan, J. M. (1956), 'Private Ownership and Common Usage: The Road Case Re-examined'. *Southern Economic Journal,* Vol. 22, pp. 305-316, January.

Buchanan, J. M. (1965), 'The Economic Theory of Clubs', *Economica,* Vol. 32, February. Reprinted in Tyler Cowen (Editor), *The Theory of Market Failure: A Critical Examination,* George Mason University Press, 1988.

Buchanan, J. M., and Gordon Tullock (1962), *The Calculus of Consent,* University of Michigan.

Button, Kenneth (1989), 'Private Provision of Roads in Europe', *Selected Proceedings of the Fifth World Conference on Transport Research,* Western Periodicals Co., Ventura, California.

Clark, J. Maurice (1923), *Studies in the Economics of Overhead Costs,* p. 304. University of Chicago Press.

Coase, Ronald H. (1960), 'The Problem of Social Cost', *Journal of Law and Economics,* Vol. 3, No. 1, pp. 1-44, October.

Congressional Budget Office (1985), *Toll Financing of US Highways,* Congress of the United States, Washington DC, December.

Creasy, Sir Edward (1877), *History of the Ottoman Turks,* Richard & Son, London.

Curry, Jerry Ralph, (1991) Testimony before the US House of Representatives Subcommittee on Energy and Power, April 16, 1991.

Deaton, Angus (1987), 'The Demand for Personal Travel in Developing Countries'. *Infrastructure and Urban Development Papers, Report INU1,* pp. 5.36-5.37, World Bank.

Deen, Thomas B. (1963) 'Fiscal Policy and Transportation Planning', *Traffic Quarterly,* Vol. 17, No. 1, January. Eno Transportation Foundation Inc., Landsdowne, Virginia.

Department of Transport (1994) 'City Congestion Charging'. Memorandum dated 6 October prepared for the House of Commons Transport Committee. (Discussed in *The Economist,* November 12, 1994, p. 71.)

Dougher, Rayola S. (1995), 'Estimates of Annual US Road User Payments Versus Annual Road Expenditures'. Research Study #078, March, American Petroleum Institute, Washington DC.

Downing, A.J., C.J. Baguley and B.L. Hills (1991), 'Road Safety in Developing Countries: An Overview'. In *PTRC Nineteenth Transport, Highways and Planning Summer Annual Meeting, Proceedings of Seminar C*. PTRC Education and Research Services, London.

Downs, Anthony (1962) 'The Law of Peak-Hour Expressway Congestion', *Traffic Quarterly*, Vol. 16, No. 3, July. Eno Transportation Foundation Inc., Landsdowne, Virginia. See also *Stuck in Traffic*, 1992, Brookings Institution, Washington DC.

Drucker, Peter F. (1993), 'The Five Deadly Business Sins', *The Wall Street Journal*, October 21, 1993.

Dupuit, J. (1844), 'On the measurement of the utility of public works', *Annales des Ponts et Chaussees*, Vol. 8. Translated from the French by R.H. Barback for *International Economic Papers* (1952), No. 2, pp. 83-110.

Economists Advisory Group (1972). 'The Belgium Intercommunale System of Road Finance', London.

EDI (1991), 'The Road Maintenance Initiative: Building Capacity for Policy Reform', Vol. 2. EDI Seminar Series, Economic Development Institute, World Bank.

Faison, Seth (1992), 'Bus-Fare Cuts Fail to Lure Queens Riders'. *The New York Times,* p. 41, November 29.

Faiz, Asif, Kumares Sinha, Michael Walsh and Amiy Varma (1990), 'Automotive Air Pollution: Issues and Options for Developing Countries', PRE Working Paper No. WPS 492, World Bank.

Farah, Joseph, and Mike Antonucci (1994), 'Strangled in the Crib: Jobs and Regulations in California'. *Regulation,* No. 3, pp. 21-27, Cato Institute, Washington DC.

Fayard, Alain (1994), 'The French Experience', *World Highways,* January/February, 1994.

Federal Highway Administration (1988), *America on the Move*, p. v, Washington DC.

Federal Highway Administration (1993), *The Status of the Nation's Highways, Bridges, and Transit: Conditions and Performance: A Summary,* P.17. Publication FHWA-PL-93-017, Washington DC.

Field, David (1995), 'Shuster vows end to pork projects', *The Washington Times*, January 23, p. A.9.

Forbes, R. J. (1934), *Notes on the History of Ancient Roads and Their Construction,* Adolf M. Hakkert, Amsterdam.

Foster, Christopher (1963, revised edition, 1975) *The Transport Problem,* p. 47, Croom Helm, London.

Francis, Philip (1963), *John Evelyn's Diary*, p. 90. The Folio Society, London.

Gage, Theodore J. (1981), 'Getting Street-Wise in St. Louis', *Reason,* pp. 18-26, Los Angeles.

General Motors (1994). *1994 GM Public Interest Report,* Detroit.

Gilliet, Henri (1990), 'Toll roads — the French experience'. Transroute International, Saint-Quentin-en-Yvelines.

Gilmour, Paul (1995), 'Did Volcanic Gas Poke a Hole in the Ozone?', *The Wall Street Journal*', January 12, p. A15.

Glaister, Stephen, and Tony Travers (1994), 'Tolls and Shadow Tolls', London School of Economics.

Goldstein, Alfred (1987), 'Private Enterprise and Highways', in *Private-Sector Involvement and Toll Road Financing in the Provision of Highways, Transportation Research Record* No. 1107, Transportation Research Board, Washington DC.

Gómez-Ibáñez, José A., and John Meyer (1993) *Going Private: The International Experience with Transport Privatization.* The Brookings Institution, Washington DC.

Guangdong Provincial Communications Department and others, 1992. *General Report on Highway Financing System: Study in Guangdong Province*. Draft report, p. 78, December.

Gunderson, Gerland (1989), 'Privatization and the 19th Century Turnpike', *Cato Journal*, Spring/Summer, Washington DC.

Hall, Jane V., Arthur M. Winer, Michael T. Kleinman, Frederik W. Lurmann, Victor Brajer and Steven Colome (1992), 'Valuing the Health Benefits of Clean Air'. *Science*, Vol. 255, February.

Hall, Peter (1980), *Great Planning Disasters,* pp. 96, 103. Weidenfeld and Nicholson, London.

Harral, Clell G. (1987), 'Road deterioration in developing countries: organization and management of road maintenance'. *Transportation Research Record* No. 1128, Transportation Research Board, Washington DC.

Harral, Clell G. (1988), *Road deterioration in developing countries: causes and remedies*. A World Bank policy study, World Bank.

Harral, Clell G. (Editor), Peter Cook, and Edward Holland (1992), 'Transport Development in Southern China'. *World Bank Discussion Papers* No. 151.

Hau, Timothy (1992a), 'Economic Fundamentals of Road Pricing', p. 56. *Policy Research Working Paper No. WPS 1070,* World Bank.

Hau, Timothy (1992b), 'Congestion Charging Mechanisms for Roads', *Policy Research Working Paper No. WPS 1071* World Bank.

Hayek, Friedrich A. (1960), *The Constitution of Liberty*, University of Chicago Press.

Heggie, Ian G. (1991), 'Improving Management and Charging Policies for Roads: An Agenda for Reform'. *INU Report* No. 92, December. World Bank.

Heggie, Ian G. (1992), 'Selecting Appropriate Instruments for Charging Road Users', *INU Discussion Paper* No. 95, February, World Bank.

Heggie, Ian G. (1995), 'Management and Financing of Roads: An Agenda for Reform'. Sub-Saharan Africa Transport Policy Program, Working Paper No. 8, World Bank.

Hibbs, John (1994), 'The true cost of planning — the lack of a market for transport land'. *Road Law,* Vol. 13, No. 1, p. 2, Barry Rose Law Publishers, Chichester.

Hibbs, John and Gabriel Roth (1992), *Tomorrow's Way: Managing Roads in a Free Society*. Adam Smith Institute, London.

Highway Loss Data Institute (1992), 'Trends in Injury and Collision Losses by Car Size: 1979-89 Model Passenger Cars', December, Arlington, Virginia.

Highways Agency (1994), *Roads DBFO Projects: Information and Pre-qualification Requirements,* Department of Transport, August.

Insurance Institute for Highway Safety (1990), 'Where is Safety in the Fuel Economy Debate? *Status Report*, Vol. 25, No. 8, September 8, Arlington, Virginia.

International Bridge, Tunnel and Turnpike Association (1992), 'Comparative Traffic Statistics', Washington DC.

Jackman, W.T. (1966), *The Development of Transportation in Modern England*, Frank Cass & Co., London.

Jannson, Jan Owen (1994), 'Accident Externality Charges', *Journal of Transport Economics and Policy,* Vol. XXVIII, No. 1, p. 42, University of Bath .

Jones-Lee, M.W. (1990), 'The Value of Transport Safety'. *Oxford Review of Economic Policy*, Vol. 6, No. 2, pp. 39-60.

Klein, Daniel (1994), 'History Holds Lesson in Toll Road Success', *Los Angeles Times,* p. B1, June 6.

Klein, Daniel B., and Gordon J. ('Pete') Fielding (1992) 'Private Toll Roads: Learning from the 19th Century', *Transportation Quarterly*, Vol. 46, No. 3, July, (pp. 321-341). Eno Transportation Foundation Inc., Landsdowne, Virginia.

Knight, Frank H. (1924), 'Some Fallacies in the Interpretation of Social Cost', *Quarterly Journal of Economics*, Vol. 38, pp. 582-606, August.

Larsen, Odd (1994), personal communication. Institute of Transport Economics, PO Box 6110 Etterstad, N-0602, Oslo.

Lave, Charles A. (1993), 'Clean for a Day: California Versus the EPA's Smog Check Mandates'. *Access* No. 3, Fall, University of California Transportation Center, Berkeley.

Lave, Charles A. (1994), 'It Wasn't Supposed to Turn Out Like This: Federal Subsidies and Declining Transit Productivity'. *Access* No. 5, Fall, University of California Transportation Center, Berkeley.

Lave, Charles A., and Patrick Elias (1992), 'Did the 65 mph Speed Limit Save Lives?' AAA Foundation for Traffic Safety, Washington DC.

Lee, Douglass B. (1982), 'New Benefits from Efficient Highway User Charges', *Transportation Research Record* No. 858, Transportation Research Board, Washington DC.

Lee, Douglass B. (1995), 'Full Cost Pricing of Highways', Paper presented to Transportation Research Board Annual Meeting, Washington DC.

Lee, Dwight R. (1993), University of Georgia. 'The Case for Decentralization as a Constraint on the Power to Tax'. Paper presented at the Mont Pelerin Society Regional Meeting, Rio de Janeiro.

Machiavelli, Niccolo (1513), *The Prince,* Translated by W.K. Marriott, pp. 47-48, Everyman Edition, J.M. Dent & Co., 1908, London.

Marcus, M.J., and Spavins, Thomas C. (1993), 'The Impact of Technical Change on the Structure of the Local Exchange and the Pricing of Exchange Access'. Paper presented at the 1993 Telecommunications Policy Research Conference. Federal Communications Commission, Washington DC.

McCleary, William (1991), 'The Earmarking of Government Revenue: A Review of Some World Bank Experience'. *The World Bank Research Observer*, Vol. 6, No. 1, pp. 81-104, World Bank.

McKenna, Michael (1994), 'Adventures in Smogocop III'. *Regulation,* No. 1, pp. 11-15, Cato Institute, Washington DC.

Meads, Chris, and Bryce Wilkinson (1993), 'Options for the Reform of Roading in New Zealand'. Prepared by CS First Boston New Zealand Limited for the New Zealand Business Round Table.

Mills, David E (1981), 'Ownership Arrangements and Congestion-Prone Facilities'. *American Economic Review*, Vol. 71, No. 3, pp. 493-502. June.

Ministry of Transport (1964), *Road Pricing: The Economic and Technical Possibilities*, HMSO, London.

Mohring, Herbert (1965), 'Relation Between Optimum Congestion Tolls And Present Highway User Charges', *Highway Research Record* No. 47, Transportation Research Board, Washington DC.

Mohring, Herbert, and David Anderson (1994), 'Estimating Congestion Costs and Optimal Congestion Charges for Large Urban Areas'. Paper prepared at the Department of Economics, University of Minnesota, for the Twin Cities Metropolitan Area Council.

Mohring, Herbert, and Mitchell Harwitz (1962), *Highway Benefits — An Analytical Framework*, Northwestern University Press.

National Defense University (1978), *Climate Change to the year 2000*, Fort Lesley J. McNair, Washington DC, February.

Newbery, David (1990), 'Pricing and Congestion: Economic Principles Relevant to Pricing Roads', *Oxford Review of Economic Policy*, Vol. 6, No. 2, pp. 22-38, Summer.

Newbery, David (1994), 'The Case for a Public Road Authority', *Journal of Transport Economics and Policy*, Vol. XXVIII, No. 3, pp. 235-253, September, University of Bath.

Niskanen, William A. (1971), *Bureaucracy and Representative Government,* Aldine Atherton, Chicago.

Oborne, Michael (1986), *China's Special Economic Zones*, OECD Development Centre, Paris.

OECD, (1987), 'Toll Financing and Private Sector Involvement in Road Infrastructure Development', Paris.

Oregon Department of Transportation (1992), *Motor Vehicle Cost Responsibility Study: Summary Report,* Table 10, p. 25. December.

Ornitz, Richard (1994), 'Hungarian Connection', *Infrastructure Finance,* p. 62, April/May.

Owen, Wilfred (1994), 'Upgrading International Aid for Roads'. *Public Works Financing*, International Supplement, p. 9, April. Westfield, New Jersey.

Paterson, W.D.O. and R. Archondo-Callao (1991) 'Estimating Road Use Costs'. Unpublished document, World Bank, September. (Much of the material in this paper was presented by W.D.O. Paterson in 'Engineering and Economic Efficiency for Highways: An Introduction to the Highway Design and Maintenance Standards Model, HDM'. *Proceedings, First Conference on Road Management Practices*, World Bank, and Colegio de Ingenieros de Caminos, Canales y Puertos, Barcelona, June 1933.)

Peters, Eric (1994), 'Clean air bracket creep for motorists', *The Washington Times,* August 9, p. A16.

Pigou, A.C. (1920), *The Economics of Welfare,* Macmillan, London.

Pisarski, Alan E. (1987), *Report on Highways, Streets Roads and Bridges,* p. 20. National Council on Public Works Improvement, Washington DC.

Pisarski, Alan E. (1992), *Travel Behavior Issues in the 90s,* pp. 70-71, US
    Department of Transportation, Federal Highway Administration,
    Office of Highway Information Management, Washington DC.
Poole, Robert W., Jr. (1992) 'Private Tollways: How States Can Leverage
    Federal Highway Funds'. Reason Foundation *Policy Insight* No. 136,
    Los Angeles.
Poole, Robert W., Jr. (1993) 'SR 91: A Triple-Header for Privatized
    Infrastructure', *Public Works Financing*, July/August, p. 8, Westfield,
    New Jersey.
Public Works Financing (July/August, 1993), 'Cofiroute: Lean, Mean,
    Cash Machine', p. 6, Westfield, New Jersey.
Public Works Financing (September, 1993), 'Dulles Greenway Ground-
    breaking', p. 2, Westfield, New Jersey.
Public Works Financing (September, 1993), 'Midlands Toll Road on
    Hold?', p. 9, Westfield, New Jersey.
Public Works Financing (February 1994), 'Kumagai Sells Thai Road
    Shares', p. 10, Westfield, New Jersey.
Public Works Financing (July-August 1994), 'Early startup for Dulles Toll
    Road', p. 1, Westfield, New Jersey.
Pyle, Thomas H. (January, 1994), 'Private Financing of Infrastructure',
    Princeton Pacific Group, Princeton, New Jersey.
Pyle, Thomas H. (February, 1994), 'The New Jersey Turnpike of China',
    Public Works Financing, February, p. 17, Westfield, New Jersey.
Quinet, E. (1989), 'Evaluations du cout social des transports', *Selected
    Proceedings of the Fifth World Conference on Transport Research*,
    Western Periodicals Co., Ventura, California.
Rae, John B. (1971), *The Road and the Car in American Life*, MIT Press.
Reason Foundation (1994), *Eighth Annual Report on Privatization.* Los
    Angeles, California.
Rees Jeffreys, W. (1949), *The King's Highway*, Batchworth, London.
Reina, Peter (1992), 'Tolled Ring Road Led the Way for Bangkok B-O-T
    Projects'. *Public Works Financing*, International Supplement, p. 5,
    July. Westfield, New Jersey.
Reina, Peter (1994), 'Hungary's M1-M15 Toll Road: Eastern Europe's
    First Go at B-O-T'. *PublicWorks Financing*, International Supplement,
    p. 1, April. Westfield, New Jersey.
Reinhardt, William G. (1993), 'Kiewit Moves SR 91 Financing to Closure
    Launching a New Era in US Toll Roads'. *Public Works Financing*,
    July/August, p. 1, Westfield, New Jersey.

Reinhardt, William G. (1994), 'First US Private Startup Toll Road is Financed and Under Construction'. *Public Works Financing*, January, p. 1, Westfield, New Jersey.

Rickard, John (1994), Department of Transport. 'Developments in Financing Highways in the United Kingdom'. Paper to the Congress on Road Financing in the European Union, Salamanca, November.

Roth, G.J. (1965), 'An Economic Approach to Traffic Congestion', *The Town Planning Review*, Vol. 36, No. 1, April, pp. 49-61, Liverpool University Press.

Roth, Gabriel (1990), 'Perestroika for US Highways: Managing Roads for a Free Society'. Reason Foundation *Policy Insight* No. 125, Los Angeles.

Schipper, Lee, Elizabeth Deakin and Daniel Sperling (1994), 'Sustainable Transportation: The Future of the Automobile in an Environmentally Constrained World'. International Energy Studies Group, Lawrence Berkeley Laboratory, California.

Semmens, John (1987), 'Using competition to break the US road monopoly'. *Backgrounder* No. 622, Heritage Foundation, Washington DC.

Semmens, John (1993), 'From Highways to Buy-ways', *Spectrum*, Fall 1993, The Independent Institute, Oakland, California.

Semmens, John (1994), 'Combining the Issuance of Vehicle Registrations, Drivers' Licenses and Auto Insurance'. In *Reinventing Government*, Goldwater Institute, Phoenix, Arizona.

Small, Kenneth A. (1992), 'Using the Revenues from Congestion Pricing', *Transportation* , Vol. 19, No. 4, pp. 359–381.

Small, Kenneth A., Clifford Winston and Carol A. Evans (1989), *Road Work. A new highway pricing and investment policy*. Brookings Institute, Washington DC.

Small, Kenneth A., and Camilla Kazimi (1995), 'On the Costs of Air Pollution from Motor Vehicles', *Journal of Transport Economics and Policy*, Vol. XXIX, No. 1, pp. 7-32, University of Bath.

Smeed, R.J. (1961), 'The Traffic Problem in Towns', Manchester Statistical Society.

Smith, Adam (1776), *An Inquiry into the Nature and Causes of the Wealth of Nations*. Page numbers refer to the two volumes ('i' and 'ii') of Edwin Cannan's edition, University of Chicago Press, 1976, which is actually based on the 1789 (fifth) edition of the *Inquiry*.

Smith, Fred L., Jr. (1990), 'Autonomy', *Reason*, Vol. 22, No. 4, Aug/Sep, Los Angeles.

Stanley, Ralph (1989), 'Reducing the Federal Role in Highway Assistance'. In *Mandate for Leadership III: Policy Strategies for the 1990s,* pp.433-434. Heritage Foundation, Washington DC.

Starkie, D. N. M. (1990), 'The Private Financing of Road Infrastructure'. *Transport and Society* Discussion Paper No. 11, Transport Studies Unit, Oxford University.

Strotz, Robert H. (1965), 'Principles of Urban Transportation Pricing', in *Highway Research Record* No. 47, Transportation Research Board, Washington DC.

Takeda, Fumio (1989), 'Evaluation of the Japanese Type of Toll Road System and Private Participation'. *Selected Proceedings of the Fifth World Conference on Transport Research,* Western Periodicals Co., Ventura, California.

Tam, Angela (June 1993), 'Thais Break BOT Expressway Contract', *Public Works Financing,* p. 1, Westfield, New Jersey.

Tam, Angela (September 1993), Thailand Expropriates Completed BOT Expressway, *Public Works Financing,* p. 18, Westfield, New Jersey.

Teja, Ranjit, Barry Bracewell-Milnes (1991), *The Case for Earmarked Taxes: Government Spending and Public Choice.* Institute of Economic Affairs, London.

The Daily Telegraph (1994), 'Drivers may be charged to enter cities', August 22, p. 1, London.

The Times (1994), 'Roadside cameras reduce death and injury by a third', August 23, p. 4.

The Times (1994), 'Police move in as M11 protesters make last stand', November 29, p. 7.

The Wall Street Journal (1994), 'Prevention May Be Costlier than a Cure', July 6, p. B1.

The Wall Street Journal (1994), 'Product Liability Suits Fare Worse Now', July 12, p. B9.

The Washington Post (1994), 'Many Va. Drivers Convicted of DWI [Driving While Intoxicated] Keep Licenses', December 18, p. B1.

Towe, Kenneth M. (1995), 'NASA jumps the gun on announcing what's causing ozone depletion', *The Washington Times,* January 10, p. A.18.

Traffic Engineering and Control (1994), 'Electronic Road Pricing: Singapore Trials Well Under Way'. June, pp 390-392, London.

Transport and Road Research Laboratory (1988), *A guide to road project appraisal,* Overseas Road Note 5, Crowthorne, Berkshire.

TRIP (1994), *1994 State Highway Funding Methods.* The Road Information Program, Washington DC.

Turner, F.C. (1975), 'The Highway Trust Fund ... Sound and Successful', *Constructor*, August, pp. 22-25.

United Nations Economic Commission for Latin America and the Caribbean (UN-ECLAC) (1993), *Roads,* Santiago.

Vickrey, W.S. (1959), Statement on the Pricing of Urban Street Use. *Hearings, US Congress, Joint Committee on Metropolitan Washington Problems,* November 11.

Voorhees, Alan M. and Associates Inc. (1973), *Caracas road user charges: opportunities and potentialities*, prepared for the Ministerial Office of Transport. Ministry of Public Works, Caracas, November.

Walters, Alan A. (1954), 'Track Costs and Motor Taxation', *Journal of Industrial Economics*, II, pp. 135-146, April.

Walters, Alan A. (1968), *The Economics of Road User Charges*, Staff Occasional Papers Number Five, World Bank.

Watkins, Alfred (1994), 'Financing Options for Motorway Projects', World Bank.

Watson, Peter L., and Edward P. Holland (1978), *Relieving Traffic Congestion: The Singapore Area License Scheme.* World Bank Staff Working Paper No. 281, June.

Webber, Melvin M. (1994), 'The Marriage of Autos and Transit: How to Make Transit Popular Again'. *Access* No. 5, Fall, University of California Transportation Center, Berkeley.

Wilson, George W. (1966), 'Case Studies of Effect of Roads on Development', in *Highway Research Record* No. 115, Transportation Research Board, Washington DC.

World Development Report 1994, World Bank.

Yerrell, J. Stuart (1992), 'Traffic Accidents — A Worldwide Problem', paper presented to the 1st International Road Safety Seminar, Mexico City, November 23-27. Transport Research Laboratory, Crowthorne.

Zahavi, Yacov (1982), 'Travel Regularities in Baltimore, Washington, London and Reading.' Technical Memorandum attached to Progress Report No. 8 on the UMOT Travel Model, presented to the US Department of Transportation, Research and Special Programs Administration, Washington DC.

Zahavi, Yacov and Gabriel Roth (1980), 'Measuring the Effectiveness of Priority Schemes for High-Occupancy Vehicles'. *Transportation Research Record* No. 770. pp. 18-21, Transportation Research Board, Washington DC.

Name index

Geographic index

The following list excludes tabulated items, such as those in Table 7.2

Subject index